THE SCRIBNER SCIENCE REFERENCE SERIES

The RENAISSANCE and the SCIENTIFIC REVOLUTION

BIOGRAPHICAL PORTRAITS

Editor

Brian S. Baigrie is associate professor of history and philosophy of science at the Institute for History and Philosophy of Science and Technology, University of Toronto, Canada. He has published numerous articles on the scientific revolution and is the editor of *Picturing Knowledge* (1996), University of Toronto Press, which looks at the role that scientific illustration plays in the creation of scientific knowledge. He is now working on a book that examines the impact of Johannes Kepler's scientific work on philosophical debates of the seventeenth century.

THE SCRIBNER SCIENCE REFERENCE SERIES

VOLUME 1

The RENAISSANCE and the SCIENTIFIC REVOLUTION

BIOGRAPHICAL PORTRAITS

Brian S. Baigrie, *Editor*

Charles Scribner's Sons
an imprint of the Gale Group
New York • Detroit • San Francisco • London • Boston • Woodbridge, CT

Developed for Charles Scribner's Sons by Visual Education Corporation, Princeton, N.J.

For Scribners
PUBLISHER: Karen Day
COVER DESIGN: Pamela Galbreath

For Visual Education Corporation
EDITORIAL DIRECTOR: Darryl Kestler
PROJECT DIRECTOR: Meera Vaidyanathan
WRITERS: Guy Austrian, John Haley, Charles Roebuck, Rebecca Stefoff
ASSOCIATE EDITORS: Eleanor Hero, Sussannah Walsh
COPYEDITING SUPERVISOR: Helen Castro
COPY EDITOR: Joanna Foster
INDEXER: Cynthia Landeen, Ph.D.
PHOTO RESEARCH: Susan Buschhorn
PRODUCTION SUPERVISOR: Paula Deverell
PRODUCTION ASSISTANTS: Susan Buschhorn, Brian Suskin
INTERIOR DESIGN: Maxson Crandall, Rob Ehlers, Lisa Evans-Skopas
ELECTRONIC PREPARATION: Cynthia C. Feldner, Christine Osborne
ELECTRONIC PRODUCTION: Rob Ehlers, Lisa Evans-Skopas

Library of Congress Cataloging-in-Publication Data

The renaissance and the scientific revolution: biographical portraits / Brian S. Baigrie, editor in chief.
     p. cm. — (The Scribner science reference series ; v. 1)
    Includes bibliographical references and index.
    ISBN 0-684-80646-0
    1. Scientists—Biography.   I. Baigrie, Brian S. (Brian Scott).   II. Series.

Q141 .R36 2001
509.2'2—dc21
[B]

00-063565

TABLE OF CONTENTS

Table of Contents

INTRODUCTION

BY BRIAN S. BAIGRIE

The biographies of scientists collected in this volume cover the period of the Renaissance and the scientific revolution, from 1500 to 1800. No other period in the history of science has generated as much scholarly interest. Until this time, science was dominated by the ideas of ancient thinkers, notably, those of Aristotle, Galen, and members of the great school that flourished in Alexandria. By the end of this period, scientists had created new and powerful forms of inquiry that gave them an unprecedented intellectual and technological mastery over nature.

The Birth of New Forms of Inquiry. In ancient times, the pursuit of knowledge had traditionally been based on reason and revelation. The new science abandoned these established forms of inquiry and turned to experience—experiment coupled with careful observation—as the underpinning and ultimate arbiter of knowledge. Consequently, scientists were no longer compelled to bow to the authority of eminent persons; any statement in principle could now be put to the test of experience.

The result was a democratization of the pursuit of knowledge and the emergence of the conviction that science—liberated from the prejudices and dogmas of ancient times—was off to a fresh start. The new science enabled an ordinary person, such as the Dutch natural scientist Antoni van Leeuwenhoek, who had little formal education and no direct ties to the centers of learning, to pursue a robust program of scientific research. During the 1600s, when Leeuwenhoek made his startling investigations using the simple microscopes of his own design, what mattered was whether he applied the proper research methods. As methodology became paramount, scientists who contributed to the growing body of literature on the scientific method, such as Francis Bacon, René Descartes, Galileo Galilei, William Harvey, Isaac Newton, and Antoine Lavoisier, received greater attention from their peers.

These new forms of inquiry based on experimentation and observation did not emerge overnight, however. They were crafted and refined by the collaboration of many scientists over many generations, and nurtured by the emergence of a new set of scientific institutions that overcame the barriers of language, nation, and religion. Prominent new institutions, such as the Royal Society of London and the Académie des Sciences of Paris, were formed so that like-minded scientists could meet to perform experiments and to hear about the latest work being conducted by scientific groups in other places. All these researchers were dedicated to the idea that science is a work in progress. To facilitate additional discoveries, and so add to the growing body of scientific knowledge, they made provisions to publish and thereby share their discoveries by creating new journals. Prizes were awarded for the most breathtaking advances. The researchers also established new observatories, laboratories, botanical gardens, and collections of every kind of thing, both living and dead.

A Metamorphosis Occurs. The period of the Renaissance and scientific revolution featured a unique moment in human history—one that witnessed the birth of modern science. In its methods and fundamental preoccupations, the new science that was created at this time is strikingly similar to present-day practices. In philosophical terms, the new science revolutionized the West's understanding of the universe and humanity's place in it. This metamorphosis, or evolution, in human thought is commonly known as the scientific revolution, and modern historians of science have expended enormous energy attempting to frame a coherent picture of this period. For the most part, their energies have been directed at identifying the causes of the scientific revolution, which has resulted in a range of opinion on the proper dating of the period.

Initially, the scientific revolution was defined as a rupture with ancient thought that occurred in the first few decades of the 1600s. This rupture was thought to have consisted in the destruction of the Greek and medieval conception of the universe as a finite and qualitatively ordered whole. It was replaced largely by the theories of Galileo and Descartes, who believed that the universe is infinite and that its fundamental components are of equal importance.

Copernicus's Revolutions. This definition of the scientific revolution proved to be too restrictive, however, and the concept was stretched to cover the period from Nicholas Copernicus in the early 1500s to Isaac Newton at the close of the 1600s. With this broader definition, the concept of the scientific revolution included much of the scientific work carried out during the Renaissance. Some scholars believe that the catalyst for the event was the publication in 1543 of Copernicus's *On the Revolution of the Heavenly Spheres*. In this work, Copernicus boldly suggested that the earth moved around a central sun—a view that became known as the heliocentric theory. This challenged the great philosophers, astronomers, and religious thinkers of antiquity, who believed in a geocentric, or earth-centered, universe.

It was a revolution-making work in the sense that it had important consequences on scientific thought about the universe and in that it was striving to break with traditional opinion. Copernicus's theory highlighted the deficiencies in the geocentric view of the world that had been inherited from antiquity and placed a premium on the construction of a new physics based on his heliocentric theory. Some historians believe that the scientific revolution was the period in which scientists came to terms with and built on Copernicus's theories.

In many respects, however, Copernicus's work looked backward—a feature that was characteristic of writing in the Renaissance, when scientific opinion was wrapped up with notions of the glory of ancient texts. He wrote *On the Revolution of the Heavenly Spheres* with the aim of removing the stain imposed on Greek cosmological conceptions by the ancient astronomer Claudius Ptolemy. Nevertheless, he generated an entirely new set of problems for the scientific imagination, which resulted in the creation of the new mathematical physics of Galileo, Descartes, Christiaan Huygens, Johannes Kepler, and Isaac Newton.

Some scholars have carried this stretching of the concept of the scientific revolution a step further, arguing that the critical developments that we now associate with the likes of Kepler, Galileo, Descartes, and Newton are all grounded in medieval achievements. Modern scholars have argued, for example, that the pivotal concept of inertia (inaction), which was elaborated by

Galileo and Descartes, was a development of the notion of impetus (thrust) advanced by French philosopher Jean Buridan in the early 1300s. Although it is perhaps an exaggeration to suggest that the new science of the 1600s was entirely original with Kepler, Galileo, Descartes, Huygens, and Newton, it is also difficult to understand what was revolutionary about this new science, especially if the concept is stretched to cover a 500-year period. What sort of revolution is it that takes so many years to come about?

The Age of Newton. To counter this difficulty, recent scholarship has focused increasingly on the scientific output of Isaac Newton. Scholars believe that what ties together the very different ideas of Copernicus, Kepler, Galileo, Descartes, and Huygens is that each of these prominent scientists made a unique contribution that was woven into the great fabric of the new mathematical physics. The new physics was formally presented by Newton in his famous treatise *Principia*. Published in 1687, *Principia* is considered the most important work of the scientific revolution. The work advanced the law of universal gravitation, which explained the motions of planets, satellites, and comets—the constituents of the universe in which we live. The work dominated the science of the 1700s, ushering in a veritable "Age of Newton."

Many of the noteworthy advances during that time consisted in the elaboration of Newton's central ideas and their application to new phenomena. Indeed, what is taught these days to university students as "Newtonian physics" has less to do with the work of Newton himself than with the extension of Newton's ideas, assisted by the development of the calculus, by new generations of mathematical physicists during the 1700s. Newton's work was held in such high esteem that it was generally presumed that the Newtonian system should be known and understood by everyone. His characteristic approach to framing problems also exerted a profound influence in fields far removed from mathematical physics.

Notwithstanding Newton's far-reaching influence and the varied applications of his theories, many extraordinary scientific developments had little to do with the revolution of Newton. However, because many historians were convinced that there was a single, all-encompassing scientific revolution, one that they identified with the science crafted by Newton, they failed to appreciate the richness and diversity of the sciences that developed during the 1600s and 1700s. Moreover, their conviction was steeped in the notion that the revolution in science was a revolution against superstition. In short, some historians of science believed that the scientific revolution consisted in the replacement of the body of philosophical dogma passed along from antiquity by a body of well-founded scientific claims. The scientific revolution, in their view, was the triumph of Newtonian science over the lore of the ancients.

Many Small Revolutions. Rather than the replacement of ancient lore by Newtonian science, what occurred during the 1600s and early 1700s was a splintering of the scientific community into distinct communities, each following distinctive patterns of inquiry. Newton, for instance, reckoned by the time the third edition of *Principia* was published in 1726 that to discourse about God was not proper to experimental science. He also regarded the practices of the physical sciences as distinct from those of the earth sciences, and perhaps rightly so, because the methods of the two fields are different from one another. The biological sciences and physical sciences also parted company at this time. By the end of the 1600s, independent fields of inquiry had emerged. The Aristotelian model, which was demolished by the investigations of Kepler, Descartes, Galileo, and others, was replaced by a medley of scientific and philosophic cultures, each developing its own distinctive practices.

If we take the view that the scientific revolution consisted of many collaborative revolutions, the concept of the scientific revolution can then be widened so that it can speak to important developments that occurred in scientific niches other than physics. Although the scientific revolution will forever be associated with Newton's universal law of gravitation, during the 1600s there were many important developments in other fields. They include achievements in optics (Descartes, Kepler, Huygens, Newton), botany (Carl Linnaeus), biology (John Ray), anatomy (Marcello Malpighi), parasitology (Leeuwenhoek), electricity (Otto von Guericke), magnetism (William Gilbert), cartography (Gerardus Mercator), and physiology (Realdo Colombo, Gabriele Fallopio, Harvey).

The diversity of these developments and the emergence of so many new sciences are proof that the scientific revolution did involve a metamorphosis in worldview, especially in the sense that it radically affected the perception of the cosmos and the place of humanity in it. At a more fundamental level, however, this revolution consisted in a massive acceleration in the production of knowledge.

Disciplines that stand at the forefront of traditional accounts of the scientific revolution, such as astronomy, physics, and mathematics, were directly implicated in the reorganization of scientific practice that resulted in the explosion of new knowledge. One reason attributed to the accelerated production of knowledge is that these sciences were intimately connected to the inventions of new instruments, such as the telescope, the microscope, the pendulum clock, and the vacuum pump. Each of these instruments was exploited by the new generation of forward-looking scientists with revolutionary zeal. For example, Galileo's telescope revealed imperfections on the moon, undermining the ancient belief that the heavens were perfect. Over time, these instruments were improved, generating new ones that helped keep astronomy, physics, and mechanics at the vanguard of an accelerating research front.

Other sciences, such as botany, chemistry, and zoology, were not as directly connected to these developments in instrumentation. However, we should not lose sight of the far-reaching changes that these sciences experienced as they discarded their attachments with ancient texts and developed their own distinctive experimental strategies for unraveling nature's secrets.

TIME LINE

1633	Galileo is condemned by the Inquisition.
1637	René DESCARTES outlines his four canons of scientific reasoning.
1642	Blaise PASCAL invents an adding machine.
1644	Evangelista TORRICELLI describes an experiment involving the invention of the mercury barometer. Descartes elaborates his vortex theory of planetary motion.
1647	Pascal publishes his work on vacuum.
1648	Pascal uses the barometer to show that the atmosphere has weight.
1651	Otto von GUERICKE demonstrates atmospheric pressure using two copper hemispheres.
1655	Christiaan HUYGENS discovers Titan, Saturn's largest moon, and correctly identifies the rings surrounding Saturn. John WALLIS publishes *Arithmetica infinitorium*, which deals with the use of negative and fractional exponents.
1657	Huygens invents the first accurate pendulum clock to determine longitude at sea.
1658	Jan SWAMMERDAM discovers red blood cells.
1660	Robert BOYLE publishes the *Sceptical Cymist*, defending a corpuscular theory of chemical reactions. Marcello MALPIGHI publishes *De plumonibus*, in which he describes the network of blood capillaries in the lungs of frogs.
1662	The Royal Society is founded in England. Boyle's Law, which states that the volume and pressure of a gas are inversely related, is published.
1664	Gian CASSINI observes the surface of Jupiter with a telescope.
1665	Robert HOOKE publishes *Micrographia*, which contains descriptions and illustrations of the organisms he studied under a microscope. Isaac NEWTON deduces the inverse square law and invents his calculus. Royal Society begins *Philosophical Transactions*, the first journal of a strictly scientific nature.
1666	Cassini observes spots on Mars and determines the rotation of that planet. Newton works on calculus and on his theories of color and light. Académie Royale des Sciences founded.
1668	Edmé MARIOTTE announces the discovery of a blind spot in the eye. Newton builds first reflecting telescope.
1669	Swammerdam publishes *Historia insectorum generalis*, which describes the anatomy and metamorphosis of insects.
1671	Antoni van LEEUWENHOEK constructs a simple microscope.
1673	Wilhelm LEIBNIZ invents his calculus.
1674	Leeuwenhoek discovers tiny one-celled animals known as protozoa.
1675	Boyle publishes first book on electricity. Construction of the Royal Observatory at Greenwich, designed by Christopher WREN, commences.
1676	Royal Greenwich observatory opened.
1677	Leeuwenhoek describes human spermatozoa.
1678	Huygens advances his wave theory of light.
1679	Hooke writes to Newton asking his opinion about planetary motion.
1684	Leibniz publishes his notations and findings on calculus. (He publishes three years earlier than Newton, leading to a dispute over who first invented calculus.)
1686	John RAY introduces the notion of species in *Historia plantarum*.

Time Line

1687	Newton outlines his laws of motion and gravity.
1704	Newton publishes *Opticks*, which sets forth the principles of light.
1705	Edmond **HALLEY** publishes his theory that comets travel on set paths and their appearances may be predicted.
1717	Daniel **FAHRENHEIT** makes a thermometer and introduces the Fahrenheit temperature scale.
1718	Halley measures proper motions of stars.
1723	Georg Ernst **STAHL** advances the phlogiston theory.
1730	Enlightenment period commences.
1734	René **RÉAUMUR** establishes the field of entomology by describing and classifying many types of insects.
1737	John **HARRISON** tests the first stable nautical chronometer, which allows for precise longitudinal determination at sea.
1738	Daniel **BERNOULLI** discusses his kinetic gas theory in *Hydrodynamica*.
1742	Anders **CELSIUS** develops the Celsius thermometer scale.
1745	Émilie du **CHATELET** begins a French translation of Newton's *Principia*.
1747	Carl **LINNEAUS** introduces binomial nomenclature for naming plants and animals and publishes his findings in 1751. Benjamin **FRANKLIN** invents the lightning rod.
1748	Maria **AGNESI** publishes *Istituzioni analitiche*, which focuses on algebra, mathematical analysis, and calculus.
1751	Franklin publishes his theories on electricity and conducts experiments on the electrification of clouds. Pierre **MAUPERTUIS** publishes his theories about heredity and his analysis of the transmission of dominant traits in humans. Jean le Rond **D'ALEMBERT** begins work on the *Encyclopédie*.
1755	Immanuel **KANT** advances his nebular hypothesis on the origins of the solar system.
1760	Bernoulli publishes a paper in which he calculates the probability of dying from smallpox for different age groups.
1764	James **WATT** develops an improved steam engine.
1772	Antoine-Laurent **LAVOISIER** experiments on combustion.
1774	Joseph **PRIESTLEY** discovers oxygen.
1780	Lazzaro **SPALLANZANI** publishes a work on digestion and the generation of plants and animals.
1781	William **HERSCHEL** discovers the planet Uranus.
1784	Henry **CAVENDISH** discovers that air contains water.
1785	Charles **COULOMB** announces his inverse square law of electrical attraction and repulsion.
1787	Lavoisier and his collaborators publish *Méthode de nomenclature chimique*.
1789	Lavoisier publishes *Traité élementaire de chimie*.
1793	Christian **SPRENGEL** discovers the role of insects in pollination.
1795	James **HUTTON** publishes *Theory of the Earth*.
1796	Pierre-Simon **LAPLACE** publishes his thoughts on celestial mechanics.
1798	Cavendish measures the density of the earth. Edward **JENNER** publishes research supporting the benefits of vaccination.

BIOGRAPHICAL PORTRAITS

Maria Gaetana
AGNESI

1718–1799
MATHEMATICS

* **mechanics** science that studies how energy and force affect objects

Maria Gaetana Agnesi, a person of remarkable intelligence and talent, was the first woman in the Western world to gain renown as a mathematician. Her primary achievement was a major book about algebra. Born in Milan, the daughter of a mathematics professor at the University of Bologna, Agnesi was tutored by distinguished professors. At age nine, she recited and published a lengthy speech encouraging higher education for women. She spoke half a dozen languages fluently by the age of 11. Notables and visiting scholars came to the Agnesi home to hear the young woman present papers on topics as varied as logic, mechanics*, chemistry, and botany. Afterward, Agnesi would defend her ideas in lively discussions. In 1738 she published 190 of her papers under the title *Propositiones philosophicae.*

Thereafter Agnesi withdrew from social life and devoted herself to mathematical study. Ten years later she published the *Istituzioni analitiche,* a clear, complete two-volume treatment of algebra and mathematical analysis that emphasized the new developments, such as calculus, that were occurring during Agnesi's lifetime. The work, which contained many original elements, was recognized as a masterpiece. Among the many honors Agnesi received were a gold medal and an appointment to teach at Bologna, both awarded by Pope Benedict XIV. Agnesi never actually taught but held the appointment as an honorary one until her father's death in 1752. After that time she gradually gave up scientific activity in favor of caring for her younger siblings, religious study, and social work.

Jean Le Rond d'
ALEMBERT

1717–1783
PHYSICS, MATHEMATICS

The career of the French mathematician Jean Le Rond d'Alembert was marked by a concern for reconciling the abstract realm of mathematics to the workings of the physical world. Unlike many of his colleagues, d'Alembert rejected the notion that an idea was valid if it could be proved mathematically. He believed that unless a mathematical model reflected actual events in the world, it was no better than abstract speculation. Consequently, his main contributions were to various fields of applied mathematics. His concern with the philosophy behind scientific knowledge is reflected in his introduction to the *Encyclopédie,* the attempt by French scholars of the mid-1700s to gather all of the world's knowledge into a single source.

Life and Career. D'Alembert was an illegitimate child whose mother, a Parisian society hostess, abandoned him as an infant. His father, a cavalry officer named Chevalier Destouches-Canon, found the child, placed him in a home, and provided for his education. However, he never acknowledged that Jean was his son. D'Alembert attended the Collège de Quatre-Nations, where he studied law and medicine before taking up a career in mathematics. When he was 22 he submitted his first paper to the French Académie des Sciences. The paper showed that with almost no scientific training, d'Alembert had familiarized himself with the work of such great scientists as Isaac NEWTON and Daniel BERNOULLI.

Two years later he was elected to the Académie des Sciences, and three years afterward he produced his most famous work, a study of the

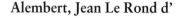

mechanics of solid bodies titled *Traité de dynamique* (Treatise on Mechanics). The book contains a statement of the famous "d'Alembert's principle," which is a generalization of Newton's third law of motion. In 1744 he published a companion work that discusses fluid mechanics, *Traité de l'équilibre et du mouvement des fluides* (Treatise on Equilibrium and the Movement of Fluids). Three years later he published a work that contained his most important purely mathematical contribution—the invention and development of partial differential equations*. He also wrote on many other topics dealing with the action of physical forces, including a paper on the cause of winds, a three-volume text on the motion of the moon, and a study of the wobble of the earth on its axis of rotation. In each of these works, d'Alembert was not just concerned with the accuracy of the mathematics that he applied to solve the problem; he also took care to ensure that his solution accounted for the observed motion of the phenomena.

During the 1740s d'Alembert became a member of the philosophes, an informal group of French philosophers and scientists who were critical of the current social and intellectual standards. Politically, the philosophe movement prepared the way for the French Revolution of the late 1700s. Scientifically, it challenged accepted ways of thinking about and searching for knowledge. When the philosophes decided to compile an encyclopedia, d'Alembert was chosen to write the introduction. His introduction was an expression of the ideas and intellectual program of the philosophes.

In 1757 d'Alembert ended his association with the *Encyclopédie* because of a controversy over an article he had written. His main work after this time was an eight-volume collection of mathematical essays, which appeared between 1761 and 1780. In 1764 the Prussian king Frederick the Great offered d'Alembert the presidency of the Prussian Academy, but he turned down the offer. D'Alembert remained in France and served as secretary of another scientific organization named the Académie Française until his death at the age of 66.

Philosophy and Accomplishments. D'Alembert embraced the new philosophy of sensationalism, according to which all knowledge comes from sense perception. Only those things that can be experienced by the five senses were valid considerations for the scientist. He rejected the notion that science could be based on intuition, speculation, or ideas not grounded in physical reality. His insistence on the importance of sense perception led him to challenge many concepts in physics and mechanics. Following Newton, his contemporaries based their theories of dynamics on the concept of force. However, because the nature and origins of force were unknown and probably unknowable, d'Alembert refused to employ it in his mechanics.

D'Alembert's greatest contribution to physics was the *Traité de dynamique*. In the introduction he states that he began by analyzing all the ideas that came to him to find a starting point for his work. He identified time and space as the only fundamental ideas and defined motion as a combination of these two ideas. He then applied these ideas to formulate his own three laws of motion as well as "d'Alembert's principle," a rule

* **differential equation** in calculus, an equation containing derivatives, which refers to the rate of change of the value of a mathematical function with respect to a change in the independent variable

Friend or Foe?

Although known for his good nature and sense of humor, d'Alembert feuded with many noted scholars, including his colleague at the Académie des Sciences, Alexis-Claude Clairaut. D'Alembert published some papers hastily to ensure that he, not Clairaut, received credit for developing the ideas first. His greatest rival, however, was the Swiss mathematician Leonhard Euler. When d'Alembert failed to win a competition sponsored by the Prussian Academy, he accused Euler of exerting influence on the judges to deny d'Alembert the prize. He later made peace with Euler by recommending that Euler be appointed president of the Prussian Academy.

* **inertia** property of matter by which it remains at rest or in uniform motion in a straight line unless acted on by an external force

for applying his laws to the motion of bodies. The first law of motion is, as Newton's is, the law of inertia*. The second is that of a parallelogram in motion. D'Alembert's third law of motion addresses the collision of bodies and states that no motion is lost even on impact. Although the velocity of each body may change on impact, the quantity of motion—the sum of the velocities and masses of the two bodies—remains constant. This law is similar to Newton's second law of motion, which deals with the conservation of energy, but omits a specific mention of mass. Newton's theory, on the other hand, incorporates a definition of mass, which is based on the work of the Dutch mathematician Christiaan HUYGENS. In the *Traité,* d'Alembert also explored the nature of matter, which he claimed consisted of perfectly hard atoms that could not penetrate each other. However, this conflicted with his laws of motion, which assumed that matter was somewhat elastic. He never resolved this conflict.

In the introduction to the *Encyclopédie,* d'Alembert outlines the philosophy of sensationalism and discusses knowledge from that perspective. However, his discussion is not confined to scientific knowledge. He states that even investigations of morality must be based on the perception of emotions and feelings that one can sense within oneself rather than on abstract ideas. He claims that knowledge is related to memory, reason, and imagination, with reason being the most important. However, anything that helps a person find the truth, even philosophical reflection, can be a useful tool. His role in changing the nature of scientific thought earned him a place among the leading figures of science in the 1700s.

Francis
BACON

1561–1626
PHILOSOPHY OF SCIENCE

Francis Bacon was a leading legal, literary, and political figure during the reigns of Queen Elizabeth I and King James I of England. He was also a philosopher of science who was deeply interested in the questions of how best to obtain knowledge of the natural world and how to use that knowledge to improve human life. Bacon's importance in the history of science rests on his theories about nature, his description of a proper scientific method, his scheme to organize the sciences, and his influence on scientific thought during the 1700s. One of Bacon's most influential works, *New Atlantis,* describes his vision of an ideal scientific society.

An Up-and-Down Career. Bacon's literary and philosophical pursuits were woven into a life devoted to public service, which in his day meant service to the royal court. Bacon was born in London into a family with court connections. His father, Sir Nicholas Bacon, was lord keeper of the great seal, and Bacon prepared and trained for similar duties. He attended Cambridge University from 1573 to 1575 and then went to France as a member of the staff of the English ambassador there. After the death of his father, Bacon returned to England.

Bacon spent the next several years acquiring legal training, becoming a barrister* in 1582. In the years that followed, he advanced steadily in the legal profession. At the same time he served as a member of Parliament and tried to win the queen's favor, in the hope that this would result

* **barrister** in the English legal system, a lawyer who argues cases in court

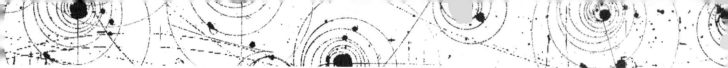

Bacon, Francis

Francis Bacon's place in the history of science rests on his natural philosophy, his philosophy of scientific method, and his projects for the organization of the principles and methods of scientific inquiry. His knowledge and philosophy were a great influence on the science and scientists of the 1600s.

in the appointment to a desirable post. In 1603, when James succeeded Elizabeth on the throne, Bacon was among the 300 men who received a knighthood.

At first Bacon's fortunes seemed to rise under James. In 1607 the king appointed Bacon solicitor general, one of the highest legal posts in the land. The appointment was a reward for Bacon's efforts to persuade Parliament to unite England with Scotland, as the king wished to do. Thereafter, Bacon's progress halted for a few years. Bacon blamed this bad turn on the jealous manipulations of his cousin, the earl of Salisbury, who was the king's chief minister. After his cousin's death in 1612, Bacon called attention to himself with papers on political issues. Bacon's position on these topics favored royal rights and privileges. Within a few years Bacon was made keeper of the great seal and lord chancellor of England. He also received the titles Baron of Verulam and Viscount of St. Albans.

Bacon's downfall came in 1621, when he was charged with accepting bribes. Always careless with money, Bacon admitted that he had received gifts from people involved in legal cases but denied that the gifts had influenced his judgments. This excuse did not save Bacon from a harsh penalty. He was stripped of his offices (but not of his titles), banned from Parliament and the royal court, fined a large sum, and imprisoned in the Tower of London for a short time. He spent his final years living near St. Albans, writing on political and scientific topics, and trying—with little luck—to regain the king's favor. During his retirement Bacon wrote *New Atlantis*, an idealistic vision of the organization of science that anticipated the scientific societies founded later in the 1600s.

Bacon's Grand Plan. Bacon lived and worked at the same time as many major scientists, including physicist Galileo GALILEI, astronomer Johannes KEPLER, and anatomist William HARVEY. Yet he was somewhat isolated from the developments they represented. Although his knowledge of the sciences came largely from literary sources, his most important original thought was that heat was a form of motion. Bacon taught that heat is caused by the motion of particles in matter and that experiments could not only show the existence of such particles but also suggest how their shapes and motions might explain the observable properties of matter. Despite this achievement, his principal interest was in natural philosophy, which is the process of forming theories about the natural world, and he had very clear ideas about how those theories should be formed.

Rather than focusing on a particular scientific discipline or area of study, Bacon took a large view, concerning himself with the organizing principles and underlying methods of science itself. To this end, he laid out a comprehensive work called the *Great Instauration* (an instauration is a restoration after a period of decline, or the act of establishing something), which contained a plan to revise the methods and goals of scientific inquiry. Although Bacon never completed this ambitious work, it provided a framework of theory for all of his scientific writings.

The *Great Instauration* was to consist of six parts. The first was a new division or organization of all sciences and fields of knowledge. Bacon accomplished this in *The Advancement of Learning*, published in 1605 and republished with additional material in 1623. The second part of the project was a description of what Bacon believed to be the proper method of acquiring knowledge about nature. He set forth this method in 1620 in the *Novum organum*, the work that Bacon regarded as his most significant contribution to science. The rest of the *Great Instauration* was to have consisted of collections of observed facts about nature, examples of how to draw conclusions from those facts, and programs for applying Bacon's methods to the realm of discovery and inquiry. However, Bacon never completed this grand plan.

In the two versions of *The Advancement of Learning*, Bacon organized knowledge, philosophy, and the sciences into a system. Although he saw no conflict between religion and science, Bacon recognized two fundamentally different kinds of knowledge: knowledge obtained from God through divine revelation and knowledge obtained from the senses. He believed that human inquiry was concerned with knowledge obtained from the senses. Bacon divided this type of knowledge into three categories: natural theology, or knowledge of God through the study of nature; natural philosophy, or the study of the principles that underlie the world and all the sciences; and the sciences of man, such as medicine, logic, morality, and the arts.

The centerpiece of Bacon's view of science was natural philosophy, which he further subdivided. One branch, natural science, concerned the formulation of theories to explain the natural world. The other branch dealt with practical uses of science to improve the human condition. Bacon

A Fatal Experiment

Bacon's fall from power depressed him and wore down his health, but it was his scientific curiosity that killed him. In March 1626 he was driving in his carriage near Highgate, north of London. Snow lay on the ground, and suddenly Bacon was seized with curiosity about whether snow would slow the process of putrefaction, or decomposition, in a dead animal. Because he approved of practical experimentation to discover the secrets of nature, he stopped the carriage, bought a hen, and filled its body with snow. Unfortunately, because of the chill, he became ill with bronchitis and died the following month.

* **Renaissance** period that marked the beginnings of modern science and the rebirth of interest in classical art and literature that occurred in Europe from the late 1300s through the 1500s

called this branch natural magic, but the term *magic* as he used it has no connection to its occult meanings. According to Bacon, natural magic, a concept that emerged during the Renaissance*, referred to the power that humans would acquire if they mastered complete knowledge of the natural world. He compared such knowledge and power to the state of Adam and Eve in the Garden of Eden before the Fall.

Bacon's Scientific Method. Once Bacon had organized knowledge and all fields of study into a system, he tried to lay new foundations for science in the *Novum organum,* which outlines his method of inquiry.

In the *Novum organum,* Bacon describes the causes of human error and false reasoning and states that both must be discarded before people can reason correctly. Bacon used the term *idols* to refer to these mental errors and pitfalls and listed four major types. Idols of the tribe are general faults shared by most people, such as the tendency to interpret natural events in terms of human motives and feelings. Idols of the cave are the particular interests and weaknesses of individuals that color how they see the world. Idols of the marketplace are errors caused by careless, vague, or imprecise use of language. Idols of the theater are philosophical systems and general beliefs received from the past. Bacon maintained that once the mind is free from these mistaken ways of thinking, it is open to true perceptions of nature.

Bacon also proposed that scientific inquiry should proceed through inductive reasoning, in which general conclusions are based on facts and observations. He also rejected the authority of many ancient philosophers, especially the deductive* logic of Aristotle and the schools of thought that developed around his writings. He pointed out the pitfalls of basing generalizations on too little information and of uncritically accepting generalizations just because they are familiar or seem obvious. He claimed that inquiry should begin with tables, or lists, of things that have properties in common and things that lack those qualities. From evaluating these tables, people would move up a ladder of reasoning to arrive at larger categories and conclusions. He believed that by this method, people would gradually accumulate well-founded knowledge and eventually understand the principles, theories, and laws of nature.

* **deductive** referring to the process of reaching a conclusion by reasoning, especially from general or universal principles

Bacon's Influence. Bacon was a major influence on the first generation of British experimental scientists, especially because of his claim that nature could be controlled by the practice of science. From his comments, such as "We need to put nature to the test" and "We need to wrest the secrets from nature," it is apparent that he regarded nature as something to be manipulated and not merely observed or worshiped. To Bacon the goal of science was not merely a passive understanding of nature but the practical application of knowledge for the good of humankind. He believed that using the system of knowledge he had mapped and the method of inquiry he had outlined, the work of science could be completed if only enough human and financial resources were devoted to the plan.

Describing a scientific college in *New Atlantis,* Bacon expressed his view of science in one sentence: "The End [purpose] of our Foundation is the knowledge of Causes, and secret motions of things; and the enlarging of the bounds of Human Empire, to the effecting of all things possible." Through this belief in science's ability to enlarge the human condition and to accomplish "all things possible," more than through theories or experiments, Bacon inspired the scientists of the later 1600s.

Joseph
BANKS

1743–1820

BOTANY

* **naturalist** student of natural history, the systematic study of natural objects, especially in their natural settings

Joseph Banks was one of the most influential men in English science during the late 1700s and early 1800s. His importance lay not in his scientific writings, which were few and insignificant, but in his role as an organizer, supporter, and promoter of scientific activity in general. As a botanist he established a major collection of plants. As president of England's Royal Society from 1778 to 1820 he encouraged close contacts among members of the international scientific community.

Banks was born in London into a family that had been prosperous and well known for several generations. He eventually inherited a sizable fortune that he used freely to fund scientific projects. He grew up at the family's country home in Lincolnshire and attended college at Christ Church, Oxford, although he left before receiving a degree. His education followed the typical upper-class pattern of his day, with emphasis on Greek and Latin. However, one summer evening when he was 15, Banks was so struck by the beauty of nature that he began to collect plants and study botany.

In 1766 Banks traveled to Labrador and Newfoundland to collect plants. The samples he brought back became the start of a botanical collection called the Banks Herbarium. Several years later he set out as ship's naturalist* on an English expedition to the South Pacific led by Captain James Cook. At his own expense Banks arranged a scientific party of eight well-equipped men to collect samples, make observations, and record the scientific discoveries of the three-year voyage. The more than 800 previously unknown plant and animal specimens that they brought back to England made Banks's reputation as a naturalist.

After Banks was introduced to King George III in 1771, the two men—both interested in plants and agriculture—became friends. Banks persuaded the king to turn Kew Gardens into a botanical research center. The king's friendship was undoubtedly one reason Banks was made president of the Royal Society. Banks considered the presidency the greatest honor of his lifetime and faithfully carried out his duties, presiding over 417 meetings. He was concerned about maintaining open and cooperative communications between English and French scientists after the two nations went to war in 1793.

Banks remained interested and involved in scientific pursuits until his death. Always modest, he called himself a botanizer rather than a botanist and would have been the first to admit that his true contribution to science was in service to the scientific community rather than in original discoveries. His extensive scientific library and his immense collection of specimens, always available to fellow scientists for research, are part of the collections of the British Museum.

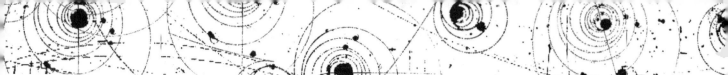

Daniel
BERNOULLI

1700–1782

MATHEMATICS, PHYSICS

Daniel Bernoulli made important contributions in the fields of medicine and anatomy, but his chief interests were mechanics, physics, and mathematics. He did a great deal of work the areas of statistics and probability as well.

* **mechanics** science that studies how energy and force affect objects

* **physiology** science that deals with the functions of living organisms and their parts

Daniel Bernoulli was a multitalented scientist who published important papers in subjects as diverse as the mechanics of breathing and the expected duration of the average marriage. Although he received his formal training in anatomy and medicine, his most important contributions were in the fields of mechanics* and physics. His interests ranged over many scientific disciplines, and his accomplishments led to the development of devices that solved many practical problems of his time.

Life and Career. Bernoulli was born into a respected family in Basel, Switzerland. His father, Johann, was a professor of mathematics at the University of Basel and his older brother, Nikolaus II, was a mathematician. As a young man Daniel received instruction in mathematics from his father and brother. After Bernoulli earned his master's degree at the age of 16, his father tried to find him a position as a commercial apprentice. When that venture proved unsuccessful, Johann allowed his son to study medicine at Basel. Daniel continued his medical education at universities in Heidelberg and Strasbourg. He later returned to Basel, where he earned his doctorate in 1721 and applied for the position of professor of anatomy and botany. However, he failed in his effort to win that position as well as in a later attempt to obtain a professorship in logic. Unsuccessful in landing a teaching position in Basel, Bernoulli left for Venice, Italy, to continue his studies in medicine. He hoped to stay in Italy to work, but he contracted a serious illness that ended those plans.

In 1724 Bernoulli published *Exercitationes mathematicae*, a book that brought him widespread recognition and an invitation to teach at the St. Petersburg Academy in Russia. The following year, the Paris Academy awarded Bernoulli the first of ten prizes he would receive from that institution. In his winning paper he discussed the best shape for hourglasses filled with sand and water as well as the best way to install them.

After his return to Basel from Venice, Bernoulli left for Russia with his brother Nikolaus. His time in St. Petersburg was perhaps the most creative period of his life, but it was not altogether a happy one. The climate was severely cold, and his brother died suddenly. While still in Russia, Bernoulli applied three times for a professorship at Basel, but he was turned down each time. In 1732 he was finally awarded the chair of botany and anatomy, and he returned to Switzerland the following year. On his trip home he toured much of Europe with his younger brother, Johann II, and was warmly received by scholars throughout the continent.

At Basel, Bernoulli lectured in medicine and botany but continued to publish papers in the fields of mathematics and mechanics. He eventually gave up his lectures in botany for those in physiology*, and in 1750 he was appointed to the chair in physics. He occupied that position for almost 30 years, presenting lectures to packed audiences on his impressive experiments. Bernoulli died in 1782 and was buried near his home.

Important Works. Bernoulli made his earliest scientific contributions in the fields of medicine and anatomy, but his chief interests were always mechanics and physics. He first explored these subjects as they related to anatomy, but later he focused on problems dealing with pure mechanical and physical phenomena. He also did a great deal of work in mathematics, including the areas of statistics and probability.

Anatomy and Medicine. Bernoulli's dissertation*, titled *De respiratione* (On Respiration), examined the mechanics of breathing. While in St. Petersburg he published a mechanical theory of muscular contraction that challenged the view that muscular contraction was caused by the fermentation of corpuscles in the blood. He also helped identify where the optic nerve enters the eye's blind spot and its shape at that location. After returning to Basel he gave a lecture discussing the mechanical work done by the heart. He later developed a method to correctly calculate the amount of work performed by the heart. Bernoulli also made significant contributions to understanding the physiology of work and determining the maximum amount of work a person can perform over a specified period.

Mechanics and Physics. Although Newton's famous book *Principia* covered the subject of mechanics, it was understood only by those who had mastered calculus*, recently independently invented by Newton and Wilhelm Leibniz. In 1738 Bernoulli founded the modern science of hydrodynamics* with the publication of *Hydrodynamica*. The book explores the reactions of fluids under varying conditions and the properties and motions of liquids and gases, also known as his "kinetic* gas theory." Bernoulli's work on gases anticipated major discoveries in this field by 100 years. The work also explores the principles behind machinery, such as pumps and lifting devices; establishes a formula that relates air pressure to altitude; and calculates the velocity, duration, and force generated by water gushing through a small opening. His other explorations in physics and mechanics included extensive work with vibrating bodies, most notably an analysis of the movement of the strings of musical instruments.

Mathematics and Statistics. Early in his career Bernoulli published a paper on the probabilities involved in the card game called faro. Although the paper contributed little new to the field of statistics, it showed his interest in the subject. He later produced some original works that were useful to economists and the insurance industry. His most important contribution was a paper that contains an unusual mathematical evaluation of capital gains* and a discussion of the moral value of income. In its basic form the theory states that the larger a person's fortune, the smaller the moral value of a given increase in that fortune. Bernoulli later looked at two other interesting statistical problems. In 1760 he published a paper in which he calculated the probability of dying from smallpox for different age groups. In this work, Bernoulli argued that if a person took an inoculation* against smallpox, his or her average life expectancy would increase by three years. In another paper he attempted to determine the expected average duration of marriage for people of various ages.

Evaluating Bernoulli's Work. Bernoulli's publications in statistics highlight his gift for finding practical applications of his studies. This is also evident in many of the prizes he won from the Paris Academy. These

* **dissertation** lengthy formal discourse presented by a student as the final requirement for receiving a doctoral degree

* **calculus** advanced form of mathematics that involves computing quantities that change as functions of different variables

* **hydrodynamics** scientific study of the motion of liquids

* **kinetic** relating to the motion of material bodies and to the force and energy of those bodies

* **capital gain** increase in the value of an asset, such as real estate, between the time of its purchase and the time of its resale

* **inoculation** treatment to protect someone from disease, sometimes by injecting the person with a bacterium or virus to produce a mild version of the disease

Bernoulli vs. Bernoulli

Although Daniel Bernoulli was highly respected by the scientific community, his father, Johann, worked to undermine his reputation. When Daniel published *Hydrodynamica* in 1738, his father published a similar work, *Hydraulica,* the same year. Moreover, to ensure priority for himself, Johann falsely dated his own work 1732. This was not the first such incident. Four years earlier, the two had shared first prize in a contest sponsored by the Paris Academy of Sciences, but Johann attempted to deny Daniel credit for his part in the work.

applications included the best practical design for an anchor, the best way to reduce sources of error in constructing a compass, a method for determining the time of day at sea when the horizon is not visible, the effects of forces other than wind on a ship's movement, and how to reduce the pitch and roll of ships at sea. Because he explored so many disciplines, he was often unable to complete projects he started. Still, his contributions and his ability to apply his findings to practical problems make Bernoulli one of the truly outstanding figures in the history of science.

Jakob BERNOULLI

1654–1705

MATHEMATICS, MECHANICS, ASTRONOMY

* **theology** study of religion

* **mechanics** science that studies how energy and force affect objects

* **calculus** advanced form of mathematics that involves computing quantities that change as functions of different variables

---

The Swiss mathematician Jakob Bernoulli, also known as Jacques Bernoulli, developed no far-reaching or influential theories, but he was noted for his clever solutions to mathematical problems. His most original work contributed to the theory of probability.

Bernoulli was born in Basel, Switzerland, to a prosperous and well-established family of merchants. His father was a druggist and member of the town council. Bernoulli received a master's degree in philosophy in 1671 and went on to study theology*, and against his father's wishes, mathematics and astronomy as well. In the late 1670s and early 1680s, Bernoulli traveled to France, the Netherlands, and England, studying the work of the leading thinkers of the day and meeting scientists such as Robert HOOKE and Robert BOYLE.

After returning to Basel, Bernoulli gave lectures, accompanied by experiments, on such subjects as the mechanics* of liquids and solids. He contributed articles on science and mathematics to journals. In 1687 the university made Bernoulli a professor of mathematics. By order of their father, his brother Johann studied medicine at the university, but Jakob secretly tutored him in mathematics. The two studied and worked together, but as Johann's reputation as a mathematician rose, their shared quality of competitiveness made them rivals. One of their main disputes involved finding the shortest path between two points on a particle moving solely under the influence of gravity. The dispute resulted in the calculus* of variations, a field that the Swiss mathematician Leonhard EULER later refined.

Jakob's contributions to astronomy, mechanics, and engineering include theories about comets and gravity, a study of the use of sliding weights to balance drawbridges, and a study of the shape and tension of watch springs. He is, however, remembered as a mathematician. He mastered the calculus that had been developed by Wilhelm LEIBNIZ and solved several mathematical problems that were current among the experts of the time, such as Leibniz and Christiaan HUYGENS. One problem that he solved in 1696 is sometimes called the Bernoullian differential equation. He popularized calculus by showing how it could be applied to several areas of mathematics.

Bernoulli left an incomplete work called the *Ars conjectandi,* which was published in 1713, several years after his death. It contains his contributions to the theory of probability, the branch of mathematics that calculates the likelihood of given outcomes within sets of possible outcomes. The book includes a knowledgeable commentary on some of Huygens's work; a discussion of the theory of combinations; examples of the expectation of profit in various games; philosophical thoughts about probability, necessity, and chance; and a detailed discussion of a game called *jeu de paume*, an early form of tennis. It also contains a statement of Bernoulli's discovery of what is now known as the law of large numbers.

Johann BERNOULLI

1667–1748

MATHEMATICS

* **differential calculus** advanced method of mathematics that finds the rate of change of functions with respect to their variables

Johann Bernoulli, an accomplished mathematician, was considered the foremost mathematician in Europe, especially after the death of Isaac NEWTON in 1727. Bernoulli was especially adept at explaining complex mathematics and solving difficult problems. He was the younger brother of the mathematician Jakob BERNOULLI and the father of Daniel BERNOULLI, who became a highly distinguished scientist.

Johann was born in Basel, the tenth child of a merchant father who was disappointed that Johann was not suited to a career in business. In 1683 the young man enrolled in the University of Basel, where Jakob, 12 years older, was a lecturer. A few years later Johann began studying medicine, but at the same time his brother privately tutored him in mathematics. The two brothers were the first to fully understand the form of mathematics known as differential calculus* that Wilhelm LEIBNIZ had presented. In 1691 Johann released his first independently published work, a solution to a problem that his brother had posed. The result placed him in the front rank of mathematicians with Newton, Leibniz, and Christiaan HUYGENS.

In 1691 Bernoulli traveled to Paris, where he met and impressed the leading thinkers of the day. For a fee, he tutored a French mathematician; their correspondence later became the basis for the first textbook in differential calculus. Bernoulli, a diligent letter writer, wrote more than 2,500 letters to more than 100 fellow scholars, including Leibniz.

In 1695, through the influence of Huygens, Bernoulli was appointed professor of mathematics at Groningen in the Netherlands. By this time relations between the Bernoulli brothers had soured. Throughout the 1690s Bernoulli published papers in learned journals and solved some difficult mathematical problems. One problem, however, baffled both Bernoulli brothers. Eventually Johann's brilliant student Leonhard EULER solved this problem, which involved the summation of reciprocal squares.

In 1696 Johann posed a mathematical problem and invited "the shrewdest mathematicians of all the world" to solve it. Leibniz, who solved it on the day he received it, correctly predicted that only four other people would do so: Newton, the two Bernoullis, and the French mathematician that Johann Bernoulli had tutored. This problem also publicly demonstrated the difference in the talents of the Bernoulli brothers. Jakob solved it with a painstaking, somewhat awkward analysis, but Johann's solution, although simpler and more ingenious, was less thorough.

After Jakob died in 1705, Johann returned to Basel to take over his brother's position as professor of mathematics. When Leibniz and Newton became embroiled in an argument over who had first formulated calculus,

Bernoulli supported Leibniz. His criticisms of some of Newton's ideas delayed the acceptance of Newtonian physics on the European continent.

Once established in Basel, Bernoulli turned his attention to applied mathematics and astronomy. In 1714 he published his only book, a treatise on navigation at sea, and in the 1720s and 1730s he wrote prize-winning papers on the motions of the planets.

Joseph BLACK

1729–1799

CHEMISTRY, PHYSICS, MEDICINE

* **latent heat** heat, usually undetectable, given off or absorbed during a process

* **specific heat** heat in calories required to raise the temperature of one gram of a particular substance by one degree Celsius

* **dissertation** lengthy formal discourse presented by a student as the final requirement for receiving a doctoral degree

The English chemist Joseph Black is best known for his discovery of carbon dioxide and his experiments that led to the discovery of latent* and specific heat*. Black was a true experimental chemist who cautioned his colleagues to reject speculation as a basis for forming scientific theories. The only way to find true answers, he said, was to perform experiments. Black's experimentation resulted in his two great discoveries and formed the foundation of his popular chemistry lectures at the University of Edinburgh.

Life and Career. Black was born in Bordeaux, France, but his parents were Scots by birth. His dual heritage was particularly appropriate, given the role that French and Scottish scientists were to play in advancing the young field of chemistry during Black's lifetime. Black, the fourth of 12 children, received his earliest education from his mother. He was sent to Ireland at age 12 to study Latin and Greek, and four years later he enrolled at the University of Glasgow in Scotland. Because he chose to enter the medical profession, Black studied anatomy and chemistry. He was particularly taken with the chemistry lectures of a professor named William Cullen, who later became his lifelong friend.

In 1752 Black transferred to the University of Edinburgh, where he received his doctorate two years later. His dissertation* was based on a series of experiments he had performed that led to his discovery of fixed air, or carbon dioxide. The following year he described his experiments to the Philosophical Society of Edinburgh, and the year after that they appeared in the society's publication *Essays and Observations*.

That same year, Black's friend Cullen moved from Glasgow to Edinburgh to take the position of professor of chemistry at the university. Black filled the professorship that Cullen had left in Glasgow, and he remained there for the next ten years. Black's course was immensely popular, attracting students who had no professional interest in chemistry. Black also ran a busy medical practice and assumed many administrative duties at the university. It was during this time that he discovered latent and specific heat, although he never published the experiments or his results.

In 1766, when Cullen retired as professor of chemistry at Edinburgh, Black was invited to take over that position. At Edinburgh, Black concentrated on his teaching duties, delivering more than 100 lectures each year. Black never married, but he was fond of company and socialized with friends and colleagues. He formed a dining club with his colleagues, and Scottish industrialists often joined them at dinner, during which time they would discuss the role of science in the development of new technologies.

Black, who suffered from poor health his entire life, stopped teaching when he was 69. He died three years later.

Discovery of Carbon Dioxide. Black's first major discovery resulted from his investigations into the medical properties of a solution of quicklime known as limewater. This substance, which had been proven effective in dissolving kidney stones, also aroused the interest of two of Black's teachers, Robert Whytt and Charles Alston, but the two professors disagreed on why quicklime is caustic*. Whytt believed that when quicklime was calcinated (heated at a very high temperature), it became caustic because it absorbed a fiery matter produced by the heat. Alston performed experiments that showed that this was not the case, and he argued that the causticity of quicklime was a property of the lime itself. Black wanted to solve this dilemma, but because he did not want to alienate either of his professors, he chose to work with another alkaline substance called magnesia alba (magnesium carbonate).

Black treated lime and magnesia alba with various acids and noted that magnesia alba effervesced* strongly when treated with acid, but lime did not. When he calcinated magnesia alba he found that, unlike quicklime, it was not caustic. Intrigued, he weighed a quantity of magnesia alba and heated it until it produced a whitish liquid and a substance called magnesia usta. He weighed the magnesia usta and the white liquid and found that together they were much lighter than the original weight of the magnesia alba. Because he knew that some alkaline substances contain air, he assumed that the difference in weight was due to loss of air. However, when he treated the magnesia usta with acid, it did not effervesce. Magnesia alba apparently lost its air when combined with acids, while magnesia usta lost its air through strong heating before combining with acids.

Black then mixed quicklime with alkali and produced a white chalk-like substance that also effervesced when treated with acid. Something in the alkali must have caused the chalklike substance to effervesce. The substance also gave off a type of air that extinguished a candle and a piece of burning paper. Other experiments showed that this air was exhaled during breathing and that it could not support life. Black called this substance fixed air because it was fixed, or trapped, in the alkaline substances he tested. The substance is known today as carbon dioxide. Later experiments by French chemists confirmed that fixed air was just one of the components of common air, which was composed of many other airs or gases. These studies also proved that air was not a basic element, as previously believed, but one that was composed of other substances.

Latent and Specific Heat. Black's experiments on heat stemmed from the observations of the German scientist Daniel FAHRENHEIT that water could be cooled below the freezing point without turning to ice. However, if the water was shaken, it froze suddenly. Because Black understood that the shaking motion generated heat, he realized that a large transfer of heat was necessary to cause the water to change its state from liquid to solid. The heat in the water was concealed and went undetected by a thermometer. Black called it latent heat and set out to measure it. He first showed

* **caustic** capable of destroying by chemical action; corrosive

* **effervesce** to emit small bubbles of gas

Black's Attractive Theory

One of Black's most interesting ideas was the theory of chemical affinity, which states that chemical reactions result from the attraction between certain chemicals. He held that simple affinities, or attractions, are produced by heat and that double attractions occur when chemicals are mixed together in a solution. Modern chemistry recognizes this affinity as the tendency of molecules of different substances to share their atomic particles, such as electrons. Although Black did not explicitly tie his theory to a belief in the doctrine of atoms, he nevertheless provided the theoretical basis for the modern understanding of chemical affinity.

that latent heat played a part not only in forming ice but also in melting it. He then demonstrated that it played a part in vaporizing water as well.

Black placed water in a tin container and heated it to 50°F. He then continued to heat that water until it began to boil, recording the amount of time this took. He continued to heat the boiling water and measured how long it took the water to boil away completely, or vaporize. After conducting three such experiments, he calculated the amount of heat absorbed during the process of vaporization. He determined that this amount of heat would have raised the temperature of the water to 810°F, if it were possible to do so without vaporizing all of the water. From these experiments he determined that the latent heat of vaporization of water measured 450 calories per gram. In later experiments he came much closer to the currently accepted figure of 539.1 calories per gram.

Another of Fahrenheit's observations led to Black's discovery of specific heat. When Fahrenheit mixed equal parts of mercury and water, each at a different temperature, he found that the temperature of the water had a far greater effect on the final temperature of the mixture. Black realized that the mercury must store less heat per volume than an equal amount of water. He concluded that all substances store different amounts of heat, which he called specific heat. Working with several colleagues, Black mixed different substances with water and measured the amount of heat each substance transferred to the water. These experiments provided the first measures of the specific heats of any substances. Black never published the results of these investigations, but his colleagues continued to work with specific heat and published the results after Black's death.

Giovanni Alfonso
BORELLI

1608–1679

ASTRONOMY, PHYSICS, ANATOMY

* **physiology** science that deals with the functions of living organisms and their parts

* **humanist** referring to humanism, a cultural and philosophical movement to revive ancient Greek and Roman works and to value individuals' capacity for reason and dignity during their earthly life

* **theology** study of religion

* **Renaissance** period that marked the beginnings of modern science and the rebirth of interest in classical art and literature that occurred in Europe from the late 1300s through the 1500s

Giovanni Alfonso Borelli was an Italian scientist and professor whose enthusiastic mind led him through several fields of study. Although his work was often interrupted by political and religious conflicts, he made important advances in astronomy, physics, and animal physiology*, with fascinating side projects to study epidemics and volcanoes. Despite his fame and expertise, he died in poverty as an elementary school teacher.

Born into Conflict. The Italy of Borelli's childhood was not yet a nation but a group of independent provinces ruled by aristocrats. The region was a stronghold of Catholicism, and dissent was viewed with suspicion. For instance, the astronomer Galileo GALILEI was condemned for defending his theory that the earth is in motion because it contradicted Catholic doctrine.

At the time, Naples was occupied by Catholic Spain, and a Spanish guard named Miguel Alonso married a local woman; the couple's son, born in 1608, was Giovanni Borelli. In 1614 Alonso was stationed at the castle where a friar named Tommaso Campanella was imprisoned for defending humanist* ideas and for attempting to reconcile Christian theology* with Renaissance* science. Sometime after that, the young Borelli came to know Campanella, and his brother became one of Campanella's disciples. It may also have been Campanella who introduced Borelli to Benedetto Castelli, an astronomer in Rome who became Borelli's first professional mentor.

In his book *De motu animalium,* Giovanni Borelli discussed the movements of humans and animals with geometric and mechanical descriptions. He explained muscular action and the movement of bones in terms of levers as seen in this engraving from his book.

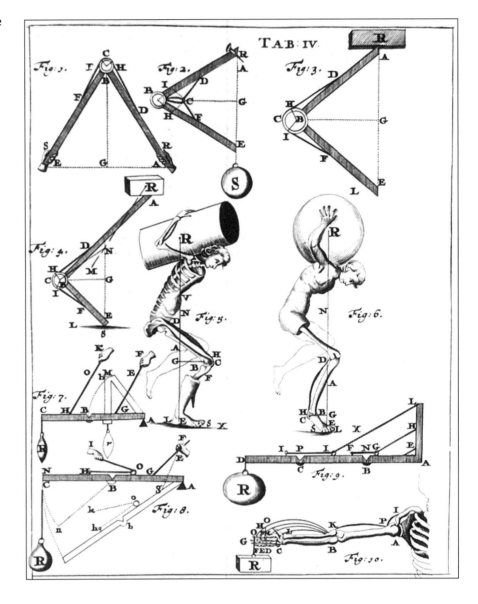

Making a Name in Sicily. Along with Evangelista TORRICELLI, Borelli studied astronomy and other sciences with Castelli in Rome. In about 1635 Castelli recommended Borelli for a position teaching mathematics in Messina, Sicily. Borelli got the job. He quickly fell in with a group of nobles and merchants who were agitating to improve Sicily's political and intellectual life, despite Spanish rule. They formed an academy, where Borelli gained respect and admiration. He was sent to other Italian cities to recruit professors, and he began to make a reputation for himself throughout Italy. Meanwhile, he published two works, one concerning geometry and the other concerning the outbreak of fevers in Sicily. Borelli proposed that the fevers were caused not by the weather or by astrological influences but rather by a chemical that entered the body.

Professorship in Pisa. In 1656, in his late 40s, Borelli was selected to be chair of mathematics at the University of Pisa. He was not greeted kindly at first: Students shouted catcalls to interrupt his first few lectures, which were long-winded, dull, and lacking in grace or eloquence. He was also known as a difficult man to get along with. But he soon won a dazzling reputation for his learning and skill as a scientist.

One of his first projects at Pisa, a rewrite of Euclid's *Elements* in a clear and concise form, was very well received. Borelli's pursuit of ancient Greek mathematics also involved him in a collaboration to revive the works of Apollonius of Perga, several of whose books existed only in Arabic versions. With the help of a scholar who knew Arabic, Borelli translated the Arabic version into Latin and published it.

Borelli moved quickly to help establish a new academy, which grew out of an informal circle of scientists at the courts of Prince Leopold and Grand Duke Ferdinand II, two powerful Tuscan nobles. The new academy, the Accademia del Cimento, included many distinguished scientists, such as Francesco REDI and Niels STENSEN. The group soon became known for publishing its reports collectively, without acknowledging individual members.

Another project presented itself in 1664, when a comet blazed prominently in the sky. Borelli took up detailed astronomical observations for more than two months. Some of his conclusions about the structure of the solar system went against the accepted doctrine, so he published his report under a fictitious name. The following year Borelli established an observatory on a nearby hill and studied the moons of Jupiter. He noted that Jupiter exerts a gravitational pull on its satellites, acting on its moons the way the sun acts on the planets. Like Galileo, Borelli viewed Jupiter and its satellites as a possible model for the solar system with the sun at its center. However, Borelli had to hide this implication by pretending to focus solely on Jupiter.

Yet all these projects sometimes seemed like mere distractions from his favored endeavor—a laboratory in his own home for the study of animal anatomy, founded almost immediately after he arrived in Pisa. Together with many talented students, including Marcello MALPIGHI, Borelli studied the movements of animals in relation to many other topics in physics and chemistry. Borelli explained muscular action and the movement of bones in terms of levers. However, he extended these mechanical explanations to the internal organs, such as the heart, stomach, and lungs, overlooking the chemical action that occurs in these organs. Consequently, his treatise on the movement of animals—*De motu animalium* (On the Movement of Animals)—is considered misguided.

Borelli also conducted years of research into gravity, magnetism, fluids, vibrations, pendulums, the properties of water, the process of fermentation, and more. Perhaps it is not surprising that he was unwilling to publish this work—which he considered his most important—under the anonymous umbrella of the Cimento. In 1667 Borelli published some of his results independently and left Pisa for his old job in Messina.

Politics and Poverty. Nearing the age of 60, Borelli returned to Messina, where he soon found a new area of inquiry. The volcano Mount Etna erupted in 1669, and he made a close study, even climbing to the volcano's rim. Borelli also returned to local politics, which was reaching a boiling point. The meeting house for his old academy was burned down in 1672, and he was declared a rebel by the Spanish authorities. Borelli fled to Rome two years before Messina broke into open revolt against the Spanish.

In Rome Borelli renewed his many professional relations and for a time enjoyed the patronage of Queen Christina. But this arrangement did not provide a sufficient salary, and Borelli wrote to an old colleague named Gian Domenico CASSINI, who was flourishing in the royal court of Paris. Borelli hoped to join Cassini there but soon felt too old to travel. A robbery left him without any possessions, and he was forced to take shelter with a local church. Borelli earned his keep by teaching mathematics in the church's elementary school. Late in 1679 Christina at last agreed to finance the publication of *De motu animalium*. Sadly, Borelli died on December 31, and a priest at the church carried out the publication over the next two years.

Robert BOYLE

1627–1691

CHEMISTRY, PHYSICS, NATURAL PHILOSOPHY

Robert Boyle was one of the most original scientific thinkers of the 1600s. He combined chemistry and physics by emphasizing that the properties of the individual particles of matter were responsible for the way matter itself behaved. He made himself an expert in creating and conducting bold experiments in chemistry and physics and made a powerful argument for rational methods of scientific work. Boyle also devoted himself to the meeting of science and religion, promoting his vision of a God who set up the universe to operate according to natural laws.

Becoming a Scientist. Boyle was born into a world of aristocratic privilege and wealth and so was able to pursue his education and scientific work without financial worries. His father was an earl, and the family was related to almost all the noble Anglo-Irish families that presided over England's rule in Ireland. Though Boyle was the youngest son among 14 children, his education was not neglected; he had private tutors, attended the academy at Eton, and traveled to the European continent, where he learned practical mathematics and other subjects. He also exposed himself to recent advances in science, such as the work of Galileo GALILEI.

Boyle returned home in the 1640s, when war broke out between England and Ireland as well as civil war between the Crown and Parliament in England. Boyle apparently sympathized with Parliament. Meanwhile, he picked up an interest in agriculture and medicine, which led him to study chemistry for the preparation of drugs. He mastered the subject while still in his 20s. At the time, however, chemistry was still tied to medicine and hindered by historical associations with mysticism and alchemy*. Nevertheless, Boyle developed a conviction that chemistry was an important physical science. He took this belief to Oxford University in 1656, where he worked with leaders of English science, such as John WALLIS.

The Study of Air and Water. Although Boyle was a chemist, his first great contribution was in pneumatics*. After learning that the German engineer Otto von GUERICKE had invented an air pump, Boyle used another

* **alchemy** medieval form of chemical science, especially one that sought to turn base metals into gold or silver or transform something common into something special

* **pneumatics** field of physics that deals with the properties and behavior of air

17

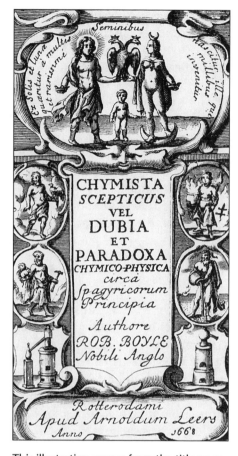

This illustration comes from the title page of Robert Boyle's book *Chymista Scepticus,* published in 1661. In this work, Boyle referred to the particles of matter as corpuscles, and in doing so, he rejected the accepted theories of matter proposed by Aristotle and Paracelsus.

* **hydrostatics** field of physics that deals with the properties and behavior of fluids at rest

* **natural philosopher** person who develops theories to explain the natural world

(designed by Robert HOOKE) to conduct a series of brilliant experiments on the physical nature of air. Boyle was assisted by Hooke in these experiments. Through these experiments, he reinforced the pioneering work of the Italian physicist Evangelista TORRICELLI. He proved that air has weight, that sound is impossible in a vacuum, that air is necessary for life and flame, and that air never loses its ability to expand or compress. He developed this last observation into what is now called Boyle's Law: that at a constant temperature, the volume and pressure of a gas are inversely related. In other words, as pressure increases, the volume of a gas decreases, and as pressure decreases, the volume of a gas increases. Boyle published this material in 1662. A few years later he published his work on hydrostatics*, in which he described his own experiments and offered insightful critiques of the Frenchman Blaise PASCAL's work on the subject.

New Ideas About Matter. Boyle's chemical theory was based on his belief that matter is composed of small, differently shaped particles, which he called corpuscles. This idea had first been proposed by ancient Greek philosophers such as Epicurus and Democritus, who called the particles atoms. In modified form, the same idea had gained popularity in Europe in the 1600s. Boyle was also influenced by Francis BACON and René DESCARTES. Bacon taught that heat is caused by the motion of particles in matter and that experiments could not only show the existence of such particles but also suggest how their shapes and motions might explain the observable properties of matter.

Boyle strove in his own work to refute the old ways of thinking and replace those ideas with rational, mechanical explanations of matter and motion. He also tried to show that this goal was best accomplished through careful, logical series of experiments. He engaged in debates with natural philosophers*, who believed that experiments were unnecessary and that theories could be proved by logical reasoning. Boyle argued that experiments were an essential ingredient of proof.

Advances in Chemistry. Boyle considered corpuscles so basic and important in the chemical and physical behavior of matter that he had little use for older theories about the elements of nature. Aristotle had made earth, air, fire, and water the elements of his system, whereas PARACELSUS proposed salt, sulfur, and mercury. Other chemists used categories of phlegm, oil, spirit, acid, and alkali. Although Boyle believed that the specific properties of corpuscles transcended these categories, he did recognize that chemicals could fall into classes.

Among his many contributions to chemistry, Boyle used experiments to study acids and alkalis (also called bases). He showed that acids turned the blue syrup of violets red, while alkalis turned the syrup green. He also showed how an acid could change the color of a solution made from a South American wood and how an alkali could restore the color. This reaction allowed him to test the relative strengths of acidic and alkaline solutions. Other experiments allowed Boyle to distinguish among different chemicals. Such experiments were a major advance in chemistry because most chemists of the time remained helplessly confused or ignorant about the identities and compositions of the substances they used. Many chemists insisted on sweeping, general theories and had little patience for the careful, detailed analyses performed by Boyle. Nevertheless, his influence eventually spread widely and his emphasis on experimentation made a strong impression on Isaac NEWTON and many other young scientists.

Public and Religious Life. Throughout his career Boyle remained active in public life. He was active in Irish politics, and beginning in 1661 he was governor of the Society for the Propagation of the Gospel in New England. He also helped anchor the scientific life of London, where he increasingly spent his time. He helped found the Royal Society, an organization of prominent scientists and physicians, and he welcomed friends and colleagues to his home and his laboratory.

Boyle's rational, scientific thought was no obstacle to his religious devotion. He wrote many lengthy, passionate papers and books about his belief that God had created a universe based on rational, natural laws that humans could discover. When he died, he left a sum of money to found the Boyle lectures, a series of addresses that used scientific reasoning to counter the philosophy of atheism*.

* **atheism** belief that no god or supernatural force exists

Tycho
BRAHE

1546–1601
ASTRONOMY

The Danish astronomer Tycho Brahe helped revolutionize the study of astronomy with his detailed and accurate observations of the stars and planets, observations that he made before the invention of the telescope. Brahe also designed and developed various astronomical instruments and used them to measure the movements of celestial bodies. His work paved the way for later discoveries and provided the basis for modern astronomical study.

Early Life and Education. Born into a noble family in the town of Skane in Denmark (now part of Sweden), Brahe was the son of a provincial governor. At an early age he went to live with his uncle, a wealthy and childless man who supervised and financed his nephew's upbringing and education. From the age of seven Brahe learned Latin and other subjects from a private tutor in preparation for attending university.

Brahe studied law at the University of Copenhagen from 1559 to 1562. As part of his education, he also studied mathematics, philosophy, natural sciences, and astrology—which combined astronomy and medicine. Through these studies he became acquainted with the ideas of ancient Greek thinkers including Aristotle and Ptolemy, whose theories about the motion of the planets and other celestial bodies dominated astronomy at that time.

In 1560 Brahe witnessed a solar eclipse that shifted his attention from law to astronomy. The observation of this phenomenon, as well as the accurate prediction of the event by scholars, fascinated the 14-year-old student. Thereafter, Brahe began to devote much of his time and energy to observational astronomy. However, astronomy was not offered as a course of study by the university, so Brahe studied the subject on his own.

He was aided by some of his teachers, who provided him with books and helped him build scientific instruments with which to make astronomical observations.

Brahe's family disapproved of his interest in astronomy because they considered it an unsuitable area of study for an aristocrat. To separate him from this interest, Brahe's uncle sent him to the University of Leipzig in Germany to continue the study of law. The change of location did little to discourage Brahe, however. Although he studied law during the day under the supervision of a hired tutor, he secretly continued his study of astronomy at night and acquired more books, mathematical tables, and instruments to help him with his observations.

While in Leipzig, Brahe witnessed another natural event, one that he later regarded as the turning point in his career. He observed and recorded a planetary conjunction—an overlapping of the paths of the planets Saturn and Jupiter in the night sky. At this time Brahe discovered that the prevailing astronomical tables and almanacs that recorded and predicted planetary positions and events were terribly inaccurate. He then decided to devote his life to making accurate observations of the heavens and to correcting the existing tables and almanacs.

Travels and Early Work. Two years later Brahe left Leipzig and began traveling throughout Europe. After a short visit home, he went to the universities at Wittenberg and Rostock in Germany, where he studied astronomy under well-known teachers. He then continued his travels, meeting several people devoted to the study of astrology and mathematics. Some of these individuals helped arrange for the manufacture of instruments to help Brahe with his observations. Brahe repeatedly emphasized the importance of making new and accurate observations before trying to explain celestial motions. Consequently, he was especially aware of the need for good instruments to obtain those observations.

After his father's death in 1571, Brahe and his brother inherited the family estate in Denmark. Brahe returned to Denmark, set up quarters at the castle of another uncle, and devoted his time to observing the heavens and conducting chemical experiments. The following year Brahe made one of his most famous observations. While observing the night sky, he looked at the constellation of Cassiopeia and noticed one star shining more brightly than all the others. He immediately realized that this star had not been there before and began taking measurements of its position. Brahe continued to observe that star for almost two years, until it was no longer visible to the naked eye, always noticing changes in its color and brightness.

Through his observations and measurements, Brahe concluded that the object was a star and that it lay beyond the moon, in the realm of the other fixed stars in the sky. Modern astronomers know that this bright star was a supernova*. Today known as Tycho's Nova, it remains one of the few supernovae recorded in the Milky Way galaxy. Many people at the time found Brahe's discovery very disturbing because, in keeping with the teachings of Aristotle, they believed that the region of the stars beyond the surface of the moon was perfect and unchanging. Brahe's idea that a star had the ability to change so dramatically challenged Aristotle's astronomical

* **supernova** star that suddenly becomes extremely brilliant because it has exploded; *pl.* supernovae

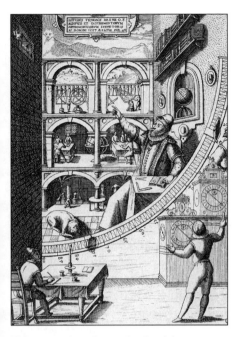

This engraving shows the Danish astronomer Tycho Brahe in his observatory on the island of Hven near Copenhagen. At the time it was built, this observatory was the finest and grandest in all of Europe. It was equipped with a library, several workrooms, and a print shop.

teachings, shook people's confidence in the laws of nature, and forced them to consider that the universe might be a chaotic and imperfect place.

Brahe published his observations of the star in 1573 in a short document called *De nova stella* (On the New Star). This work transformed him from an unknown Danish amateur to a professional astronomer known throughout Europe. In the years that followed, Brahe gave a series of lectures at the University of Copenhagen. During these lectures he discussed his work and also spoke of the great skill of Nicholas COPERNICUS, whose revolutionary idea that the earth and other planets revolved around the sun challenged the ancient theory of Ptolemy, which placed the earth at the center of the universe. Although Brahe did not accept all of Copernicus's ideas, he admired that scientist's reasoning and the mathematical principles on which his findings were based.

A Grand Observatory. Brahe traveled throughout Europe again, meeting with scholars and scientists and looking at scientific instruments that might be useful for his work. Meanwhile, his fame attracted the attention of King Frederick II of Denmark. When Brahe returned to Denmark in 1576, he received an offer from the king, who hoped that the astronomer would pursue his astronomical studies in his homeland. The king offered to grant Brahe title to Hven, a small island near Copenhagen, pay him a salary, and build an observatory and other buildings needed for his work. Brahe readily accepted the king's offer. For the next two decades, he spent much of his time at Hven, studying the heavens, building astronomical instruments, writing about his findings, teaching students, and training assistants.

At the time, the observatory at Hven was the finest and grandest in all of Europe. Located near the center of the island at its highest point, it was called the Uraniborg (heavenly castle). The large three-story building housed observatories on the upper level, with living quarters, a great library, workrooms, and storage areas below. The building also contained a printing shop, which enabled Brahe to produce manuscripts according to his own specifications and desires. In 1584 Brahe supervised the construction of a second, smaller observatory—the Stjerneborg (castle of the stars)—a short distance from the Uraniborg. With income from his landholdings and financing from the king, Brahe was able to live a life of luxury on Hven and devote all his attention to his astronomical studies.

Brahe filled his observatories with some of the finest astronomical instruments of the day. Some he brought from Europe. Most were designed by Brahe and built with the help of artisans from around Europe. The instruments included a large globe engraved with the zodiac and on which he could mark the positions of stars, and a large quadrant, a measuring device used to calculate the angles of stars in relation to each other and to the earth. These instruments enabled Brahe to achieve a level of accuracy in his observations that was unsurpassed from the time of ancient Greece to the invention of the telescope a few years after his death.

Work in Denmark. Brahe spent 21 years observing the heavens. He often required the help of trained assistants and students because some of the larger, more complex scientific instruments could not be operated by

Foretelling the Future from the Stars

Like many people of his time, Brahe believed in astrology and the idea that the heavens affect the earth and human lives. He criticized astrologers for drawing improper conclusions based on error and superstition. Instead, he argued that accurate knowledge of the stars and experience gained from signs in the heavens could be used to foretell events reliably. Through his own studies Brahe predicted the death of Sultan Suleiman the Magnificent, ruler of the Ottoman empire, but he later learned that Suleiman had died before the predicted date. Brahe also calculated horoscopes for the sons of King Frederick II and prepared annual predictions for the king.

one person. Brahe also carried on an extensive correspondence with other scholars throughout Europe. These contacts helped Brahe spread his ideas to the scholarly world. The scientists also provided Brahe with their own records and observations, enabling him to compare his own work to theirs.

Brahe's work at Hven made a significant impact on the field of astronomy. One of his contributions involved a comet that he began observing in 1577. Based on his observations and measurements of the comet, Brahe rejected Aristotle's notion that comets are formed of material drawn up from the earth. Instead, he suggested that they are formed far out in space and that their tails are composed of solar rays transmitted through the head of the comet. Brahe emphasized that he based his conclusions on observation, detailed measurement, and mathematical calculations. He contrasted this approach to that of the ancients, who based their ideas largely on logic and reason. Brahe's observations on the comet were published in 1588 in a book called *De mundi aetherei Recentioribus Phaenomenis* (Concerning the New Phenomena in the Ethereal World).

Brahe's main occupation on Hven was observing and measuring the positions of the stars, the planets, the sun, and the moon to improve the almanacs and astronomical tables and charts. Although he recorded the positions of 777 fixed stars in his lifetime, his work with the planets and moon was perhaps more important. Earlier astronomers had observed the positions of these celestial bodies only at certain points in their orbits. Brahe, however, observed the positions of the objects throughout their orbits. In doing so, he discovered several abnormalities that led to new views about the nature of the solar system.

New Model for the Solar System. In 1583 Brahe proposed a new model for the solar system, one that combined the ideas of Ptolemy and Copernicus. Like Ptolemy, Brahe believed that the earth lay fixed at the center of the universe and that the sun revolved around an imaginary point called the eccentric, located near the earth. He rejected the Ptolemaic idea that the planets revolved around the earth. Instead, he accepted Copernicus's notion that the planets revolved around the sun.

Brahe's model of the planetary system enjoyed limited success. Although it did not offend religious thinkers whose support for an earth-centered view of the universe stemmed from the Bible, it did not attract the support of leading astronomers of the day. Brahe's student Johannes KEPLER supported the Copernican system instead. Brahe's model was observationally equivalent to the Copernican system, with the motion of the earth attributed to the sun. However, it did not have the advantage of Copernicus's bold theory of a moving earth, which called for a new physics of planetary motion and challenged the accepted theories of Aristotle.

Later Life. After the death of Frederick II in 1588, Brahe began to lose his favor at the royal court. This was due partly to his arrogant behavior, his carelessness in maintaining the public buildings on Hven, and his neglect of the island's other residents. The new king, Christian IV, was reluctant to continue providing large sums for astronomical studies.

In 1597 Brahe stopped work at Uraniborg and moved his scientific instruments to a house in Copenhagen. When attempts to regain the support of the king failed, Brahe left Denmark and went to Germany, where he stayed for two years. In 1599 Emperor Rudolph II, ruler of the Holy Roman Empire, offered financial support to Brahe and invited the astronomer to Prague (in the present-day Czech Republic). With the emperor as his new patron, Brahe installed his instruments in a castle and resumed his observations and studies. One of his young assistants was Johannes Kepler.

Brahe died in 1601, after a brief illness. On his deathbed he asked Kepler to complete a series of tables based on observations that Brahe had been working on for some time. Kepler agreed and later published the Rudolphine Tables, which summed up Brahe's observations of the positions of the fixed stars and the motions of the sun, moon, and planets. This work helped fulfill Brahe's goal of making accurate observations and measurements of the heavens and correcting the errors of earlier astronomers. The tables also served as a basis for Kepler's own work, which resulted in laws of planetary motion that helped explain the true movements of the planets around the sun and added to the Copernican model of the solar system. Brahe's data also helped Kepler lay the groundwork for the discoveries by Isaac NEWTON on the laws of gravitation.

Otto
BRUNFELS

ca. 1489–1534
BOTANY

* **theological** referring to theology, the study of religion

O tto Brunfels was the earliest of the three "German fathers of botany" (the others were Jerome Bock and Leonhart FUCHS). He is known primarily for *Herbarum vivae eicones* (Pictures of Living Herbs), the first printed book in which the illustrations of botanical specimens had as much value as the text. The accuracy, detail, and realism of the drawings revolutionized botanical illustration.

The son of a barrelmaker, Brunfels was born in Mainz, Germany, and educated at the university there. He later entered a monastery in Strasbourg as a priest of the very strict and austere religious order of the Carthusians. Brunfels remained at the monastery until 1521, a few years after the Protestant Reformation had begun to sweep through Europe. Influenced by the religious upheaval, he fled the monastery and converted to the new Protestant faith of Martin Luther. For the next three years, Brunfels served as a Lutheran pastor in the town of Steinau and engaged in the theological* controversies raging in Germany. In 1524 he returned to Strasbourg, opened his own school, and married Dorothea Heilgenhensin.

While in Strasbourg, Brunfels demonstrated a growing interest in medicine by editing and translating older medical texts. He also wrote one of the earliest medical bibliographies, the *Catalogus* (Catalog), published in 1530. That same year, the first volume of the *Herbarum* was published. Between 1530 and 1532 Brunfels supervised the publication of the second volume of the *Herbarum* while writing several other books as well. Among his other writings are texts on medicine and pharmacology* designed for use by physicians and apothecaries*.

* **pharmacology** science that deals with the preparation, uses, and effects of drugs

* **apothecary** individual trained to fill prescriptions; pharmacist or druggist

Around 1532 Brunfels moved to Bern, Switzerland, and received a degree in medicine from the university there. The following year he accepted

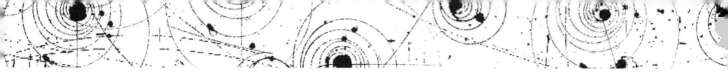

a position as town physician of Bern, but about a year later he became seriously ill and died. Brunfels's wife, Dorothea, helped prepare his remaining manuscripts for publication after his death.

Brunfels's major work, the *Herbarum*, is a curious combination of old and new. The text is a collection of descriptions compiled from earlier works. The illustrations by artist Hans Weiditz, however, are strikingly different from those in older works. The *Herbarum* is divided into several chapters, each devoted to one plant. The text identifies plants and discusses their medicinal properties, providing information about preparation, dosage, and the ailments for which the plants are most beneficial. Identified by their Greek and Latin names as well as common German names, the plants are not arranged in any systematic order. Most of the plants described are local to Strasbourg and surrounding areas.

The *Herbarum* contains 238 detailed and accurate illustrations that depict the entire plant and its typical habitat. Some illustrations show leaves damaged by insects and drooping stems and leaves, suggesting that Weiditz illustrated the plants after they had been dug up and begun to wilt. The illustrations in the *Herbarum* mark the first time that an artist assumed a recognized place in botanical literature.

Georges-Louis Leclerc
BUFFON

1707–1788

NATURAL HISTORY

* **naturalist** student of natural history, the systematic study of natural objects, especially in their natural settings

The French naturalist* Georges-Louis Leclerc Buffon is probably best remembered for his work *Histoire naturelle* (Natural History). He brought together for the first time all existing knowledge in the fields of natural history, geology, and anthropology. Widely praised for its clearly written descriptions and illustrations, *Histoire naturelle* became one of the most widely read scientific works of the 1700s.

Born in Montbard, France, Buffon came from a solidly middle-class family. His father was an official in the state of Burgundy, and his mother was related to a wealthy banker. The eldest of five children, Buffon studied at the Collège des Jésuites in Dijon. Although only an average student, he displayed a marked talent for mathematics. However, because his father wanted him to have a legal career, Buffon studied law as well. In 1728 he traveled to Angers in western France, where he studied medicine, botany, and mathematics. Forced to leave Angers because of a duel, Buffon traveled through southern France and Italy with a young English nobleman and his tutor for two years.

Buffon returned to France in 1732 and received an inheritance from his mother, who had died during his absence. Settling down on the family estate at Montbard, he began doing research in botany and forestry and continued his studies of mathematics. He later became interested in chemistry and biology as well, and he conducted some microscopic research on animal reproduction. Buffon also translated into French a number of works by other scientists, including Isaac NEWTON. In 1734 Buffon gained admission to the French Académie des Sciences.

Beginning in 1740, Buffon divided his time between Montbard and Paris. While in Paris he met with scientists, politicians, and other elite scholars and worked on his writings. He also worked as keeper and director of the Jardin du Roi (king's garden), which he turned into an important center of botanical research. Returning each spring to Montbard, Buffon administered his estates, continued his research, and edited his writings.

Buffon's first original work was a report presented to the Academy of Sciences on calculus* and the theory of probability. It was probably Buffon's interest in mathematics that drew him to science in the first place. He focused on the practical application of mathematics and its use as a way to clarify reality rather than as an abstract discipline. Buffon's other works may be grouped into two main categories: the various reports, or *Mémoires,* presented to the Royal Academy, and the *Histoire naturelle.* The *Mémoires,* which appeared between 1737 and 1752, dealt with mathematics, astronomy, physics, forestry, and other subjects. Many of these subjects appeared again in the *Histoire naturelle.*

Of the proposed 50 volumes for the *Histoire naturelle,* Buffon published only 36 before his death. The rest were published later. The *Histoire naturelle* covers a range of subjects related to biology, including birds, reptiles, fish, humans, and other animals. Several volumes dealt with geology, astronomy, chemistry, and anthropology. The work contained not only scientific observations and descriptions but also philosophical discussions about the nature and value of science. Breaking with the spirit of the times, Buffon attempted to separate science from metaphysics* and the religious ideas that had dominated science for centuries. His goal was to construct a science derived solely from nature.

One of the best-known sections of the work is the *Époques de la nature* (Epochs of Nature), which presents a new theory about the history of the earth. Buffon believed that the earth was a piece of the sun that had torn away and then gradually solidified and cooled. As the earth solidified, mineral deposits and mountains were formed, and as the planet cooled, water vapor condensed and covered the planet with great oceans. Forces of erosion gradually shaped the planet, and life eventually appeared through the action of heat on certain substances. This work was the first to present geologic history in a series of stages. It also introduced the idea of lost species (represented by the fossils found in rock), which paved the way for the development of paleontology*.

Buffon studied humans with the same methods that he applied to animals. Although he believed that humans had the same history as animals, he proclaimed the absolute superiority of humans over animals because of their ability to reason. He maintained that because of their intelligence, humans have been able to adapt to different environments.

Buffon also studied the vestigial organs* of animals, arguing that this reduction of organs could be applied to the degeneration of species. For instance, Buffon believed that an ape was a degenerate man and a donkey a degenerate horse. This suggestion played a role in the rise of evolutionary thought because it implied that certain species have common ancestors.

Buffon's work is of exceptional importance because of its diversity, richness, originality, and influence. Among the first to create a science free of religious influence, he also was one of the first to understand the important roles that other areas of science play in natural history.

* **calculus** advanced form of mathematics that involves computing quantities that change as functions of different variables

* **metaphysics** branch of philosophy that deals with the fundamental principles or ultimate nature of existence

* **paleontology** science that deals with prehistoric plants and animals through the study of fossils and other remains

* **vestigial organ** organ that is deformed or degenerate in appearance and no longer has any recognizable function in comparison to one that is more fully developed in a past generation or closely related life-form

Rudolph Jakob
CAMERARIUS

1665–1721

BOTANY, MEDICINE

The German botanist Rudolph Jakob Camerarius was the first to demonstrate that plants reproduce sexually. Camerarius, who came from a family of physicians, carefully observed and described the structures of plants in a long letter to a fellow professor of medicine. In the same letter he also reported his observation that a female mulberry tree bears fruit in the absence of a male plant but that the fruit contains only empty seeds. He repeated this experiment by isolating two female flowers from other plants. The plants bore fruit that soon dried up and contained no seeds as well.

In another experiment he cut off the structures of a flower just below its pollen-producing organ (known as the anther). Again, the plant produced only empty fruit. From these experiments Camerarius concluded that the anther is the male organ of a plant and that the seed-bearing parts of the plant—the style and stigma—are the female organs. Camerarius also published other works on botany. In the most famous of these, he showed that plants with similar flower structures have similar healing properties and are thus made of similar substances.

Girolamo
CARDANO

1501–1576

MEDICINE, MATHEMATICS, PHYSICS

Girolamo Cardano's searching intellect brought him encyclopedic learning, and he wrote more than 200 works on medicine, mathematics, physics, music, religion, and philosophy. Yet his progress was often affected by his unstable personality, as he was subject to fears and delusions of grandeur.

Cardano had a difficult childhood, born out of wedlock to a prominent judge and a widow. He endured illness and mistreatment as a youth, but his father also encouraged him to study classical texts, mathematics, and astrology. Cardano received a doctorate in medicine at Padua in 1526 and practiced medicine in a small town for six years that he called the happiest of his life. He married Lucia Bandareni in 1531 and had two sons and a daughter.

Cardano's career began in Milan in 1534, and his success at teaching and practicing medicine aroused great envy from his colleagues. His first published work was an attack on his colleagues. Even so, he became famous, perhaps second in Europe only to the Flemish scientist Andreas VESALIUS.

Although he was primarily a physician, Cardano's principal achievements were in the field of algebra. His *Ars Magna* (The Great Skill), published in 1545, was the first printed text in algebra. It contains solutions to two long-standing algebraic difficulties—the general cubic and the general quartic—that defied solution by the ancients. Using the following example of a cubic equation, $x^3 + 6x = 20$, Cardano solved the problem by showing that it could be reduced to a quadratic equation, which has a squared term. He then proved that a quartic equation, a fourth-degree equation with one unknown, could be solved by reducing it to a cubic equation. New mathematical techniques were needed to solve fifth-degree and higher equations. The solution to the cubic equation problem was revealed to Cardano by Niccolo TARTAGLIA in confidence. Consequently, when Cardano published the solution, it led to a bitter feud between the two. Cardano also studied games of chance, but Pierre de FERMAT and Blaise PASCAL's work on the subject was published sooner, so Cardano's had no influence.

In 1543 Cardano accepted the chair of medicine at Pavia, where he remained for much of his career. Yet he also found time to make major contributions to other fields. He published two encyclopedias of natural science, in 1550 and 1557, which included everything from the construction of machines to the study of codes, from notes on the state of the sciences to opinions on the evil influence of demons.

In physics Cardano studied the lever and the inclined plane in new ways, observed that the course of a projectile* launched through the air is a parabola, and affirmed that perpetual motion is impossible except for astronomical bodies. He also studied running water and vacuums. In one famous experiment he compared the densities of air and water by firing a bullet through each and recording how far it traveled in each. In geology he proposed, correctly, that mountains are shaped by running water. He also presented the novel idea that water travels in a cycle: running from streams to the sea, evaporating to the atmosphere, and falling as rain to replenish streams.

However, Cardano encountered trouble in 1560, when his elder son was executed for having poisoned his own wife. Upset as well by his younger son's decadent lifestyle and offended by the criticisms of his enemies, Cardano moved to Bologna in 1562. His respite was short-lived, for in 1570 he was imprisoned for several months by the Inquisition, which accused him of heresy against the Roman Catholic Church. After his release Cardano went to Rome and found favor with the pope. He died in Rome five years later.

* **projectile** body projected by an external force and continuing in motion by its own inactivity

---

Gian Domenico
CASSINI

1625–1712

ASTRONOMY

Gian Domenico Cassini gained fame and prestige among high-ranking Italian nobles and scientists, yet his greatest work took place after he moved to Paris, France. As an astronomer his gifts were as an observer rather than as a theoretician, and he stubbornly clung to many ideas that his colleagues were proving false.

Cassini was raised by an uncle and educated in Catholic schools. He showed a keen interest in poetry, mathematics, and astronomy. At first he was attracted to astrological predictions, and although he soon rejected this type of study, he took a job with a wealthy astrologer who was making astronomical observations. He completed his education under two excellent scientists who showed him the importance of precise and systematic observations. They may also have instilled in him his resistance to new theories, such as the heliocentric theory proposed by Nicholas COPERNICUS, according to which the sun, not the earth, was at the center of the universe.

Cassini's early observational work was so exceptional that at the age of 25 he was named chair of astronomy at the University of Bologna. He made valuable and precise studies of comets—one of his favorite subjects—

and of the positions and motions of the earth and sun. He drew heavily on the work of other astronomers, including the Dane Tycho BRAHE and the German Johannes KEPLER. Cassini also presented the first major theory of how light is disturbed as it passes through the atmosphere; however, his ideas were based on an incorrect model of the atmosphere. Even so, the many observations and charts he compiled were so precise that other astronomers relied on them to develop their own theories.

Cassini also served the pope and officials of Bologna as a scientific expert on the flow of rivers and the strength of the city's defenses. But his main work flourished again in 1664, when he began to collaborate with two Italian lensmakers, who built for him a series of very sophisticated telescopes. Over the next few years, Cassini made remarkable observations of the shadows cast by Jupiter's moons on Jupiter's surface as well as of the bands and spots on Jupiter itself. Thanks to the telescopes and his skill in using them, he succeeded where Galileo GALILEI had failed, in establishing tables of the movements of Jupiter's moons.

These tables increased his fame yet again, and in 1668 he accepted an invitation to help set up an observatory at the Académie des Sciences in Paris. Thinking that he would only stay for a short while, Cassini made little attempt to adjust to the French lifestyle and language, and his bossy, stubborn personality earned him the hostility of his colleagues. Yet his ambitions and skills were enough to win him the support he needed. He moved into an apartment built into the observatory and was so delighted with France and his work there that he soon became a French citizen. He also married and had two sons, the younger of whom followed in his footsteps as an astronomer.

The observatory enjoyed generous funding from the French king, and Cassini used the best available instruments to continue his work. He discovered four moons of Saturn and saw that Saturn's rings are divided into two main parts, separated by a narrow gap now called Cassini's division. He also prepared an atlas of the moon.

Cassini's greatest project was directing efforts to compare astronomical measurements made at Paris and at Cayenne, a French colony on the northern coast of South America. With these observations he worked out the parallax* of Mars, which enabled him to calculate the astronomical unit—the mean distance between the earth and the sun—at 87 million miles. Earlier, Kepler had reckoned this distance at 15 million miles. Although Cassini's figure was a little lower than the actual mean distance of nearly 93 million miles, it gave astronomers a reasonably accurate idea of the size of the solar system for the first time.

* **parallax** in astronomy, apparent angular difference in direction of a heavenly body as measured from two points on the earth's orbit

Henry
CAVENDISH
1731–1810
NATURAL PHILOSOPHY

Although Henry Cavendish published only a small fraction of his work, by the end of his 50-year career, the international scientific community considered him the most distinguished British scientist of his day. The phrase *natural philosophy* reflects the wide range of Cavendish's interests—he performed experiments concerning many aspects of the natural world. Some of his notable researches in physics and chemistry involved studying the properties of air, heat, water, and electricity. Cavendish also designed and performed an experiment to weigh the earth, an achievement that was the most important addition to the science of gravitation since Isaac NEWTON had launched that field of study, in the late 1600s.

Living for Science. Cavendish was born into an aristocratic family in Nice, France. He attended school in England and entered St. Peter's College at Cambridge University in 1749. After leaving Cambridge, Cavendish settled in London with his father, who was interested in science and had performed experiments that earned the approval of the American inventor and experimenter Benjamin FRANKLIN. First as his father's assistant, and then following his own interests, Henry Cavendish immersed himself in the world of science, which became his sole passion for the rest of his life. After his father died in 1783, he moved to a different London house, where he lived alone, except for servants, until his death.

Cavendish never had to work for a living because he received a large inheritance. In fact, a French scientist called him "the richest of all learned men, and very likely also the most learned of all the rich." Yet Cavendish lived modestly, spending his money mainly on scientific equipment and on a collection of books that he allowed other scientists to use. Shy and quiet, Cavendish had little to do with his fellow aristocrats. He was, however, quite active in various scientific organizations, including the British Museum, the Society of Antiquaries*, and especially the Royal Society, Britain's leading association of scientists and scholars.

Interests and Experiments. Cavendish investigated nearly all the physical sciences known in his day, including optics*, geology, magnetism, and mechanics*. He was also a mathematician. During his lifetime, however, he was known principally for the fewer than 20 papers he published between 1766 and 1798. Inspired by Newton's discoveries in physics and gravitation, Cavendish sought to understand the forces that cause particles of matter in the universe to move, interact, and change. All his researches in various fields were unified by this search for underlying physical principles.

One early body of work concerned heat, which Cavendish, like Newton, explained as the result of the vibration of particles. Cavendish conducted experiments to study the heat properties of various materials. He refined the concept of specific heat*, but this work was not published. He also studied the composition of airs (gases), distinguishing hydrogen (inflammable air) and carbon dioxide (fixed air) as gases separate from ordinary air. Cavendish's work involved the synthesis of water. He exploded (ignited with an electric charge) hydrogen with oxygen and air, concluding that air is a mixture of oxygen and nitrogen. He also discovered that when hydrogen and oxygen were mixed in proportions of 2:1, the weight of the product—water—was equal to their own combined weight.

In 1771 he published a theory of electricity. Although some of his ideas about electricity were later proved incorrect, Cavendish determined that particles followed set laws of electrical attraction and repulsion, but he did not publish this insight.

The English physicist and chemist Henry Cavendish performed experiments that concerned many aspects of the natural world. He studied the properties of air, heat, water, and electricity.

* **antiquary** person interested in the history, objects, and texts of earlier times

* **optics** scientific study of the properties of light

* **mechanics** science that studies how energy and force affect objects

* **specific heat** heat in calories required to raise the temperature of one gram of a particular substance by one degree Celsius

* **meteorological** pertaining to weather

During the 1780s Cavendish conducted experiments proving that air contains water. He also published several papers on the freezing points of mercury, certain acids, and other liquids. This work was related to his study of the Royal Society's instruments for meteorological* measurements. During this time he discovered that the extremely low temperatures that some mercury thermometers had recorded were due to the shrinkage of the mercury and not because of cold weather.

In 1798 Cavendish successfully measured the density of the earth. He used an instrument called a torsion balance to measure the gravitational force of the earth. The apparatus consisted of two movable lead balls arranged on either end of a suspended beam. The two movable balls were attracted by a pair of stationary lead balls. Cavendish calculated the force of attraction between the balls by measuring the extremely tiny movements of the balls. From that force he deduced the density of the earth. Cavendish calculated that the earth had a density 5.48 times greater than that of water. This achievement was the most important addition to the science of gravitation since Newton.

Cavendish left most of his work unpublished. In the years following his death, scientists impressed with his work published some of it, giving additional weight to Cavendish's reputation as the first British physical scientist after Newton to possess comparable talents in mathematics and experimentation. However, his career marked the peak and the end of the original British tradition in mathematical physics.

Anders
CELSIUS

1701–1744
ASTRONOMY

* **dynamics** study of the relationship between motion and the forces affecting motion

During his brief life the Swedish astronomer Anders Celsius published a number of important papers in various sciences. These included works on the shape of the earth, the brightness of stars, and the water level of the Baltic Sea. However, he is best known for devising the thermometer scale that bears his name.

Celsius was the son of a professor of astronomy at the University of Uppsala, Sweden. He studied astronomy, mathematics, and experimental physics. In 1725 he became secretary of the Uppsala Scientific Society, and he served several years as professor of mathematics at the university there. In 1730 he was appointed professor of astronomy, and two years later he embarked on extensive foreign travels to gain more knowledge in his chosen field. He visited astronomers and astronomical observatories in Germany, Italy, and France. Celsius subsequently joined a French expedition that traveled to northern Sweden to measure the length of a meridian—an imaginary circle that passes through the North and South Poles, at right angles to the equator—in the north. This expedition supported Isaac NEWTON's theory that the earth is flatter at the poles than at the equator, which was one consequence of the English scientist's work in dynamics*. After the expedition, Celsius returned to Uppsala to resume teaching.

In the last few years of his life, Celsius made several important scientific findings and developed the Celsius thermometer scale. He based his scale on two fixed points—the boiling point and freezing point of water.

He set the upper limit (boiling water) at 0° and the lower limit (melting ice) at 100°. The modern centigrade scale has the opposite fixed points. Although earlier scientists had used a 100-degree scale, that scale gained acceptance only after Celsius published his paper discussing the fixed points. Three years after his death, the astronomical observatory in Uppsala introduced a version of the scale that set the upper fixed point at 100° and the lower point at 0°. That scale was called the Swedish thermometer until about 1800. Thereafter, people began to refer to it as the Celsius thermometer, the name by which it is still known.

Émilie du CHÂTELET
1706–1749
SCIENTIFIC COMMENTARY

* **optics** scientific study of the properties of light
* **mechanics** science that studies how energy and force affect objects

Émilie du Châtelet was the daughter of a high-ranking nobleman at the French royal court. Thanks to his position Émilie received an education in literature, music, and science. At the age of 18, she married an aristocrat, Florent-Claude. They had three children, but Florent-Claude pursued a military career abroad and visited the family only occasionally.

In her husband's absence Châtelet enjoyed a glittering life among the wealthy nobles and intellectuals of Paris. She formed an intimate friendship with the philosopher Voltaire, who passionately supported the new scientific worldview of the English physicist Isaac NEWTON. From 1734 she and Voltaire lived on her estate and made it a brilliant center of French literary and philosophical life.

Châtelet guided and advised Voltaire's work and undertook her own, which included writing essays on optics* and fire. Inspired by Newton, she worked on a book about physics and mechanics*, designed for her son's education, but she interrupted this effort to study the recent ideas of Gottfried Wilhelm LEIBNIZ. Her strong defense of Leibniz led her into a series of heated arguments with other French physicists and philosophers.

In 1745 Châtelet began her major work, a French translation of Newton's *Principia*. She collaborated with Alexis-Claude CLAIRAUT on commentary and supplements to accompany the translation. However, an unexpected pregnancy forced her to leave Paris in 1749; before she could give birth, she died of a fever at the age of 42. Her translation of the *Principia* was not published in its entirety for ten years.

Alexis-Claude CLAIRAUT
1713–1765
MATHEMATICS

* **geodesy** scientific measurement of the size and shape of the earth

The youngest person ever elected to the Paris Académie des Sciences, the French mathematician Alexis-Claude Clairaut was a prodigy who made important contributions to mathematics, physics, and geodesy*. A close friend of the French mathematician Pierre-Louis MAUPERTUIS and the philosopher and writer Voltaire, he was also a supporter of the English physicist Isaac NEWTON.

Early Life and Career. Born in Paris, Clairaut was the son of a mathematics teacher. His father educated Clairaut at home in his early years and probably taught him the alphabet using *Elements,* the famous book of geometry by the ancient Greek mathematician Euclid. When Clairaut was nine years old, his father had him study *Application de l'algèbre à la géométrie* (Application of Algebra to Geometry), a well-known textbook that was a good introduction to the pioneering mathematics of the era.

In the early 1720s Clairaut began his research on geometric curves, which culminated in a work that led to his election to France's scientific academy. Thereafter, Clairaut allied himself with Maupertuis and a small group of scholars who supported the work of Isaac Newton.

In 1736 Clairaut went on an expedition led by Maupertuis to Lapland, in northern Scandinavia. The purpose of this trip was to measure a degree of longitude. The mission was a success, and Clairaut and the others returned to Paris the following year. At this time his work turned increasingly toward celestial mechanics*, and he published several studies on the subject.

Accomplishments. Clairaut's primary contribution to science lies in his own works. One of his early works, published in 1733, was noteworthy in the history of calculus*, and a subsequent work made important contributions to the study of differential equations*. In 1742 Clairaut published a book on dynamics*, which dealt with the relative movement and dynamics of a body in motion, and presented a method for attacking problems related to the acceleration of moving bodies.

In 1743 Clairaut published *Théorie de la figure de la terre* (Theory About the Surface of the Earth), a work that resulted from his trip to Lapland. Considered a scientific classic, it confirmed the belief of both Newton and the Dutch physicist Christiaan HUYGENS that the earth was flatter at the poles. He also introduced a formula that expressed gravity as a function of latitude. This work in geodesy, combined with his work on a French translation of Newton's *Principia*, helped gain the widespread acceptance of Newton's theory of gravitation.

At around this same time, Clairaut suggested revising Newton's law of attraction, which led to controversial arguments with the French naturalist* Georges-Louis BUFFON. Out of this controversy arose one of Clairaut's major accomplishments—the first approximate resolution of the three-body problem in celestial mechanics. This problem concerned disparities in the orbits of the moon and planets. His ideas on the subject appeared in *Théorie de la lune* (Theory of the Moon), published in 1752, and *Tables de la lune* (Tables of the Moon), published in 1754. Clairaut also became involved in the study of comets, and he competed in the attempt to calculate the timing of Halley's comet. He announced several approximations, each one more accurate than the last. Although none was completely accurate, his predictions came closer than those of any other scholar.

Clairaut's other works were on geometry and algebra. In his work on geometry, he compiled a history of mathematical thought. His aim was to let beginners discover geometry. In his work on algebra, he first set out elementary problems that students could solve using common sense. Gradually, Clairaut increased the level of difficulty, introducing algebraic symbolism and techniques to solve the problems. This work influenced the educational techniques adopted by schools at the time of the French Revolution.

* **mechanics** science that studies how energy and force affect objects

* **calculus** advanced form of mathematics that involves computing quantities that change as functions of different variables

* **differential equation** in calculus, an equation containing derivatives, which refers to the rate of change of the value of a mathematical function with respect to a change in the independent variable

* **dynamics** study of the relationship between motion and the forces affecting motion

* **naturalist** student of natural history, the systematic study of natural objects, especially in their natural settings

Looking into Light

One of Clairaut's interests was the behavior of rays of light and the role of lenses in transmitting and changing images. He undertook precise experiments with lenses and presented his findings to the Paris Académie des Sciences. He began to write a technical work on the subject of lenses that would be useful to artisans, but he did not complete the work in his lifetime.

Realdo COLOMBO

ca. 1510–1559

ANATOMY, PHYSIOLOGY

* **physiology** science that deals with the functions of living organisms and their parts
* **apothecary** individual trained to fill prescriptions; pharmacist or druggist

* **ventricle** chamber of the heart

* **theology** study of religion

During the 1500s many European scientists turned their attention to the structure and function of animal and human bodies. One such researcher was Realdo Colombo, an expert in anatomy and physiology*, who made the significant discovery that air enters the bloodstream in the lungs. His work contributed to an understanding of how the heart and the lungs work.

Little is known about Colombo's life. He was born in Cremona, Italy, the son of an apothecary*. After a period of following his father's trade, Colombo became an apprentice to Giovanni Antonio Lonigo, a surgeon in Venice. By 1538 Colombo was studying at the University of Padua, also in Italy. A few years later Colombo became an instructor of surgery and anatomy at Padua, taking a position formerly held by Andreas VESALIUS, one of the foremost anatomists of the day. Vesalius and Colombo appear to have been friends and colleagues at this time, but later, after Colombo pointed out some errors in Vesalius's work, their relationship soured. Colombo, who settled in Rome in 1548, hoped to work with the artist Michelangelo on an illustrated book of anatomy that would replace that of Vesalius. The artist's advanced age made this impossible, but in 1559 Colombo published his unillustrated text, *De re anatomica* (On Anatomy).

This work reveals Colombo's attention to detail and the depth of his experience in surgery, anatomical dissection, vivisection (the practice of dissecting or cutting into the body of a living animal), and autopsy. Because *De re anatomica* contains a good account of human anatomy in brief but clear terms and reflects Colombo's wide experience and attention to detail, the 15-volume text was popular in the later part of the 1500s.

Colombo's best-known achievement was his discovery of the pulmonary circuit, the process by which blood passes from the right ventricle* into the lungs, where it absorbs oxygen, and then passes into the left ventricle, from which it is pumped through the body. Before Colombo, anatomists thought that blood moved between the two ventricles through tiny pores in the tissue wall that separates them. They also believed that air entered the heart through a large vein and then mixed with the bloodstream. By studying the breathing and blood flow of live animals, Colombo correctly determined that air enters the blood in the lungs, not the heart, and that the heart distributes the enriched, life-giving blood to the body.

Colombo was not the first to describe the pulmonary circuit, however. Michael SERVETUS had done so a few years earlier in a work on theology*, but it is most likely that Colombo made his discovery independently, with no knowledge of Servetus's work. He also pursued the discovery in greater detail than Servetus did. Colombo also made significant progress in understanding the heartbeat. His observations led him to believe that the contraction phase of the heartbeat, in which the heart briefly becomes smaller and pushes blood out into the arteries, is more strenuous than the dilation phase, in which the heart expands and draws blood in from the veins. Colombo's observations on the heartbeat were the starting point for the later studies of William HARVEY, who discovered the circulatory system.

Nicholas COPERNICUS

1473–1543

ASTRONOMY

Dance of the Planets

Since ancient times, observers watching the night sky have noted that the planets Mercury, Venus, Mars, and Saturn follow paths consisting of a series of lines, loops, and arcs. They move eastward, decrease speed, stop, reverse direction briefly, stop again, and then resume their eastward course. Before Copernicus, astronomers thought that this "dance of the planets" was a real phenomenon and that the planets actually moved in this manner. Copernicus showed that the planets only appear to move in such a way because of the relationship between their orbits around the sun and the changing position of the earth.

Considered the founder of modern astronomy, Nicholas Copernicus is best known as the scientist who questioned the model of the universe put forth by the ancient Greeks and accepted by most scholars for more than 1,400 years. The Greeks—in particular the philosopher Aristotle and the astronomer Ptolemy—had believed that the earth was at the center of the universe and that everything else revolved around it. By suggesting that the sun was at the center of the universe and not the earth, Copernicus made a bold break with the ideas accepted in his time. In this manner he helped bring about a dramatic change in astronomy and stimulated a revolution in scientific thought.

Early Life, Education, and Work. Born into a middle-class family in Torun, Poland, Copernicus was the son of a prosperous merchant who died when Nicholas was just ten years old. After his father's death Copernicus went to live with his uncle, the bishop of Varmia, who supervised the boy's education and began preparing him for a career as a church official.

In 1491 Copernicus entered the University of Cracow, where he studied Latin, mathematics, philosophy, drawing, and astronomy, subjects for which the school was famous. However, he left Cracow before earning a degree, and at his uncle's urging he went to Italy to attend the University of Bologna. Although enrolled as a student of church law, Copernicus privately pursued an interest in astronomy.

While in Bologna, Copernicus lived for a time at the house of Domenica Maria de Novara, the principal astronomer at the university. Because Novara was responsible for making annual astrological predictions (astrology at this time was closely associated with astronomy) for the city of Bologna, Copernicus learned much about astrology from him. Novara also introduced Copernicus to the most important books on astronomy of the time. One of these, the *Epitoma in Almagestum Ptolemaei* (Epitome of Ptolemy's Almagest), written by Johannes Müller, summarized the geocentric, or earth-centered, astronomy of Ptolemy. It also contained other observations that may have led Copernicus to consider alternate models of the universe.

In 1497 Copernicus recorded his first astronomical observation—a lunar eclipse in Bologna. Three years later he observed another lunar eclipse while visiting Rome and lecturing on mathematics and astronomy. After a short stay in Poland, he returned to Italy and resumed his studies in medicine and law at the universities of Padua and Ferrara. He received a degree in church law from the University of Ferrara in 1503.

Copernicus returned to Poland, where he began practicing medicine in Heilsberg, gaining a favorable reputation as a physician. He eventually settled in the city of Frauenberg (present-day Frombork) in northern Poland and accepted a position at the palace of the bishop. His responsibilities were primarily administrative and included collecting rents from church-owned lands, supervising church finances, managing the bakery and mills, and caring for the medical needs of other church officials.

Copernicus as Astronomer. Copernicus spent the remainder of his life in the service of the church; he continued to make astronomical observations in his spare time. Using the towers of churches and other buildings as observatories, he studied the movements of the sun, moon, stars, and planets. His reputation as an astronomer grew, and in 1514 he received an invitation to attend a church council to give his opinions about revising the church calendar based on his astronomical studies. Copernicus chose not to attend the council, but his observations served as a basis for the development of the Gregorian calendar some 70 years later.

The same year, Copernicus issued a manuscript titled *Commentariolus,* in which he challenged Ptolemy's geocentric astronomical system, which had dominated Western thought for more than 1,000 years. He announced that the sun, rather than the earth as previously believed, was the center of the universe. He described how the rotation of the earth appeared to make the heavens rotate in the sky and explained how the earth's revolution around the sun accounts for the motion of the other planets in the night sky.

Copernicus released *Commentariolus* anonymously to shield himself from criticism and because he did not wish to take full credit for devising a new astronomical system. In fact, he mentions certain ancient Greeks and others who had questioned the Ptolemaic system and had suggested other models for the universe. The *Commentariolus* resolved many of the difficulties that scholars had been experiencing with the Ptolemaic system. However, it also raised new problems, some of which were answered in Copernicus's later works. The startling idea proposed in the book spread quickly through Europe, bringing both admiration and condemnation.

Nicholas Copernicus revolutionized scientific thought with his idea that the sun, not the earth, stood at the center of the universe. This engraving shows the earth revolving around the sun.

Borrowing from the Past

The idea of a sun-centered universe was not entirely new when Copernicus proposed it in the 1500s. As early as the 200s B.C., Greek astronomer Aristarchus of Samos argued that the earth revolved around the sun, and German scholar Nicholas de Cusa proposed a similar idea in 1440. These theories never took hold, however, partly because they were only ideas—little supporting evidence was offered. In providing his model of a sun-centered system with data and mathematical proofs, Copernicus moved beyond the mere ideas proposed by Aristarchus and de Cusa and developed a model that combined theory and scientific evidence.

* **theologian** person who studies religious faith and practice

Copernicus spent more than 25 years making astronomical observations and measurements and refining his ideas before publishing a full version of his heliocentric, or sun-centered, model of the universe. Even then he published the main elements of his theory under the name of another individual—his 25-year-old assistant and enthusiastic supporter, George Joachim RHETICUS.

A mathematician, Rheticus left a teaching post in Germany in 1539 to work with Copernicus in Poland. In fact, Rheticus convinced Copernicus that it was time to publish his ideas. *Narratio prima* (First Narration) appeared in 1540 under Rheticus's name. The work summarized the main principles of Copernicus's theory and emphasized their use in calculating new tables on planetary movements. Although the ideas marked a dramatic break with the Ptolemaic system, Rheticus took pains to praise Ptolemy and others who supported the earth-centered view. *Narratio prima* contains an argument, based on scientific observation and measurement, for the new heliocentric theory. Although Copernicus and Rheticus knew that they could not definitely rule out other theories, they could provide the most logical possibility based on existing knowledge.

In 1542 Rheticus returned to his teaching position in Germany. He took with him the finished manuscript of the Copernican theory in its final form, which Copernicus finally agreed to have published. Rheticus took the work to Nürnberg, where he left it with Andreas Osiander, a theologian* experienced in publishing scientific manuscripts. Osiander, aware of religious attitudes against the heliocentric system, added an anonymous preface in which he insists that the idea of a moving earth is only a mathematical hypothesis and that astronomy is incapable of explaining heavenly phenomena. However, Osiander did this without permission from either Rheticus or Copernicus, and in doing so dramatically changed the intended emphasis of the work.

Published in 1543, *De revolutionibus orbium coelestium* (On the Revolutions of the Heavenly Spheres) presents the Copernican theory and astronomical system. Although opposition to *De revolutionibus* was not as great as was expected, some people feared that changing the natural order of the universe might result in chaos. By presenting the idea as a hypothesis, Osiander might have minimized the opposition to the new theory.

The Copernican System. Drawing on his observations and measurements, Copernicus rejected many of the ideas of Aristotle and Ptolemy. Copernicus placed the sun, not the earth, at the center of the universe. He also proposed that the earth rotates on its axis once every 24 hours, that the moon orbits the earth, and that the earth revolves around the sun once each year. Copernicus also enlarged our conception of the size of the universe, arguing that it is much greater in size than Aristotle and Ptolemy imagined. Although he suggested that the universe might be infinite, he left it to philosophers to determine the answer to that problem.

Copernicus argued that his basic ideas about the structure of the universe and solar system explained the movements of the planets and stars in a simpler and more elegant way than the Ptolemaic system. For example, the rotation of the earth on its axis is responsible for the apparent movement of the sun and stars through the sky. The Copernican system also offered a simple explanation for the changes in brightness of the planets—they vary in brightness because as they travel around the sun, they are not always the same distance from the earth.

However, Copernicus did not reject all of Ptolemy's ideas. His system still placed the planets in uniform circular orbits. It took later astronomers, such as Johannes KEPLER, to discover that the orbits of the planets are elliptical (oval shaped). Consequently, Copernicus had to rely on mathematical constructions associated with Ptolemy's system to reconcile the observed motions of the planets with the notion that they move in circular orbits. He relied on the idea of epicycles* and on the idea of an eccentric, whereby the earth is situated not at the center of the solar system but at a distance from the center. However, the Copernican system contained fewer epicycles than the Ptolemaic system.

Copernicus also retained Aristotle's idea that every body has a natural place in the universe. However, he limited this notion to the earth and used it to help explain why objects are not swept away by the rotation of the earth. He also proposed a new explanation for the movement of objects on earth. He argued that heavy objects everywhere tend toward their own center of gravity—stones or other objects on earth fall toward the center of the planet. This idea opened the door for the studies of universal gravitation by Isaac NEWTON and other scientists.

Many scholars of the time considered the Copernican system implausible. However, his ideas set in motion a chain of events that led to a revolution in scientific thought as scholars and scientists began to question traditional beliefs and to use observation, experiments, and mathematical calculations to uncover explanations for natural phenomena.

* **epicycle** in Ptolemaic astronomy, circle within which a planet moves and which has a center that is simultaneously carried around the circumference of a larger circle

Charles Augustin
COULOMB

1736–1806

PHYSICS, MECHANICS

* **mechanics** science that studies how energy and force affect objects

Charles Augustin Coulomb's career encompassed two distinct but closely related scientific disciplines. Between the ages of 25 and 45, he was perhaps the world's premier engineer. Thereafter he devoted his energies to the study of physics, applying much of his engineering expertise to the newly emerging fields of electricity and magnetism. His contributions to these fields extended the mechanics* developed by Isaac NEWTON into the world of physics. His work also helped establish these and other practical areas of physics as separate disciplines worthy of specialized study.

Life and Career. Coulomb was born in the town of Angoulême, France, and moved to Paris as a child. After graduating from college he moved to Montpellier to live with his father and joined the local scientific academy there. At the age of 22, he returned to Paris to enroll in engineering school. Three years later he graduated as a lieutenant in the French corps of engineers. He was first assigned to the port city of Brest, and in 1764 he transferred to the Caribbean island of Martinique. He remained there for eight years, overseeing the construction of Fort Bourbon. The work he did on the fort would prove extremely valuable in his later studies of mechanics.

During his stay in Martinique, he suffered from several serious illnesses that had a lasting effect on his health.

In 1772 Coulomb returned to France, and five years later he submitted a paper on magnetic compasses that shared first prize in a competition sponsored by the Paris Academy of Sciences. This paper incorporated several ideas central to all his later studies in physics. In 1781 Coulomb was elected to the academy for a paper about his experiments in friction. Election to the academy ensured Coulomb a permanent residence in Paris and enabled him to retire from active participation in engineering projects. He devoted the rest of his life to investigations in physics, particularly in the areas of electricity and magnetism.

Coulomb was later appointed to oversee management of the water systems of all the royal properties in France, including the water supply to Paris. He was also a member of the committee that developed the metric system. During the last four years of his life, he served as inspector general of public instruction. In this position he played a leading role in establishing the system of French high schools known as *lycées*. For many years Coulomb suffered from the long-term effects of health problems he had first encountered in Martinique. In 1806 his health declined rapidly, and he died in Paris the same year.

Mechanics and Engineering. Coulomb's service in the corps of engineers exposed him to practical problems in all areas of mechanics. His efforts were devoted to the study of friction and cohesion, which formed the basis of contemporary engineering mechanics. Coulomb spent a great deal of time examining the strength of masonry materials, the design of retaining walls, and the design of arches. In his first and most important paper on mechanics, he developed a theory on the flexibility of beams and on the shearing and rupture of brittle materials. He then turned to cohesion, or the ability of materials to hold together under stress.

By experimenting with different materials, he determined the strength of mortar, stone, and brick under tension and strain. In the same paper Coulomb discusses earth pressure and a theory of soil mechanics that is still in use in modern engineering practices. The paper that won him election to the academy examines both static and dynamic friction, taking into account differences in load, materials, lubrication, velocity, and other factors. This work was so important that some modern commentators credit Coulomb with founding the science of friction.

Physics. Coulomb's work in physics was largely a continuation of his earlier work in mechanics. His concern with friction and cohesion in structural mechanics led him to study torsion, the stress produced when one end of an object is fixed and the other end is twisted. These subjects also played a part in his studies of electricity, magnetism, and the properties of matter. Coulomb developed a theory of torsion in thin silk threads and strands of hair that showed physicists how to measure very small forces. He also invented a torsion balance based on his principles that allowed them to make such measurements. The balance provided him an instrument with which to pursue his investigations into electricity and magnetism. He also used it to explore the elasticity of substances and to formulate principles to determine when torsion will cause an object to rupture.

Coulomb felt that it was necessary to determine the exact nature and strength of the forces of electric and magnetic attraction and repulsion. Using his torsion balance, he found that the attraction between bodies with opposite magnetic or electrical charges is inversely proportional to the square of the distance separating them; the farther apart the objects, the weaker the attraction. He extended this principle to both attractive and repulsive forces. Although he showed that electrical and magnetic phenomena follow the same law, he did not question the prevailing opinion of the day that the underlying causes of electricity and magnetism were unrelated.

Coulomb also studied the leakage of electric charge from various bodies and proposed a theory of electrical conductivity. He argued that there are two classes of objects: perfect conductors and nonconductors, or dielectrics. He established that the distribution of an electric charge in an object depends on mutual repulsion of like charges (for example, two positive charges) and the shape and relative position of the objects. Earlier scientists had argued incorrectly that other factors, such as chemical similarity, played a role in charge distribution.

Coulomb's theory of magnetism disregarded the accepted idea of magnetism as a fluid that carried a charge and flowed around and through objects. Instead, he said that each magnetized particle is a separate polarized molecule that carries its own charge. His later studies focused on the nature and extent of the magnetic properties of matter. The scope and precision of his researches in these areas led a colleague to remark that Coulomb was largely responsible for the rebirth of physics in France.

René du Perron
DESCARTES

1596–1650

SCIENTIFIC METHOD,
MATHEMATICS, PHYSICS,
PHYSIOLOGY

* **analytic geometry** field of mathematics that uses algebra to study the properties and relations of points, lines, and shapes on a coordinate grid

* **optics** scientific study of the properties of light

* **empirical** based on or derived from observation and experiment

The French philosopher René du Perron Descartes was one of the earliest champions of what is known as the scientific method. As a philosopher he was motivated to discover basic principles by which he could explain all natural phenomena. However, Descartes also realized that these principles were only a starting point for deeper investigations into the workings of nature. True knowledge, he believed, could come only from testing the principles against experience. Descartes applied his philosophical and scientific methods to study problems in a variety of scientific disciplines. The practical results of his efforts included the invention of analytic geometry* and the formulation of some of the basic laws of optics*. Just as important, his insistence on empirical* study, rather than mere philosophical speculation, helped lay the foundations of modern science.

Life and Career

As a member of a wealthy and intellectual French family, Descartes received a modern education that included training in mathematics, physics, philosophy, and the classics. He studied law at the University of Poitiers, and after his graduation he enlisted as a volunteer in the army of Prince

* **mechanics** science that studies how energy and force affect objects
* **acoustics** branch of physics that deals with sound and sound waves

Small Gland, Big Emotions

Descartes was one of the first scientists to offer a mechanical explanation for human moods and emotions. He argued that when especially pure blood enters the heart, it vaporizes quickly. This in turn stimulates those nerves in the heart that the soul associates with the feeling of joy. According to Descartes, the organ most closely associated with the soul is the tiny pineal gland, which is located deep within the brain and produces secretions that are distributed in the body through the bloodstream. Descartes believed that the soul can cause the pineal gland to redirect the animal spirits from one set of nerves—nervous channels—to another. These spirits are then interpreted as emotions as they are transmitted through the pineal gland.

Maurice of Nassau. When Descartes was 22, the Dutch philosopher Isaac Beeckman challenged him with problems in several subjects, especially mechanics* and acoustics*. This encounter with Beeckman was a major stimulus to Descartes's development as a scientific thinker. A year after their meeting, Descartes wrote Beeckman a letter in which he outlined his ideas for an "entirely new science"—analytic geometry.

Later the same year, Descartes had an experience that shaped the course of his thinking for the rest of his life. During a solitary night in a *poêle*, a French word meaning "stove" or "well-heated room," he arrived at two conclusions. The first was that he had to work on his own to discover true knowledge, without relying on the efforts or discoveries of others. The second was that he must begin by questioning the accepted ideas of philosophy and seeking the basic principles with which he could explain all the natural sciences. These principles had to be self-evident, not derived from existing ideas or observations. According to one biographer, Descartes had a series of dreams that night that convinced him of the validity of his conclusions. However, Descartes did not pursue the ideas he formulated in the *poêle* until many years later.

Around the same time, Descartes defeated a fellow philosopher in a public debate by using his philosophical method to draw distinctions between probability and true scientific knowledge. One of the spectators at the debate challenged Descartes to improve the human condition by applying his methods to medicine and mechanics. Descartes accepted the challenge and retired to Holland, where he spent the next 20 years working out his philosophy and publishing the results of his speculations. In 1649 he traveled to Stockholm to become the court philosopher to Queen Christina of Sweden. He died during his first winter in Sweden, shortly before he turned 54.

Philosophy and Scientific Achievements

Descartes began his investigations by first developing a theory and then observing to see how his theory compared with experience. This was a decidedly different approach from that taken by such scientists as Francis BACON and Isaac NEWTON, who insisted that theories should be firmly grounded in experimentation and observation. His approach testifies to the great authority that he placed in the power of human reason. He was so confident in his use of reason as a tool for uncovering truths about nature that he once admitted that it would be the worse for experience if it were to conflict with a self-evident truth furnished by reason.

Descartes's Philosophy. In 1637 Descartes published a single volume containing a series of papers that outlined his basic theories. At the heart of his thinking was the notion of mind-body dualism. That is, he believed that all creation was divided into two separate substances—matter and mind. Matter was conceived as extended material, which was indifferent to its state of motion or rest and bereft of thought or reason. For Descartes the suggestion that matter could acquire the capacity to think or reason was a contradiction in terms. Mind was conceived as a substance that

The French philosopher René Descartes stressed the importance of supporting theories with experiments and observations. He also developed algebraic notation, the law of inertia, and ideas about mind-body dualism.

thinks and reasons but which has no physical presence. Consequently, it was impossible for a mind to affect a body at a distance. From this basic premise Descartes argued that the origin and operation of the universe result from matter in motion and that the only properties of matter that are appropriate in scientific explanations are magnitude, shape, and motion. Descartes even went so far as to say that people and animals behaved simply as mechanisms, operating according to mechanical principles. This was a dangerous idea to promote in a Catholic country such as France, because the idea disregarded the soul in its explanation of behavior. The Catholic Church had recently punished the Italian scientist Galileo GALILEI for advancing ideas that went against its teachings. Consequently, Descartes left the more radical ideas out of his work; they did not appear in print until after his death.

Descartes felt that the only scientific knowledge that was valid was that which could explain experience. However, he felt that a theory was not valid simply because it could explain how a phenomenon occurred. It also had to prove that no other explanation could account for the phenomenon. He criticized the work of other scientists who failed to place their discoveries in a larger theoretical framework. For example, Galileo outlined the basic mathematical laws that govern the movement of falling bodies. However, Descartes criticized him for simply explaining one type of motion but failing to account for the mechanism that underlies all motion.

This mechanistic philosophy was at the heart of Descartes's investigations into the natural world. He was concerned with discovering the mechanisms that were responsible for producing observable phenomena. To this end he stressed the need to observe and experiment. He dissected adult animals and animal embryos, studied chemistry and anatomy, and performed experiments on the weight of air and the vibration of strings. Interestingly, however, he often failed to live up to the scientific standards he set. For example, he said that physics had to be mathematically proved, yet he supplied no proof for his own basic ideas about the operation of the universe. In fact, it was Newton who used mathematics to show that Descartes's theory of planetary motion could not account for the velocity relations that are implied in Johannes KEPLER's laws of planetary motion. Descartes also stressed observation, but many of his theories on motion and impact were completely reworked after the more careful observations of Christiaan HUYGENS and Wilhelm LEIBNIZ. However, the questions raised by his philosophy and methods were more important than the results of his scientific investigations. His insistence on rigorous experimentation and observation set the tone for the scientific revolution.

Mathematics. Descartes's groundbreaking work in mathematics was stimulated by his dissatisfaction with the prevailing methods. He wished to revive the pure mathematics of the ancient Greeks without the "multiple numbers and inexplicable figures that overwhelm it." At the time, the accepted method for solving numerical problems was a type of algebra, but Descartes felt the need to separate algebraic reasoning from the specific types of problems it was used to solve. His goal was to develop a purely symbolic algebra to analyze and classify all types of problems in terms of the techniques needed to solve them. To this end he replaced all the symbols in the algebra he was using with letters of the alphabet. He also eliminated verbal expressions, such as *square* and *cube,* and replaced them with numerical notations, such as x^2 and x^3. Using his new system of notation, he applied algebra to solve geometric problems, such as determining the area under a curve. In addition to creating the discipline of analytic geometry, Descartes's mathematical methods formed one of the bases on which Leibniz and Newton invented calculus*.

Physics. Descartes used his work in mathematics to supply proofs for his work in physics, especially in optics. By combining mathematical proofs and his ideas about motion, he formulated basic laws of reflection and refraction of light. He used these findings to analyze the structure and functioning of the eye. Descartes explained various distortions of vision, such as nearsightedness, and discussed the types of lenses that could be used to correct each defect. He also demonstrated the application of his ideas to develop better lenses for telescopes. Using his optical theories, Descartes explained that a rainbow is created by the refraction of sunlight passing through raindrops and its reflection inside the drops of rain.

Descartes also studied the physics of motion. He developed the first modern formulation of the law of inertia, according to which a body's state of rest or of motion is conserved in a straight line. Earlier, Galileo had argued that motion and rest are states of matter, but it was Descartes who explicitly declared that the motion that is preserved is rectilinear (moving in or forming a straight line). Descartes was also the first to outline the law of conservation of motion, which states that during a collision between bodies, the total quantity of motion remains unchanged. For example, if object A has an amount of motion equal to "a", and it strikes object B, which has an amount of motion equal to "b", the combined amount of motion of both objects after the collision is "a + b" even if the collision causes them to change their speed and direction of movement. Descartes proposed other theories of motion dealing with such subjects as impact and centrifugal force, although they were later proven incorrect. Huygens, who supported many of Descartes's ideas, found the correct solutions to many of these problems.

Physiology. Like so many of his areas of study, Descartes's thinking about physiology* owed much to his mechanistic philosophy and ideas on mind-body dualism. He stated that all involuntary motions in humans and animals are controlled by unconscious mechanisms. He flatly rejected the popular philosophical idea that human activities were caused by unseen "vegetative souls" or "innate spirits."

In outlining his principles of physiology, he stated that to understand how the human body works, it is important to study its inherent mechanical processes. Descartes applied his mechanistic theories to general physiological processes, such as digestion, as well as to the workings of the nervous system. He believed that the nerves were hollow tubes filled with a fine substance called animal spirits—quick-moving particles of blood that travel from the heart to the brain, where they separate from the other parts of the blood to become "a wind or very subtle flame." This wind

* **calculus** advanced form of mathematics that involves computing quantities that change as functions of different variables

* **physiology** science that deals with the functions of living organisms and their parts

then flowed into the muscles, inflating them and causing the muscles to contract. The spirits also played an important role in sensation. Descartes believed that the sense organs, such as the eyes, nose, and ears, were "jiggled" by external stimuli, causing animal spirits to flow to the brain. As the spirits passed the pineal gland in the brain, it interpreted them as sensations. Descartes also explored sleep, dreaming, memory, and the imagination as they relate to the actions of animal spirits.

Although later investigators disproved most of his physiological theories, his work was of major importance. His ideas of mind-body dualism and the mechanical nature of animal activity were adopted and used by later scientists. These ideas led later physiologists to study anatomy carefully when formulating ideas about the workings of the body. In this manner, one of Descartes's main goals was realized: to create a method of investigation that bypassed the speculative philosophical explanations for natural processes in favor of observation and experimentation. For that, he earned a place as one of the architects of the modern scientific world.

Leonhard EULER

1707–1783

MATHEMATICS

* **calculus** advanced form of mathematics that involves computing quantities that change as functions of different variables

* **mechanics** science that studies how energy and force affect objects

* **theology** study of religion

Leonhard Euler was one of the greatest mathematicians of all time. One of the founders of pure mathematics, he was one of the first to develop the methods of calculus* on a wide scale. He also made significant contributions to algebra, geometry, trigonometry, mechanics*, and number theory, and he developed methods for problems related to observational astronomy. Euler was also one of the most prolific mathematicians of all time, with written works collected in more than 70 volumes.

Early Life and Career. Born in Basel, Switzerland, Euler was the son of a Protestant minister. Shortly after Euler's birth his family moved to the village of Riehen, where his father gave Leonhard an elementary education, including studies in mathematics. Euler later spent several years with his grandmother in Basel, studying at a local school. Mathematics was not taught at the school, but Euler studied it privately with Johann Burckhardt, an amateur mathematician.

In 1720 Euler entered the University of Basel, a small college that had only about 100 students. One of his teachers was the well-known Swiss mathematician Johann BERNOULLI. Euler received a bachelor's degree from the university in 1722 and a master's degree in philosophy the following year. His studies included theology*, Greek, Hebrew, and other subjects, but he devoted most of his time to mathematics. Although Euler originally planned to become a minister like his father, he gave up that idea to pursue mathematics instead.

At the age of 18, Euler began his independent investigations into mathematics. His first work, *Acta eruditorum* (Records of Instruction), published in 1726, dealt with the construction of geometric curves. The following year Euler participated in a competition announced by the Paris Académie des Sciences, which proposed a problem about the most efficient arrangement of masts on a ship. Although he did not win that competition, Euler received 12 prizes from the academy between 1738 and 1772.

For mathematicians beginning their careers in Switzerland in the mid-1700s, the conditions were difficult. There were few positions for professors in the country and little chance of finding a suitable job. Moreover, there were no scientific magazines, and publishers were reluctant to publish books on mathematics, which were considered financially risky. With few opportunities in Switzerland, Euler was willing to look elsewhere. At the time, the newly organized St. Petersburg Academy of Sciences in Russia was looking to hire faculty. In 1725 Nikolaus and Daniel BERNOULLI, the sons of Johann, went to Russia, and they persuaded the authorities there to invite Euler as well. Two years later Euler left for St. Petersburg. From this time on, his life and work were closely connected with the St. Petersburg Academy of Science and with Russia. He never returned to Switzerland, but he maintained his Swiss citizenship.

Euler in Russia. Although Euler had been invited to St. Petersburg to study physiology*, he was soon appointed to the mathematics section of the academy there. He became professor of physics in 1733 and two years later succeeded Daniel Bernoulli as professor of mathematics. Although the young academy faced many hardships, the presence of well-known and respected scientists provided an atmosphere that was beneficial for the development of Euler's genius. Also important was the academy's generous publication program, which published many of Euler's works.

During the 14 years that Euler spent in Russia, he made brilliant discoveries in many mathematical fields, including analysis, number theory, and mechanics. He worked in other areas as well. After 1733 he began to work on maps in the department of geography. From the mid-1730s he studied problems of shipbuilding and navigation, which were especially important to the rise of Russia as a great seafaring power. Euler also tested scales, fire pumps, saws, and other technological tools and devices.

By 1741 Euler had prepared nearly 90 works for publication, of which 55 were published, including the two-volume *Mechanica*. Because he carried on an extensive correspondence with scientists from many countries, his work and discoveries often became known long before they were published, and this contributed to his growing fame. The only mishap that marred Euler's life during this time was a disease that caused the loss of sight in his right eye in 1738. Around 1740 the political atmosphere in St. Petersburg grew troubled. At that time Frederick the Great took the throne of Prussia (in present-day Germany) and decided to reorganize the Berlin Society of Sciences. Euler was invited to work in Berlin, and because of the growing turmoil in Russia, he accepted the offer.

Euler in Berlin. Euler arrived in Berlin in late 1741 and remained there for the next 25 years. He became actively involved in transforming the old Berlin Society of Sciences into a large academy, which was founded in 1744 as the Royale des Sciences et des Belles Lettres de Berlin (Royal Academy of Sciences and Fine Letters of Berlin). Euler had many administrative duties at the academy. He supervised the observatory and botanical gardens, selected personnel, oversaw finance, and managed the publication of calendars and maps. King Frederick also engaged Euler with practical

* **physiology** science that deals with the functions of living organisms and their parts

Leonhard Euler, one of the greatest mathematicians of all time, introduced many of the symbols used in mathematical notation today. He also made significant contributions to the fields of astronomy and navigation.

problems, such as projects to correct the level of canals and supervising work on the hydraulic system at Sans Souci, the royal summer residence. He also served as a consultant to the government on problems of insurance and widows' pensions, out of which grew his studies on demography*.

Euler's influence on scientific life in Germany was not restricted to the academy. He maintained a large correspondence with professors at numerous German universities and promoted the teaching of mathematical sciences and the preparation of university texts. Euler also maintained a close relationship with the St. Petersburg Academy of Science, editing the mathematical section of its journal, keeping the academy informed of scientific and technological thought in Western Europe, and recommending candidates for positions at the academy. His participation in the training of Russian scientific personnel was especially important and contributed to the establishment of mathematical education in Russia.

Euler transformed the science of mechanics into a discipline to which analytical techniques could be applied. He also laid the foundations of mathematical physics, helped advance the theory of lunar and planetary motion, created the mathematical tools for hydrodynamics*, developed the geometry of surfaces, and made extensive studies in optics*, electricity, acoustics*, and magnetism. He also pondered various problems related to the use of technology.

Between 1741 and 1766 Euler prepared nearly 380 works, of which about 275 were published, including *Institutiones calculi differentialis* (Institutions of Differential Calculus), a fundamental work on calculation of orbits, a work on artillery and ballistics*, and an essay on navigation and shipbuilding. His works on mathematics contain formulas and methods, many invented by Euler, that remain a foundation of modern calculus.

In the 1740s and 1750s, Euler participated in philosophical and scientific arguments that were important to the development of mathematical sciences. One of these arguments, with French mathematician and philosopher Jean le Rond d'ALEMBERT, involved problems dealing with negative numbers and exponents. Another argument, on the solution of the equation of a vibrating string, was with d'Alembert and Daniel Bernoulli. Still another dealt with various optical problems.

After 1759 Euler managed the Berlin Academy under the direct supervision of King Frederick. By this time, however, relations between Frederick and Euler had deteriorated greatly. In 1763, when it became known that the king wanted to appoint d'Alembert to the position of president of the academy, Euler began to think about leaving Berlin. During the next few years, conflicts over philosophical and financial matters arose between Euler and Frederick. In 1766 Euler left Berlin and returned to St. Petersburg at the invitation of Catherine the Great, the ruler of Russia.

Last Years. Soon after returning to Russia, Euler suffered a brief illness that left him almost completely blind in the left eye. He could only see outlines of large objects and write in large letters with chalk and slate. An operation in 1771 temporarily restored his sight, but Euler did not take adequate care of himself and within a short time became totally blind. However, the loss of sight did not lessen his scientific activities. In fact, his

* **demography** science that deals with social statistics, such as births, deaths, marriages, income, and population

* **hydrodynamics** scientific study of the motion of liquids

* **optics** scientific study of the properties of light

* **acoustics** branch of physics that deals with sound and sound waves

* **ballistics** study of the dynamics of projectiles

Applied Mathematics

Many of Euler's mathematical findings were applied to practical matters, such as improving shipbuilding techniques and methods of navigation. A good example of the relation of his work to applied mathematics involved his studies of lunar motion. From his investigations and calculations on the motion of the moon, he developed a new theory of lunar motion. A German astronomer used Euler's formulas to create lunar tables that enabled navigators to calculate the position of the moon and use that information to determine the longitude of a ship at sea more accurately than before.

literary output increased, and he attended academic meetings regularly until the last years of his life. Nearly half of his written works were produced after 1765. Euler had a remarkable memory, and he carried on his plans and studies with the help of his two sons, Johann Albrecht and Christoph, and various colleagues and students.

Among the writings he published during his second stay in St. Petersburg were works on algebra, integral calculus, optics, lunar motion, and naval science. One of his works, a manual for naval cadets, was translated into English, Italian, and Russian and earned Euler large sums from the Russian and French governments. He died in 1783 and was buried in St. Petersburg. A massive monument was erected at his grave in 1837.

Accomplishments in Mathematics. Euler was one of the most important creators of mathematical science after Isaac NEWTON. His work in mathematics was linked with other sciences, to problems in technology, and to public life. He developed mathematical solutions for problems in astronomy, mechanics, physics, navigation, geography, hydraulics, and demography. He sought to solve problems using simple solutions, ensuring accurate results.

Euler was first and foremost a mathematician. He tried to express all problems in mathematical terms. When he found a mathematical idea for a solution, he developed that idea systematically and drew generalizations from it. The primary focus of his work was analysis. In *Introductio in analysin infinitorum* (Introduction to the Analysis of Infinities), he developed the idea that mathematical analysis is a science of functions in which variables are related to one another. His mathematical treatises collectively systematized and developed the accomplishments of mathematicians of the 1700s.

Unsurpassed in his formal calculations, Euler was also a creator of new and important ideas and methods, some of which were not properly understood until after his death. He also introduced many of the symbols presently used in mathematical notation, including the modern signs for trigonometric functions, the symbol Σ for the sum of an equation, and the symbol π for the ratio of circumference to diameter in a circle.

The 1700s can be fairly labeled the Age of Euler because of his enormous influence and contributions to mathematics. However, Euler's influence on the development of mathematical sciences extended beyond that time as well. The work of many outstanding mathematicians in the 1800s stemmed directly from the works of Euler. Unsurpassed in his productivity as well as in his imaginative solutions to problems, Euler is counted among the greatest mathematicians of any era.

Bartolomeo
EUSTACHI
ca.1500–1574
MEDICINE

The Italian scientist Bartolomeo Eustachi is often considered the founder of modern anatomy. A practicing physician and medical researcher, he conducted important research on various parts of the human body, including the kidneys, the adrenal glands, the heart, and other internal organs. He is perhaps best known for his research on the structure of the ear and for his descriptions of the Eustachian tube, which bears his name.

* **medieval** relating to the Middle Ages in Europe, a period from about 500 to 1500

* **cadaver** dead body, especially one intended for dissection

Eustachi was born in the town of San Severino in central Italy. The son of a physician, he received a good education that included training in the Greek, Hebrew, and Arabic languages. Later in his life, Eustachi used his knowledge of Arabic to translate the works of the great medieval* physician and philosopher Ibn Sīnā. After completing his basic education, Eustachi appears to have studied medicine in Rome. He began practicing medicine in about 1540 and became the personal physician of a duke and a high church official. By the end of that decade, he had settled in Rome and become a professor at the Archiginnasio della Sapienza (College of Learning). His position permitted him to dissect cadavers* from several local hospitals, which enabled him to pursue his research on human anatomy.

In 1552 Eustachi prepared a series of 47 anatomical illustrations based on his research with cadavers. He was assisted by an artist named Pier Matteo Pini, who was also his relative. The illustrations, engraved on copper plates, were supposed to appear in a book on anatomy, but the book was never published. Eustachi used eight of the illustrations two years later in a work titled *Opuscula anatomica* (Small Anatomy Work). These included drawings of the kidneys, various veins, the heart, and the Eustachian tube.

The other illustrations were temporarily lost after Eustachi's death. During the 1600s many scholars, including the Italian physician and anatomist Marcello MALPIGHI, looked for them unsuccessfully. The missing illustrations were eventually found in the early 1700s. These drawings, along with the eight published in 1554, appeared in a 1714 work titled *Tabulae anatomicae* (Anatomical Drawings) and credited to Eustachi. Eustachi's anatomical illustrations were not the first such works to be produced, but compared to other early illustrations, they were strikingly modern in appearance. Moreover, the accuracy of many of the illustrations far surpasses any others produced in the 1500s.

Eustachi produced various other written works during his lifetime. His work on the kidney, which contains the first description of the adrenal glands, displayed a detailed knowledge of that organ superior to that of any earlier work. One of his works on the ear provided the first correct account of the tube that bears his name. Eustachi was also the first to make a detailed study of the structure, development, and growth of the teeth. His work on the heart revealed a relatively advanced knowledge of the structure of that organ.

Most of Eustachi's written works focused on his scientific research. However, he also wrote two works directed against his contemporary, the Flemish anatomist Andreas VESALIUS, whose ideas overturned traditional views of anatomy established by the ancient Greek physician Galen. Like many other anatomists of the time, Eustachi was highly critical of Vesalius.

Girolamo FABRICI

ca. 1537–1619

ANATOMY, PHYSIOLOGY, EMBRYOLOGY, SURGERY

The Italian medical scientist Girolamo Fabrici, also known as Geronimo Fabrizio or Fabricius ab Aquapendente, dominated the study of anatomy at one of Europe's foremost universities for many decades in the late 1500s and early 1600s. Fabrici was a pioneer in embryology, the study of how animals and humans develop before birth, and his researches into the structure of veins helped lead one of his students, William HARVEY, toward an understanding of the body's circulatory system.

Life and Career. Fabrici was born in Aquapendente, Italy. The year of his birth is unknown, but it was possibly around 1537. Fabrici was the oldest son of a noble family that had once been wealthy. As a young man he studied Greek, Latin, logic, and philosophy at the University of Padua in northeastern Italy. He then went on to study medicine, and sometime around 1559 he received a degree in both medicine and philosophy.

Fabrici studied anatomy under Gabriele FALLOPPIO, and when Falloppio died in 1562, Fabrici took his place as teacher of anatomy. A few years later the university appointed him as a lecturer in both anatomy and surgery. He held that position until 1609, when anatomy and surgery became separate subjects and were taught separately. Fabrici continued as the head of anatomical study until his retirement in 1613, after nearly 50 years of service to the university.

Those years did not pass without strife. In addition to quarrels with some of his colleagues, Fabrici had troubled relations with his students. In 1588 his students publicly accused him of neglecting his teaching. There was probably some truth to this charge—Fabrici was frequently ill, and he devoted much time to scientific research. Trouble arose again when Fabrici ridiculed the manner in which his German students spoke, and they resented the insult. German students in Italy seem to have been a lively lot, for in later years, Fabrici defended one from a charge of murder and helped others who had gotten into trouble for carrying weapons. Despite his sometimes difficult character, Fabrici's excellent reputation as a surgeon and physician brought him many famous and wealthy patients, including several dukes and the physicist Galileo GALILEI.

Contributions to Medical Science. As a scientist Fabrici was a careful and exact observer. His shortcoming, however, was that he often interpreted his observations in ways that fit traditional ideas or broad principles rather than let each new observation suggest new theories.

Fabrici intended to publish a monumental work that would encompass all of his researches, discoveries, and ideas. Although he never completed this masterwork, he did publish a series of shorter volumes, beginning in 1600. They dealt with such topics as vision, voice, and hearing; the valves of the veins; and the eggs and embryos of birds, animals, and humans. Among other notable discoveries, Fabrici was the first to describe how the larynx produces speech and to show that the pupil of the eye can grow larger and smaller to admit more or less light. In 1600 Fabrici also completed a set of 300 color plates illustrating various anatomical features.

One of the best-known and most thoroughly studied of Fabrici's works is *De venum ostiolis* (On the Valves of the Veins), published in 1603. It gives the first clear description of structures that regulate the flow of blood within the veins, although Fabrici did not understand their function. Perhaps the most important feature of Fabrici's work on the veins is that one of his students, William Harvey, later drew on it when he described the system by which blood circulates within the body. Harvey, who not only studied under Fabrici but also lived for a time in Fabrici's house, first became interested in the heartbeat and circulation while observing Fabrici's anatomical dissections at Padua.

A Room with a View

Medical students have long learned anatomy by observing skilled anatomists at work as they operate on the living or cut up (dissect) the bodies of the dead. In Fabrici's time the University of Padua recognized the need for a chamber designed so that students could clearly see and hear the anatomist. Thanks largely to Fabrici's efforts, the university built a new, oval-shaped anatomy theater, which Fabrici inaugurated in 1595. It became famous as a seat of advanced anatomical study. The theater still stands and bears Fabrici's name.

Fabrici's other important contribution to medical science concerned life before birth. In 1604 he published *De formato foetu* (On the Formation of the Fetus), which dealt with fetal development in birds, sharks, mice, rabbits, cats, dogs, horses, pigs, and humans. Fabrici described the umbilical cord and provided the first clear description of the placenta*. Fabrici's insistence on fitting his observations into a framework of inaccurate traditional beliefs (such as the notion that the fetus's bloodstream was the same as the mother's) meant that he did not fully understand the meaning of some of his findings. Nevertheless, he can still be considered the founder of embryology.

* **placenta** flattened organ in pregnant mammals that connects the fetus to the maternal uterus and facilitates the exchange of nutrients

Daniel Gabriel
FAHRENHEIT
1686–1736
EXPERIMENTAL PHYSICS

Daniel Fahrenheit, the German maker of scientific instruments, is best known for devising the temperature scale used for thermometers in most English-speaking countries. He also contributed greatly to experimental science by designing precise instruments that allowed scientists to make exact measurements during their observations.

Fahrenheit was the oldest of five children of a wealthy merchant in the German city of Danzig. In 1701 his parents died unexpectedly, and Daniel's guardian sent him to Amsterdam to learn business. There he became acquainted with and interested in designing and building scientific instruments. He also roamed across Germany, meeting and observing the work of many scientists and instrument makers. He corresponded with the mathematician Wilhelm LEIBNIZ about designs for a clock to determine longitude at sea.

In 1717 Fahrenheit returned to Amsterdam and began making his own scientific instruments, including thermometers. He was the first to use mercury in the reliable thermometer that he designed. Based on a misreading of the work of the Danish astronomer Olaus Roemer, Fahrenheit fixed the high temperature on his instruments at 22½°. (He believed this to be the temperature of human blood, but it was actually several degrees lower). He fixed the lower point at 7½°, or the temperature of a mixture of ice and water. He then divided each degree on his scale into four parts so that the upper limit became 90° and the lower limit, 30°. He later changed these to 96° and 32° to dispense with difficult fractions.

Using this thermometer, Fahrenheit measured the boiling point of water at 212°, which was actually several degrees higher than it should have been. After his death the upper limit on Fahrenheit thermometers was set at the boiling point of water (212°) rather than 96°. Consequently, normal body temperature became 98.6° instead of Fahrenheit's 96°. Britain and Holland soon adopted this version of his temperature scale that is now widely used in the English-speaking world. Fahrenheit also invented a thermometer to measure atmospheric pressure based on the temperature at which water boiled. Shortly before his death, he also designed a device to pump water from low-lying lands.

Fahrenheit's work required him to solve many practical scientific problems, such as measuring the rate at which glass expands, determining how mercury and alcohol react to changes in temperature, and describing

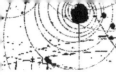

how atmospheric pressure affects the boiling point of various liquids. His attention to these details enabled him to construct accurate instruments that made the work of other scientists easier and more precise. Although he had no formal scientific training and made few direct contributions to science, London's Royal Society recognized his importance by electing him to its membership in 1724.

Gabriele
FALLOPPIO

ca. 1523–1562

MEDICINE, ANATOMY

This portrait shows Gabriele Falloppio, a distinguished scholar of medicine and anatomy. Falloppio discovered many parts of the human body, including structures of the ear and of the female reproductive system.

* **clitoris** small organ that is part of the external reproductive system in female mammals

Gabriele Falloppio was among Italy's most distinguished scholars of the human body and the first to discover many parts of human anatomy. After his father's death Falloppio studied to be a clergyman, but when his family's finances improved, he turned to medicine. Around the age of 20, he dissected a human body for his teacher, Andreas VESALIUS. Fallopio was appointed to the chair of pharmacy in Ferrara, and in 1549 he accepted the chair of anatomy at the University of Pisa. His career as a professor hit a bump in Pisa, where he was wrongfully accused of performing dissections on living humans. Overcoming this controversy, he became the chair of anatomy at Padua, succeeding the celebrated anatomist Realdo COLOMBO.

Falloppio's major work, published in 1561, is an unillustrated commentary on an anatomical text written by Andreas Vesalius. While clearly admiring Vesalius's work, Falloppio sought to correct his former teacher's errors and to add new observations of his own, based on dissections of human fetuses and the bodies of newborn infants, children, and adults. One major contribution was his description of how the many bones of infants join into the fewer bones of adult bodies. He also wrote detailed descriptions of the structure of the ears, the muscles of the scalp and face, and the tissues called nictitating membranes at the inner corners of the eyes. Falloppio went on to make important discoveries about the structure of blood vessels, kidneys, and the urinary bladder. He also traced the circulation of blood in the brain and the arrangement of nerves in the head.

Falloppio's name is best known today from the term *fallopian tubes*, also called uterine tubes, which connect the ovaries to the uterus. In his studies of the female reproductive system, he was the first to describe the clitoris* and introduced the term *vagina* into anatomy, disproving the belief that the penis enters the uterus during sexual intercourse.

Pierre de
FERMAT

1601–1665

MATHEMATICS

The French mathematician Pierre de Fermat is considered one of the inventors of analytic geometry*. His work also included early achievements in the areas of number theory and probability. In spite of his accomplishments, Fermat had little immediate influence on the field. It was only many years after his death that the full importance of his work became apparent. This was partly due to the nature of the subjects to which Fermat had turned his attention, and partly due to Fermat's reluctance to publish his work.

Life and Career

Very little information is available about Fermat's private life. Most of what is known about him has been gathered from official records. These sources portray a man who led a very conventional life, and they provide few clues about his personality. Even his scholarly writings are often vague about how he developed his ideas.

Early Life. Fermat was born in the town of Beaumont-de-Lomagne, where he apparently spent most of his childhood and early adult years. His father had a successful leather business and held high political office in the town. His mother's family belonged to the French nobility and so enjoyed both high social status and a good deal of wealth. With such a background the natural course of study for young Pierre was training in the law. After finishing his studies at a local secondary school, Fermat may have enrolled at the University of Toulouse. However, the records from this period of his life are sketchy, and Fermat's whereabouts are uncertain. He definitely spent some time in France's Bordeaux region in his late 20s. In 1631 he graduated from the University of Orleans with a bachelor's degree in Civil Laws, which was the conventional academic preparation for a career in law and government service.

Shortly before his graduation Fermat purchased several government offices in Toulouse, a standard practice among the noble class that dominated French government of that time. He returned to that city after his graduation and almost immediately married his mother's cousin. The marriage produced five children, none of whom inherited their father's gift or passion for mathematics. His oldest son, Clément-Samuel, was later responsible for publishing his father's papers posthumously*.

Later Life. Fermat led a very conventional family life for a man of his station. His political life was equally mundane. Serving as a member of the local assembly, Fermat distinguished himself by his longevity more than by his ability as a lawmaker. He eventually rose from relatively minor offices to the highest chambers of the assembly. However, it appears that the deaths of his colleagues had a great deal to do with his promotions. In fact, a letter from a local official to France's chief government minister strongly criticizes Fermat's abilities. In private correspondence Fermat questioned his own performance in office. Nevertheless, he continued to serve in official positions until his death. Fermat was buried in the town of Castres, but his remains were brought back to Toulouse and placed in his family's burial vault in 1675.

Scientific Accomplishments

Only a few documents exist that provide clues to the development of Fermat's ideas. Most of these are letters and papers written to friends in Paris many years after Fermat first began his work in mathematics. From these writings one can trace the rough outlines of Fermat's investigations of algebra and analytic geometry.

* **analytic geometry** field of mathematics that uses algebra to study the properties and relations of points, lines, and shapes on a coordinate grid

* **posthumous** occurring after the death of an individual

Developing Fermat's Mathematics. While in Bordeaux, Fermat undertook research that had a significant impact on his approach to mathematics and his later accomplishments in that field. Fermat was an avid disciple of the mathematics of François VIÈTE, who developed symbolic algebra and the new theory of equations. But it was Viète's idea of algebra as a tool for analysis that captured Fermat's imagination. This concept of algebra as the analytic art deeply influenced the kinds of problems Fermat chose to tackle as well as his approach to their solutions.

Viète saw symbolic algebra as a tool that could unite the fields of geometry and arithmetic. His theory of equations was not concerned with solving specific equations. Rather, it attempted to discover and clarify the relationships between the solutions to problems and the structures of the equations that had generated those problems in the first place. Viète's theory was also concerned with examining the relations between the solutions of one equation and those of another. Fermat saw himself as carrying on the mathematical tradition of Viète and building on his foundation. He focused on using algebra to explore the relations between problems and their solutions. The tool he used most often to do this was called reduction analysis. This technique facilitated the reduction of any one problem to another problem, or to a whole class of problems whose general solution was already known.

Fermat sought clues to mathematical analysis in the writings of the ancient Greeks. Like Viète, he hoped to restore lost texts written by classical scholars, such as Euclid, Apollonius, Diophantus, and Archimedes. Fermat began with a problem discovered in one of these texts and attempted to solve it, using the new techniques of algebra developed by Viète and others. Using his reduction analysis, Fermat restated the problem in its most general terms. He often ended up defining a whole class of problems, and in most cases his solutions were even more general than the problems with which he started. Fermat rarely offered proofs for the results that he obtained, providing instead just the algebraic equations by which he derived his answers. He felt that readers who wished to do so could always provide the proofs.

This unfinished nature of his work was characteristic of Fermat's approach to his field of study. He presented most of his ideas in letters and essays to his friends, and he never wrote for publication. In fact, he strongly resisted attempts by colleagues to convince him to edit or publish his work. The few pieces that were printed during his lifetime were published anonymously. He often sent original papers to friends without keeping a copy. The most important part of his work on number theory was drawn from notes he wrote in his copy of a work by Diophantus, and was only published after his death by his son.

Fermat's reluctance to publish is hard to understand, since he apparently knew of and valued his reputation in academic circles. Whatever its cause, it cheated him of the recognition he deserved for many of his accomplishments, and it eventually cut him off from the main areas of mathematical research. Fermat and his work were largely forgotten until the mid-1800s, a time of new interest in the number theory that had occupied much of his time. Some 200 years after his death, he finally received recognition for his work.

Different Paths, Same Results

Fermat always insisted that knowledge of the physical world must be grounded in experience and observation. For this reason he criticized René Descartes for attempting to use just mathematics to make assumptions about the physical world. Fermat also criticized Descartes's law of the refraction of light for the same reason. Notwithstanding these criticisms, Fermat himself later tried to derive a theory of refraction based solely on mathematical methods. To his surprise, when he applied mathematical formulas to the problem, he came up with the same law of refraction that Descartes had proposed earlier.

The French mathematician Pierre de Fermat made great achievements in the areas of analytic geometry, number theory, and probability. Unfortunately, much of his work gained importance, and was published, only after his death.

* **calculus** advanced form of mathematics that involves computing quantities that change as functions of different variables

Analytic Geometry. The main fruit of Fermat's work was the development of a system of analytic geometry. Interestingly, the philosopher and mathematician René DESCARTES made the same discovery at virtually the same time. The letter in which Fermat outlined his ideas was completed in 1636, and Descartes's work, *Géométrie,* was published the following year. All the evidence suggests that the two systems developed completely independently of each other. Although Fermat established the algebraic basis for analytic geometry, he never found the geometrical framework for it.

Despite the fact that they produced such similar ideas, Fermat and Descartes were never on friendly terms. Descartes considered Fermat his rival, and he severely criticized Fermat's methods. These criticisms, coming from a highly respected figure such as Descartes, tarnished Fermat's reputation as a mathematician. Fermat's friends finally succeeded in publishing some of his methods, but the development of calculus* by Isaac NEWTON and Wilhelm LEIBNIZ made Fermat's work largely obsolete.

Number Theory and Probability. Fermat's other principal area of work was in number theory, but it had even less influence on his contemporaries than did his work in analytic geometry. Few people understood or appreciated this field of study at the time, and it too lay largely forgotten for many years. Fermat's ideas form much of the basis for modern number theory, and in a sense it can be said that he invented it as a separate branch of mathematics. However, his methods remain a mystery because he left no indication of what they were. Lacking any evidence of Fermat's methods, number theorists of the 1800s were forced to devise their own. This may have been a blessing in disguise, for their efforts led to the development of new concepts that underlie modern algebra.

Along with Blaise PASCAL, Fermat was one of the pioneers whose work led to the mathematical theory of probability. Their efforts in this field were stimulated by a question posed to Pascal by a gambler. The gambler wanted to know how the money in a game of chance should be divided among the players if the game were to end prematurely. Fermat and Pascal together determined how many favorable outcomes each player experienced as a percentage of the total number of outcomes in the game. Although Fermat calculated solutions for specific problems, he did not develop any general formulas for solving them. A few years later Christiaan HUYGENS published more sophisticated findings on this topic, making Fermat's work obsolete.

Number theory occupied Fermat's attention for the last 15 years of his life. However, during this time his contemporaries were more concerned with applying analytical mathematics to problems in physics. This resulted in Fermat's isolation from the scientific community and prevented him from receiving immediate notice. Fermat left one of the most celebrated unsolved problems of mathematics, known as "Fermat's last theorem." This theorem states that the algebraic analog of Pythagoras's theorem has no whole number solution for a power greater than 2. In other words, the equation $a^n + b^n = c^n$ has no whole solution for n greater than 2, if *a, b,* and *c* are all integers. Although Fermat believed that he had devised a proof for this result, the difficulty that subsequent mathematicians experienced in proving the last theorem make it unlikely. This theorem is Fermat's most important scientific legacy.

John
FLAMSTEED
1646–1719
ASTRONOMY

* **posthumous** occurring after the death of an individual

Father Doesn't Know Best

Flamsteed's father never supported his son's choice to become an astronomer. Flamsteed wrote that his studies were "discountenanced by my father as much in the beginning as they have been since." Even at the age of 27, he received his mail through a friend so that his father would not see all of the letters that came to him, especially those of a scientific nature. Flamsteed even questioned his father's motives in pulling him out of school. On the surface, the reason was Flamsteed's health. However, he always suspected that his father had done so in the hope that John would be available to help care for the family home and business.

The English astronomer John Flamsteed is known for his commitment to precise observation, which revolutionized the field of astronomy. His measurements of the positions of the stars and planetary motions were significantly more accurate than those of earlier astronomers. This enabled Flamsteed and others to unlock secrets that had challenged observers for thousands of years. The most important product of his efforts was the publication of his monumental work, the *Historia coelestis Britannica* (British Celestial Record), published posthumously* in 1725.

The only son of a prosperous businessman, Flamsteed was born and raised in Derby, England. He attended the local school in preparation for university study, but he never attended any university. He suffered a serious illness at age 14 that affected his health throughout his life and caused his father to keep him at home. Given the poor state of astronomical instruction at the English universities of the day, this might have been a positive move in his career. Flamsteed spent his teens and early adult years teaching himself astronomy, and at age 24 he submitted a table of predicted lunar eclipses to the Royal Society, bringing himself to the attention of the scientific community. Five years later King Charles II appointed Flamsteed to be England's astronomer royal and built the Royal Observatory at Greenwich for him. Flamsteed's task was to produce accurate tables of the positions of the stars and motions of the planets to help solve the long-standing problem of determining longitude at sea.

At the time, the most accurate star catalog was one produced by Tycho BRAHE some 100 years earlier. Two months after his appointment as astronomer royal, Flamsteed began to record observations to update Brahe's findings. Over the next 13 years, Flamsteed devised precise measuring instruments to use in his work, making some 20,000 observations of the heavens. Flamsteed's measurements proved to be about 15 times more accurate than those taken by Brahe, enabling him to make significant advances in theories concerning the motions of the moon, sun, and planets. The culmination of his efforts was the 3,000-star catalog that comprises the third book of the *Historia*. At his death Flamsteed left a lifetime of practical observations and information that provided a firm basis for the dramatic advancement of astronomy by future generations of scientists.

Bernard Le Bouyer de
FONTENELLE
1657–1757
MATHEMATICS, ASTRONOMY

Writing about the early schooling of Bernard Le Bouyer de Fontenelle, one biographer summed up the young Fontenelle's feelings about the study of logic and physics: "He did not find nature in them, but rather vague and abstract ideas which, so to speak, skirted the edge of things but did not really touch them at all." Having found the sciences so mystifying as a child, Fontenelle spent his adult life demystifying them for others.

Bernard Fontanelle was the first writer to explain scientific ideas in terms that the average person could understand. His most popular work, *Entretiens sur la pluralité de la monde,* discusses the different systems of astronomy.

Fontenelle's greatest accomplishments were not scientific theories or technical papers but a series of works in which he explained scientific ideas in laypersons' terms. He helped spread interest in science beyond the scientific community and challenged the average person to question accepted beliefs about the nature of the universe.

Early Life and Career. Fontenelle was born to a minor official in Rouen, France. His mother was a very intelligent woman whose two brothers had a great influence on young Bernard. Fontenelle often visited them in Paris, where they introduced him to the social and intellectual world. Although a good student, Fontenelle had no direction. After completing school he followed his father into the law, but he had little taste for the profession and left it after arguing only one case.

His true loves were literature and philosophy, and he competed for poetry prizes as early as age 13. He also wrote plays and operas, but his greatest success would come from writings of a more scientific nature. Despite his lukewarm feelings toward logic and physics, Fontenelle displayed a talent for science and mathematics. In 1683 he published his first major work, the *Nouveaux dialogues des morts* (New Dialogues with the Dead), in which he presented fictional conversations between modern scientists and their ancient, deceased counterparts. The book touches on the nature of scientific investigation and the difficulty of discovering truth. Two years later he published an article on the properties of the number 9 that, though rather simple, shows his interest in the field of mathematics.

In 1686 Fontenelle published his most popular work, *Entretiens sur la pluralité de la monde* (Talks on the Plurality of the World). The book takes the form of a conversation between Fontenelle and a fictional noblewoman who asks him to explain the different systems of astronomy that were popular at the time. Fontenelle outlines the systems proposed by Ptolemy, Nicholas COPERNICUS, and Tycho BRAHE, discusses the moon and planets, and raises the possibility that they may contain life. He also explains recent discoveries about the stars in a nontechnical manner that an educated but untrained individual could understand.

The *Entretiens* was the first scientific work in French written specifically for a nonspecialized audience. It established Fontenelle's reputation and helped dictate the course of his future work. In 1686 Fontenelle also published a history of myths, legends, and religions titled *Histoire des oracles* (History of the Oracles). He attacked superstitions and ideas based solely on religious beliefs and unsupported by scientific evidence. This, and other works in which he attacked religion as being narrow-minded and superstitious, provoked the hostility of the church and the clergy serving at the court of Louis XIV. Only the intervention of a highly placed friend protected Fontenelle from harsh reprimand by the government.

Life and Career in Paris. Fontenelle moved to Paris in 1687 and became acquainted with the scientific community there. He was a champion of the new men of science and wrote works supporting their ideas against the forces of tradition and conservatism. Fontenelle continued his nonscientific writing, and four years after his move to Paris, he was elected to the Académie des Sciences. The members of the academy admired Fontenelle's popular writings and elected him the academy's secretary for life in 1697. This position required him to publish an annual history of the academy's proceedings, including a report of all the papers presented by its members during each year.

Fontenelle was also responsible for writing the eulogy for each member of the academy who had died during the year. His ability to understand and explain complex topics in a clear and undistorted way made him ideal for the position. For some 40 years he devoted himself to editing and publishing the yearly history of the academy. In his introductions to the histories, Fontenelle outlined the state of contemporary science and introduced new ideas to his nonscientific readers. For example, the introduction to the history for 1699 includes the first statement that the sciences are interdependent. Fontenelle states that scientific progress results from the sharing of knowledge between disciplines and that discoveries in one field form the foundations for discoveries in other fields.

Some of Fontenelle's greatest contributions to scientific literature were the eulogies he wrote for deceased members of the academy. He had a unique ability to summarize and evaluate accurately the accomplishments of his colleagues. His eulogies also offered subtle psychological and moral observations that made them more than merely reports on the lives and works of their subjects. They made for very popular reading material—Fontenelle issued five separate collections of the eulogies between 1708 and 1742.

In addition to his popular works, Fontenelle published scientific work of his own in mathematics. His *Élémens de la géométrie de l'infini* (Elements of Infinite Geometry), published in 1727, presented a theory of the concept of infinity in mathematics, something he claimed that no mathematicians who invented or worked with the calculus* had ever offered to their readers. Although it generated much discussion in scientific circles, most who read it found Fontenelle's ideas difficult to follow.

In 1731 Fontenelle contributed to a dictionary of arts and sciences published by his uncle, Thomas Corneille, and wrote two brief articles dealing with freedom of thought. These were in keeping with his belief that all knowledge is relative, that truth is never set in stone, and that only through continuing to ask questions can humankind progress. He had faith in the unlimited progress of knowledge, and throughout his life he worked to spread that faith by increasing the average person's awareness of and enthusiasm for the world of science.

* **calculus** advanced form of mathematics that involves computing quantities that change as functions of different variables

Benjamin
FRANKLIN

1706–1790

ELECTRICITY, GENERAL SCIENCE

* **meteorology** science that deals with the atmosphere, especially the weather and weather predictions; also known as atmospheric science

Benjamin Franklin, one of the most remarkable men in American history, made important contributions in many fields, including politics, education, and literature. However, he first gained fame for his pioneering work in electricity, a field of science that was in its infancy when he began his investigations. Before Franklin undertook his experiments with electricity, few scientists considered it an area worthy of exploration. According to one member of London's Royal Society, it was "a neglected subject which not many years since was thought to be of little importance . . . nor was anything of much notice expected to ensue from it."

Franklin's efforts led to a blossoming of scientific and popular interest in electricity. Electricity, however, was not the only scientific field in which he made significant contributions. His boundless curiosity and keen mind led him to investigate and achieve breakthrough discoveries in physics, meteorology*, oceanography, and medicine.

Life and Career

Unlike most great scientists, Franklin had no formal training in any of the fields he explored. But he had a great natural intelligence, a thirst for knowledge, and a practical turn of mind that served him well throughout his life.

Early Life. Franklin was born in Boston, Massachusetts. His father, Josiah, came from a family of British artisans, and his mother, Abiah, was the daughter of a weaver, miller, schoolmaster, and poet. Franklin inherited traits from both sides of his family that proved invaluable in his scientific career. The young Benjamin was sent to grammar school at age eight, but he stayed there less than a year. Afterwards, according to his autobiography, he attended "a School for Writing and Arithmetic" but failed in the latter subject. In later life Franklin taught himself mathematics by making "magic Squares, or Circles" that involved complex computations. Like many boys of the time, he left school to help his father with his candle- and

* **indenture** to bind one person into the service of another for a period of time specified by a written contract

soap-making business. Although he was finished with formal education, Franklin was a passionate reader who spent all of his money on books. Recognizing his son's interest in the printed word, Josiah indentured* him to a printer. Years later Benjamin broke the indenture and left Boston for New York. After a short and fruitless stay there, he made his way to Philadelphia, where he eventually gained both fame and fortune.

Shortly after Franklin's arrival the governor of the Pennsylvania colony offered financial backing for the youth's printing business. The governor sent Franklin to London to purchase equipment and establish contacts in England. Shortly after he set sail for England, the young Franklin realized that the governor had cruelly sent him off with neither money nor letters of introduction that would open doors for him. Franklin was forced to find work in a London printing house, where he stayed for two years before returning home. During his time in London, however, Franklin learned the printing trade, which enabled him to set up a printing shop when he returned to Philadelphia in 1726. Franklin and a partner started the *Pennsylvania Gazette* newspaper, and in 1733 he published the first edition of *Poor Richard: An Almanack*. This series of almanacs went on to become some of the most popular books of all time. Franklin soon became a major figure in the colony, serving in several public offices and making many contributions

One of Benjamin Franklin's most important contributions to history was his pioneering work in electricity. This illustration shows Franklin flying a kite in a thunderstorm to test the electrification of the clouds.

to public life. He helped organize Philadelphia's first library, the city's first fire company, and the Academy of Philadelphia, which eventually became the University of Pennsylvania. At the age of 42, Franklin retired.

Later Life and Career. In the early 1740s, Franklin began a series of experiments that would forever connect his name to the field of electricity. Although he was deeply involved in this research for several years, he continued to pursue other activities. In 1751 he became a member of the Pennsylvania Assembly, and he spent five years in London as its agent. He was also appointed deputy postmaster general for Britain's North American colonies. When the colonies declared their independence, Franklin was at the forefront of the revolution. He served on the committee that drafted the Declaration of Independence and was one of three diplomats sent to Paris in 1776 to negotiate an alliance with France. He was also a member of the commission that negotiated the final peace treaty with Britain. Afterwards, he remained in Europe for several years and became one of the world's first true international celebrities. He became the darling of French society. He enjoyed contact with many political and social figures as well as several prominent European scientists. Franklin returned to Pennsylvania in 1785 and participated in the convention that drafted the United States Constitution. He died five years later in Philadelphia.

Scientific Achievements

Franklin's experiments in electricity were only the first of his many scientific explorations. He made several contributions that had practical as well as scientific benefits. He also became the principal founder of the American Philosophical Society, the first permanent scientific organization in the "New World."

Electricity. In 1743 Franklin attended lectures on experimental science and saw experiments performed by Adam Spencer. The following year he sponsored a series of lectures by Spencer in Philadelphia. Franklin also purchased some of Spencer's apparatus. A year later the Library Company of Philadelphia received a gift from an English scientist—a glass tube along with instructions on how to use it to perform experiments with electricity. Franklin and three colleagues set to work and soon hit upon an important discovery. They charged the tube by rubbing it with silk and then held both pointed and blunt conductors near the tube. The pointed conductor drew a charge from the tube while it was several inches away, but the blunt conductor produced such an effect only when brought within an inch or so of the tube. This finding eventually led Franklin to invent the lightning rod. However, at the time it was merely one of several observations that caused him to formulate a new theory about the nature of electricity.

Before this time Franklin believed that the friction created by rubbing the silk against the glass tube actually created electricity. Franklin later realized that the rubbing action merely enabled the tube to harness electricity that already existed in it. He then concluded that all things possessed a natural amount of electricity, or "electrical fire." Franklin believed that

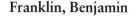

Franklin's Handiwork

During Franklin's day a scientist not only had to conceive of the type of equipment needed to conduct an experiment but often had to make it as well. Franklin's skill and his fondness for working with his hands served him well in his scientific pursuits. He not only constructed many of his own scientific instruments; he also used his talents to create several noteworthy inventions. These include bifocals, the rocking chair, and the Franklin stove. However, one of Franklin's innovations that did not require manual skills is one that affects almost every person in the world today: summer time, or—as it is now called—daylight savings time.

this fire, or electrical charge, was transferable from one object to another. He also noted that water and metals were particularly good at attracting electrical charge from other objects. An object that attracted charge in this manner was electrically positive (or plus); an object that gave up charge to another was negative (or minus). Franklin was the first to use these terms—*plus* and *minus*—when referring to electricity. He also realized that the electrical charge lost by one object was balanced by the charge it transferred to another object. Known as the law of conservation of charge, the idea is the core of one of the basic principles of the science of electricity.

Franklin then conducted a series of experiments with a device called a Leyden jar, named after one of its inventors, Musschenbroek of Leyden. The device consisted of a glass bottle (nonconductor) coated with metal (conductor) and filled with a conducting substance, usually water or lead shot. Electrical contact was made with the water or lead shot by means of a wire running through an insulating cork stuck into the neck of the bottle. When the bottle was grounded and the wire was connected to a charged object, the bottle could accumulate a large electrical charge. The first observation made by Franklin was that if the wire and the bottle's contents were "electrised positively," the outer coating simultaneously became minus in exact proportion. Franklin's work with the Leyden jar confirmed his hypothesis of the balancing of plus and minus charges. He demonstrated that the bottle itself collected the charge, and not the wire, the conducting material within, or the metal coating the jar, as previously believed. He proved the point by using a brass chain to join a series of glass panes separated by lead plates. When exposed to a charged body, the device could accumulate a large charge just as the Leyden jar did.

Franklin's most famous experiments with electricity came from his study of the electrical charge of clouds. He hypothesized that lightning is a form of electricity, but he was puzzled by how clouds acquired an electrical charge. His experiments with pointed conductors led him to conclude that a long, pointed rod fixed to a structure and grounded would attract lightning from passing clouds. He believed that this was a way to draw electrical charge from a cloud before lightning struck. He drew up an experiment to test this theory, which was successfully proven by a French scientist in 1752. Franklin realized that such lightning rods, when mounted on buildings or ships, could conduct lightning from a cloud and direct it safely to the ground. The famous incident in which he attached a key to the string of a kite and flew it in a thunderstorm was another experiment to test the electrification of clouds.

Franklin's theories on electricity were published in 1751. In this book, titled *Experiments and Observations on Electricity, made at Philadelphia in America,* he outlined his theory that electricity is a special fluid that can travel through all substances. He argued that electrical particles always repel one another, whereas particles of other types of matter attract electrical particles. Thus, regular matter soaks up electricity like "a kind of spunge" until it can hold no more. Excess electricity accumulates on the surface of such an object, forming an "electrical atmosphere" around it. Consequently, when two positively charged bodies are brought close together, the excess electrical particles cause them to repel one another. Franklin also showed that one could induce a negative electric charge in a conductor by exposing it to a positively charged object, and vice versa. Franklin's work in electricity earned him the Royal Society's Copley gold medal in 1753 as well as honorary degrees from several universities.

Other Discoveries. Franklin had a fascination for seamanship and the sea, both of which led him to make important oceanographic discoveries. When Boston's Board of Customs noted that mail ships took two weeks longer than merchant ships to sail to England, Franklin decided to investigate the situation. He talked with local fishermen, who pointed out that ships traveled faster when sailing on the edge of a warm eastward current called the Gulf Stream. He requested the captain of one ship to plot the course of the stream and later published the first chart of its course. Franklin also devised the idea of using a thermometer to help navigators determine whether they were in the stream, and he even invented a device to measure temperatures up to 100 feet below the ocean's surface.

In the field of physics, Franklin was an opponent of the widely accepted idea that light is a particle. He argued that even if the mass of light particles was very tiny, their sheer number should produce enormous pressure on whatever they struck. However, it was clear that light does not even disturb the lightest bits of dust. Franklin's arguments were cited years later to support early wave theories of light. In another foray into physics, he designed an experiment to prove that different metals conduct the same amount of heat at different rates.

Throughout his life Franklin showed a concern for health and exercise that found expression in a number of writings on medical subjects, including lead poisoning, deafness, the temperature of blood, and infant mortality. He invented bifocal glasses and a flexible catheter*. Although he was an early opponent of inoculation to prevent disease, he later reversed his position and published a pamphlet in support of the effectiveness of inoculations against smallpox. He also experimented with electric shock as a possible cure for paralysis but concluded that its benefits, if any, were only temporary. Franklin was also a member of a royal commission that investigated the Austrian Anton Mesmer's claims to cure illness with electrotherapy (treatment using electricity). The commission concluded that the treatment had no effect and that any improvement was due to the patients' belief in its effectiveness. He thus unknowingly endorsed the idea, now widely accepted, that the mind plays a large part in physical health and wellness. In this, as in so many fields, Franklin blazed a trail that led to many later scientific discoveries.

* **catheter** slender tube inserted into the body through a vein or other channel and used to maintain an opening to an internal cavity such as an organ

Leonhart
FUCHS

1501–1566

MEDICINE, BOTANY

Leonhart Fuchs was an important professor of medicine in the German universities of the 1500s. As a boy he learned the names of flowers during walks in the countryside with his grandfather. This interest guided him through his academic career. He received a doctorate in medicine at the age of 23, marrying Anna Friedberger shortly afterwards. He practiced and taught medicine in several places and then served as physician to a

German noble in Ansbach, where he gained respect for his treatment of an epidemic of English sweating sickness.

In 1535 Fuchs became professor of medicine at Tübingen, where he remained for the rest of his life. He had a strong influence on those around him, and he was a powerful conservative force for the study of ancient Greek and Roman medical texts by such men as Galen and Hippocrates. His main talent was the organization and presentation of knowledge, and he produced major medical textbooks and a valuable book in which he described 400 native and 100 foreign plants.

Galileo
GALILEI

1564–1642

PHYSICS, ASTRONOMY

The scientific methods, observations, and conclusions of Italian scientist Galileo Galilei are generally considered to mark the beginnings of modern science. Credited with establishing the effectiveness of mathematical laws to explain and predict experimental observations, Galileo was a revolutionary thinker whose ideas were often in direct conflict with the accepted theories of his time. In addition to groundbreaking work in physics, he made significant contributions in astronomy. His views on the nature of the solar system and universe brought him into conflict with the Catholic Church, which found him guilty of heresy and banned his works.

Early Life and Work. Born in Pisa, Italy, Galileo was the eldest child of Vincenzio Galilei, a musician and musical theorist who was descended from an aristocratic family from the city of Florence. Educated by a private tutor in his early childhood, Galileo began studying at a monastery when his family resettled in Florence in about 1575.

In 1581 Galileo enrolled at the University of Pisa to study medicine. He also became very much interested in mathematics and began studying the subject privately. Although Galileo's father wanted him to become a physician, he decided to pursue a career in mathematics and philosophy.

In 1585 Galileo left the University of Pisa to study in Florence. During the next four years, he gave private lessons in mathematics in Florence and the nearby city of Siena, and he became deeply interested in problems concerning the centers of gravity of solid bodies. Galileo developed formulas on gravity that brought him widespread recognition. His writings on this topic and others in physics helped him secure a position as professor of mathematics at the University of Pisa in 1589.

Galileo versus Aristotle. While at the University of Pisa, Galileo found himself at odds with many scholars. His studies discredited traditional ideas in physics established by the ancient Greek philosopher Aristotle. Although Galileo found and demonstrated the many errors in Aristotle's work, most scholars continued to oppose his new ideas. For instance, Aristotle had suggested that heavy objects fall faster than light ones. From observations and experiments, Galileo demonstrated that objects of different weights actually fall with equal speed. According to one legend, Galileo demonstrated his findings by dropping objects from the Leaning Tower of Pisa. There is little evidence, however, that this story is true.

From these experiments Galileo developed new laws about motion that undermined Aristotelian ideas. For instance, Aristotle believed that all motions were either natural or forced and that one of these forces had to be applied continually to keep a body in motion. Galileo proposed that a moving body could be influenced by two forces simultaneously—a horizontal force that would keep a body moving horizontally, and a vertical force that would cause a body to drop downward. Working together, the two forces could produce a neutral motion that would keep a body moving in a circular path.

Galileo presented his ideas in a manuscript called *De motu* (On Motion), which revealed his rejection of Aristotelian ideas and made him unpopular with his colleagues at Pisa. Shortly thereafter, Galileo left Pisa and accepted a position at the University of Padua, which was well known as a gathering place for the best scholars in Italy. Because Padua was under the control of the Venetian government, the university and its faculty enjoyed virtually total academic freedom. Galileo remained in Padua for 18 years, gaining fame because of his work. He delivered public lectures on geometry and astronomy and gave private instruction on engineering and mechanics*. During this period he published *Le meccaniche* (Mechanics), an important work on the mathematical analysis of problems of dynamics—a branch of mechanics that deals with bodies in motion.

Turning Point. In 1597 Galileo wrote a letter to a former colleague at Pisa, defending the heliocentric, or sun-centered, model of the universe developed by astronomer Nicholas COPERNICUS more than 50 years earlier. Soon afterward he received copies of a book by Johannes KEPLER that supported the Copernican system, which was opposed by many scholars because it went against the ideas of Aristotle and the ancient Greek astronomer Ptolemy.

Galileo wrote a letter to Kepler expressing his belief in the Copernican system, but he then turned his attention from astronomy to other matters. With the appearance of a supernova* in the night skies in 1604, Galileo again became involved in astronomy and attacked some of Aristotle's ideas about the heavens. Although physics remained his main interest, he found himself drawn to the controversy over the nature of the universe.

Galileo's career took a dramatic turn in 1609, when he learned about a Dutch lens-grinder who had developed a lens that could make distant objects appear closer. Intrigued by the possibilities that a lens such as this could offer, he experimented with similar lenses and constructed a simple refracting telescope. Although there is controversy over whether this was the first telescope ever, it is certain that Galileo was the first to use the telescope as an instrument in scientific research. He continued to improve his new device, and soon his telescope could magnify objects about 30 times greater than normal.

In 1610 Galileo turned his telescope to the skies, with startling results. When he observed the moon, he saw hills, valleys, craters, and other features similar to those on earth. Looking at the Milky Way, he realized that it consisted of millions of stars. He also turned his telescope toward

* **mechanics** science that studies how energy and force affect objects

* **supernova** star that suddenly becomes extremely brilliant because it has exploded; *pl.* supernovae

The Pendulum Can Tell Time

According to some accounts, while Galileo was a student at Pisa, he went to the cathedral one day and noticed the oil lamps swinging overhead, some making higher arcs than others. Galileo assumed that the lamps with higher arcs would take longer to complete a full swing than those with smaller arcs. However, when he timed the swings against the beats of his pulse, he discovered that they all took the same amount of time. After experimenting at home, Galileo used mathematics to work out the laws that govern a pendulum. Years later he used his findings to invent a practical timing device.

* **theologian** person who studies religious faith and practice

Jupiter and discovered four small satellites traveling in orbit around the planet. Galileo published his findings in *Sidereus nuncius* (Starry Messenger), which created a sensation among scholars. Galileo's discovery of satellites orbiting Jupiter, in particular, offered proof in support of the Copernican system and against the earth-centered system of Ptolemy, which had dominated astronomy for more than 1,400 years. However, Galileo's findings demonstrated that there could be more than one center of motion in the solar system, contrary to the teachings of Ptolemy.

Many scholars attacked Galileo's discoveries, but he did not enter the controversy and instead applied himself to further research. His telescope was inadequate to resolve Saturn's rings, which he assumed were satellites very close to that planet. While observing Venus, Galileo discovered that the planet experienced phases such as those of the earth's moon.

Through his discoveries Galileo became a firm believer in the heliocentric system proposed by Copernicus. Reluctant to continue teaching the old astronomy, he left the University of Padua and returned to Florence, where he became the official mathematician and philosopher of Cosimo II de Medici, the grand duke of Tuscany, who became his patron.

Growing Controversy. In 1611 Galileo traveled to Rome to exhibit his telescopic discoveries to church officials. While there, he was made a member of the Lincean Academy, the first truly scientific society in Europe. Shortly after returning to Florence, Galileo became involved in a controversy about the laws of floating bodies. Returning to physics, he published a book on the behavior of bodies floating on water that supported the ideas of the ancient Greek scientist Archimedes and rejected the ideas of Aristotle. He renewed his attack on Aristotle, angering many scholars.

In 1613 Galileo published another book, *Letters on Sunspots,* in which he first supported the Copernican system in print. This time, officials of the Catholic Church came out in opposition, condemning the Copernican system as an attack on church doctrine. Learning of the growing opposition, Galileo wrote a letter to a friend and former pupil, Benedetto Castelli, in which he argued against the interference of theologians* in scientific matters. The following year Galileo was publicly attacked for his views, and soon afterward a copy of his letter to Castelli appeared in Rome at the Inquisition, a special court established to investigate and prosecute heresy. Alarmed for his safety and academic freedom, Galileo expanded his previous letter into a defense of free scientific inquiry. In his 1615 *Letter to Christina* (the Grand Duchess), Galileo argued that neither the Bible nor nature could speak falsely. The responsibility of the scientist, he said, was to investigate nature, while that of the theologian was to reconcile scientific facts with the Bible.

The same year, Galileo went to Rome to argue for the Copernican system and try to clear his name. However, by questioning biblical interpretation, Galileo had angered Pope Paul V, who then appointed a church commission to examine the Copernican theory. The commission determined that the theory was contrary to biblical teaching, and in 1616 Galileo was ordered to abandon the idea. Otherwise, no action was taken against him.

Renewed Studies. Returning to Florence, Galileo applied himself to less controversial issues, including the use of telescopes for navigation at sea and renewed studies of motion and mechanics. He also studied magnetism and perfected the compound microscope: a type of microscope with two separate lenses that offers greater magnifying power than a single-lens device.

In 1618 Galileo became involved in controversy again, this time regarding three comets that had attracted the attention of Europeans. Although Galileo was ill at the time, he discussed his views with his pupil, Mario Guiducci, who then delivered lectures on them. Guiducci later

In his work *Dialogue Concerning the Two Chief World Systems,* Galileo discussed three different views of the universe. This title page shows an imaginary debate between Aristotle, Copernicus, and Ptolemy. Each scientist supports his own system.

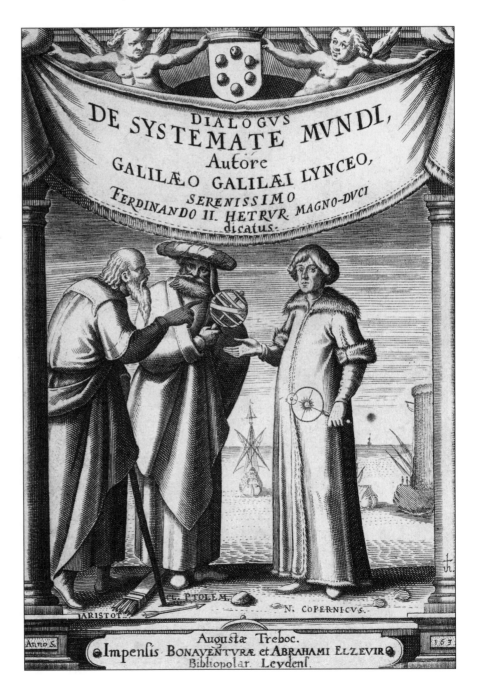

published the lectures in his own name. Galileo finally entered the controversy in person in 1623 with publication of *Il saggiatore* (The Assayer). One of the most celebrated arguments in science, *Il saggiatore* sets forth a general scientific approach to the investigation of celestial phenomena. Without supporting the Copernican theory (which he was forbidden to do) or offering any proof about comets, Galileo argues that the truth can be determined only through the language of mathematics. This work was important because it explains and defends the scientific method, an approach to answering scientific questions that combines observation, experimentation, and mathematical proofs.

While *Il saggiatore* was being published in Rome, a new pope came to power. A patron of science, Pope Urban VIII was an old friend of Galileo's. The scientist traveled to Rome to visit Urban and to obtain permission to write a new book discussing both the Copernican and Ptolemaic systems. Urban agreed to let Galileo write such a book, provided that he treated each system equally and fairly.

Trouble With Rome. Galileo spent the next several years writing his most famous and controversial work—*Dialogue Concerning the Two Chief World Systems.* Published in 1632, the work consists of a witty conversation among three men with very different ideas about the universe. Although Galileo pretended not to take sides, the character supporting the Copernican view clearly has the strongest argument. Galileo also discussed the laws of motion, falling bodies, acceleration, and other physics concepts, relating them to his overall argument in favor of the Copernican system. In doing so, he not only rejected the old astronomy of Ptolemy and Aristotle but also much of traditional physics and philosophy.

Many scholars were wounded by the ruthlessness of Galileo's writings. He was never inclined to take a charitable view of the claims of others, and many were waiting for their chance to get even. This chance was offered by Galileo's open defense of the Copernican system. He openly ridiculed the Aristotelian scholars and supporters of the Ptolemaic system, many of whom became high-ranking church officials. The church officials were outraged by the book, including Pope Urban, who became persuaded that one of characters in it, the simpleminded supporter of Aristotle, was modeled after himself. In 1632 Galileo was ordered to Rome to face the Inquisition on charges of heresy. Tried by the court in 1633, he was threatened with torture and forced to renounce any views contrary to church doctrine. Although sentenced to life imprisonment, he was put under permanent house arrest instead, first in Siena and then in the village of Arcetri near Florence. The church also banned the *Dialogue* and ordered copies of it to be burned.

Later Years and Influence. Although initially crushed by severity of the sentence, Galileo soon recovered and resumed his work on noncontroversial topics in physics. His final work, *Discourses and Mathematical Demonstrations Concerning Two New Sciences,* deals with such topics as acceleration, the nature of matter, the nature of sound, the speed of light, the nature of mathematics, and the place of experiment and reason in science.

"And Yet It Moves!"

According to legend, Galileo stood up for his beliefs even as he faced the wrath of the Inquisition. Stories say that as the scientist rose from his knees after renouncing the Copernican theory, he quietly muttered the words, *"Eppur si muove!"* ("And yet it moves!"). He was referring to his belief that the earth rotates on its axis and revolves around the sun, despite the church's opposition to that idea. Although the church forced Galileo to reject the ideas publicly, it could not change what he believed was the truth. The church had merely silenced a man, not changed the nature of reality.

Through a series of experiments involving inclined planes, Galileo showed that the speed at which bodies fall is independent of their weight. On this basis he formulated the law of falling bodies.

By the time this final work was published in 1638, Galileo had become blind. He spent his remaining years in seclusion at his home in Arcetri, visited occasionally by friends and former pupils. He died in 1642, but the pope refused to allow the grand duke of Tuscany to erect a suitable tomb for the great scientist. Nearly a century later, however, his remains were placed in the cathedral in Florence with a monument and an inscription.

Galileo had a tremendous impact on the history of science and scientific inquiry. He showed that the formulation of scientific theories must be based on observations and supported with mathematics. In addition to providing rules and reasons for scientists to gather data, he also made important contributions in nearly every area of science and paved the way for later scientists. Equally important, Galileo established the right of scientists to question old ideas and search for the truth, and he became a symbol for those who challenged authority.

Konrad
GESNER

1516–1565

NATURAL SCIENCES, MEDICINE

* **theology** study of religion

Konrad Gesner, an observer of the natural world, authored influential early works in botany and zoology. Surprisingly, most of his academic preparation was in theology*. It was not until relatively late in his studies that he turned to medicine, which prepared him for a career in the sciences.

The godson of Ulrich Zwingli, a prominent Protestant reformer, Gesner very naturally studied theology from an early age. As a child he attended theological seminaries in Zurich, Switzerland. Zwingli died when Gesner was 15, and the following year young Konrad left Zurich for France. He took up the study of Hebrew at the Strasbourg Academy and became a scholar in that field. By the time he turned 20, Gesner had compiled a Greek-Latin dictionary. Shortly thereafter, he took a position teaching Greek at the Lausanne Academy. Gesner achieved several notable successes as a language scholar. Among his successes was the publication of *Bibliotheca universalis,* a four-volume index to the works of ancient Greek, Latin, and Hebrew writers, which established him as the founder of the field of bibliography.

By the time he finished his studies in Hebrew, however, Gesner had lost interest in theology. Turning to the field of medicine, he attended the Universities of Bourges, Paris, and Basel and received his doctorate in 1541. Following the advice of his close friend Christophe Clauser, Gesner decided to pursue work in botany, which had fascinated him as a boy. He returned to Zurich and was named chief physician of the city, a position he inherited from Clauser. In addition to his duties as chief physician, Gesner devoted a great deal of time to preparing his manuscripts on botany and zoology. He traveled widely and collected a wealth of information that he incorporated into his two important scientific treatises, the *Opera botanica* (Botanical Works) and the *Historia animalium* (History of Animals).

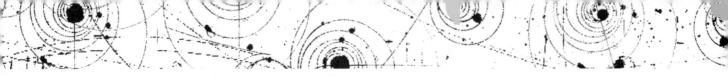

The *Historia animalium,* published by the Swiss natural scientist Konrad Gesner in the 1550s, contains thousands of pages devoted to the classification of animals. The work also contains several detailed illustrations such as this drawing of a flat fish called a ray.

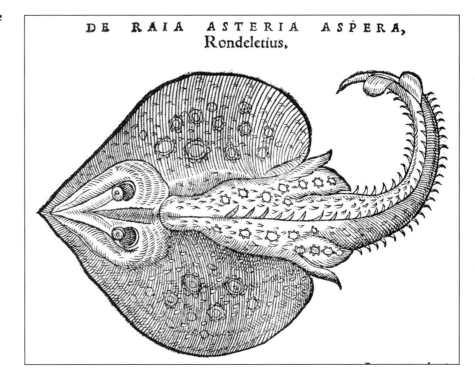

DE RAIA ASTERIA ASPERA, Rondeletius.

* **posthumously** occurring after the death of an individual

The *Opera botanica,* a massive two-volume work published posthumously*, contained nearly 1,500 detailed illustrations drawn by Gesner. He collected more than 500 plant species that were not described in ancient texts. He was one of the few botanists of his day to realize that plants could be classified according to the structure of their flowers. He was also able to establish the relationships among plants by studying and comparing their seeds. The great Swedish botanist Carl LINNAEUS, who later created the classification system that is still in use, frequently admitted that his work owed much to Gesner's efforts.

The *Historia animalium,* which was published during Gesner's lifetime, ran more than 4,500 pages in length and remained popular hundreds of years after his death. He proposed a classification system for animals based on his similar efforts to classify plants. Gesner's interest in animal life included studies of animal physiology and pathology*, and in fact, some consider him the father of veterinary science. Gesner also studied fossils and wrote memoirs on extinct forms of vegetable life. An epidemic that struck Zurich in 1565 claimed Gesner's life. He was not yet 39 years old.

* **pathology** study of diseases and their effects on organisms

William
GILBERT

1544–1603

ELECTRICITY, MAGNETISM

A pioneer researcher into the mysteries of magnetism, William Gilbert was the first to distinguish between magnetic and electrical phenomena. Considered the father of electrical studies, he was the first to use the term *electricity* to describe a certain force of attraction. Gilbert's discovery that the earth acts like a giant magnet, with magnetic poles located near the geographic North and South Poles, influenced Johannes KEPLER in his attempt to furnish a physics to supplement the Copernican model of the universe.

Life and Career. Born in the town of Colchester, England, Gilbert came from a middle-class family. Although nothing is known of his early life and education, it is known that in 1558 he entered St. John's College at Cambridge University to study medicine. He also held a number of appointed positions at the college, including mathematical examiner and senior bursar. Again, little is known about his life during the first years after he left Cambridge. It is possible that he went abroad for further study.

In the mid-1570s Gilbert settled in London, where he practiced medicine and eventually became a member of the Royal College of Physicians. By 1581 he had become one of London's most prominent physicians, and influential members of the English nobility looked to him for medical advice. In 1600 he was appointed official physician to Queen Elizabeth I, and after her death in 1603 he became physician to King James I.

Gilbert played an active role in the Royal College. Over the years he held various positions at the college, including president. He never married, and little is known of his private life in London. After his death in 1603—from the plague, perhaps—the Royal College received all his books, globes, scientific instruments, and other possessions. These were all destroyed in the Great Fire of London in 1666.

Scientific Works. Gilbert's studies on various magnetic phenomena were published in 1600 in a book titled *De magnete* (On the Magnet). Considered his first great British scientific work, the book presents the first fully developed theory dealing with all known magnetic movements and the first comprehensive discussion of magnetism since the 1200s. It is critical of many popular beliefs about magnetism. For example, Gilbert demonstrated that the widespread belief in the ability of diamond to magnetize iron was groundless.

De magnete is divided into six books. The first book deals with the history of magnetism, from the earliest legends about the lodestone* to the theories proposed by Gilbert's contemporaries. Gilbert discussed the nature, properties, and behavior of the lodestone and suggested ways of demonstrating them. He concluded the first book by introducing a new idea to explain all terrestrial* magnetic phenomena. Gilbert suggested that the earth is a giant magnet and has magnetic properties. To support this idea, he compared the earth and a lodestone—each has poles, each draws objects to itself—and suggested that iron, the main magnetic substance, can be found in great quantities deep within the planet.

The remaining books of *De magnete* deal with the five known magnetic movements: coition (drawing together, or attraction), direction (pointing north), variation (deviation from true north), declination (bending), and revolution. Drawing on many experiments, Gilbert explains these movements in relation to the magnetic properties of the earth. His findings not only advanced scientific knowledge of magnetic movements but also introduced terms and ideas that laid the basis for the study of electricity.

In the final book, Gilbert extended his theory to the cosmos. One of his conclusions—that the earth rotates on its axis—supported Nicholas COPERNICUS's claim that the earth has a diurnal (daily) rotation on its

* **lodestone** substance that possesses magnetic properties and attracts iron

* **terrestrial** relating to land or the earth

axis. Gilbert's theories about the cosmos were developed further in another book, *De mundo* (Concerning Our World), which was published after his death.

In *De mundo* Gilbert presents a number of ideas about the planets, stars, and other celestial bodies. Many of these ideas were based on his theories of magnetism. Gilbert believed, for example, that all the planets were held in their orbits around the sun by a magnetic force. He also explained the relationship between the moon and the earth in terms of a magnetic attraction. *De mundo* also contains ideas about springs, rivers, and tides on earth. Gilbert explained the motions of springs and rivers in terms of water returning to its natural source. He believed that tides were the result of the combined actions of the motion of the earth and the magnetic relationship between the earth and moon.

Many scholars praised Gilbert's work on magnetism but found his ideas on the cosmos less acceptable. His idea about the earth's magnetic power was incorporated into arguments in support of the Copernican theory. Kepler used the magnetic theory to help develop and support his own theories of the universe and solar system.

Otto von GUERICKE

1602–1686

ENGINEERING, PHYSICS

Otto von Guericke is best known for his exploration of vacuums and the properties of air, studies that led him to develop the first air pump. The eldest son of a prominent German family, Guericke devoted most of his time and energies to politics. However, during his leisure time he engaged in scientific experimentation and speculation about the nature of space. Guericke attended universities in Leipzig, Helmstedt, and Jena, where he studied law, engineering, and mathematics. Thereafter, Guericke held several public offices in his hometown of Magdeburg, including alderman (council member), mayor, and city contractor. During his career he traveled to many of the seats of government and royal courts of Europe, where he gained exposure to the new scientific ideas of René DESCARTES, Evangelista TORRICELLI, and others.

Guericke's interest in the definition of space dated from his days as a student. His acceptance of the system of the universe proposed by Nicolas COPERNICUS led him to ask three basic questions about space. He asked if empty space exists or whether it is always filled with some substance. His second question pertained to the movement of heavenly bodies and whether they interact with each other. Guericke's third question asked whether space and the bodies that occupy it are infinite or if they have a limit.

Guericke's first exploration into these matters was an attempt to discover whether a vacuum could exist in the physical world. To answer this question he constructed a closed vessel and invented a device to pump the air out through an opening in the vessel. According to Descartes, the resulting vacuum should cause the vessel to implode (burst inward). However, the vessel remained intact, proving that a vacuum could exist. His later experiments also showed that while air was being pumped out of the vessel, the air that remained inside was evenly distributed throughout the vessel. In this manner Guericke discovered the elasticity of air, perhaps the most important finding from his work.

In another experiment Guericke demonstrated the power of air pressure to King Ferdinand III by joining two copper hemispheres and pumping the air out of the sphere they formed. Teams of horses, hooked up to the sphere, could not pull the two halves apart. His investigations led him to explore the density of air at high altitudes. He constructed an early type of barometer, with which he made successful weather forecasts based on changes in air pressure.

Regarding his questions on the nature of space beyond the earth, Guericke believed that each star was a sun surrounded by a system of planets that border on, but do not interact with, each other. He rejected the widely accepted notion that because only God was infinite, all of God's creation must be finite. Guericke overcame this argument by redefining nothingness. He claimed that because empty space is nothingness, God could not have created it; rather, it is just the vessel to contain God's creation. Moreover, because empty space is independent of God and existed before God created the universe, it cannot be finite. It would then follow that the number of worlds is also limitless. Other scientists had speculated on the possibility of an infinite universe, but Guericke offered an explanation that took into account current ideas about the nature of God. Although not widely accepted at the time, Guericke's ideas about an infinite universe are now accepted by many scientists and astronomers.

Stephen
HALES

1677–1761

PHYSIOLOGY, PUBLIC HEALTH

* **physiology** science that deals with the functions of living organisms and their parts

* **naturalist** student of natural history, the systematic study of natural objects, especially in their natural settings

Many English scientists of the 1700s were clergymen who spent their free time in study and experimentation. One such scientific clergyman was Stephen Hales, whose experiments with plants made him the founder of plant physiology*. Hales also investigated the nature and chemistry of air, the circulation of blood in animals, and various medical problems. Hales also invented the ventilator, which helped improve the quality of air in confined spaces, such as prisons, and made him famous as a contributor to public health.

Education and Career. Hales was born in Bekesbourne in Kent County, England. Nothing is known about his childhood, but in 1696 he entered Benet College (now Corpus Christi College) at Cambridge University. He received a Master of Arts degree in 1703. Six years later he was made a deacon in the Church of England and left Cambridge for Teddington, Middlesex County, where he served as a minister. Hales spent the rest of his life in Teddington and carried out most of his scientific work there.

Hales's interest in science awakened during his time at Cambridge because the university was undergoing something of a scientific renaissance during those years. The renowned mathematician Isaac NEWTON and the naturalist* John RAY were associated with the university, which also established new professorships in astronomy and chemistry and built an astronomical observatory and a chemistry laboratory. Cambridge's energetic air of scientific inquiry and progress inspired Hales and other students to delve into the sciences.

At Cambridge Hales became friendly with a medical student named William Stukeley, who was interested in botany and anatomy. With other like-minded students, the two men collected plants in the countryside, dissected frogs and small animals, performed chemical experiments, attended lectures on scientific topics, and read books on physics and mathematics. Hales also demonstrated his knowledge of celestial physics and his mechanical ingenuity by building an orrery, a machine to show the motions of the planets. Stukeley's drawing of this device survives in the Bodleian Library in Oxford, England.

Plant Physiology. Almost ten years after Hales settled in Teddington, he was elected to England's Royal Society, an organization of scientists and people interested in science. Stukeley, by then a doctor in London, had recommended him for membership. It was a few years, however, before Hales displayed any of his work to the society.

After leaving Cambridge, Hales continued his animal experiments for a time, studying the flow of blood. During this time he wrote: "I wished I could have made the like Experiments, to discover the force of the Sap in Vegetables." In early 1719, however, by mere accident he hit on a method of measuring the volume and pressure of the flow of sap by attaching a glass tube to a cut in the stem of a plant. He proceeded to carry out a systematic

Stephen Hales investigated the nature of air, the circulation of blood in animals, and the physiology of plants. He also discovered the harmful effects of alcohol and ways to remove kidney stones.

program of plant experiments, using his own garden as well as plants and trees from a nearby royal garden at Hampton Court.

Hales was guided by the belief that the life processes of plants—such as breathing and circulation—are similar to those of animals. His principal method of studying living things was called "staticks," the weighing or measuring of substances that flow through organisms, including blood, sap, air, and water. Hales believed that by determining when, where, and how organisms use these substances, he could arrive at insights into how they function. Consequently, he devised experiments that focused on precise measurements.

To measure the sap pressure, Hales employed a "mercurial gage," a bent tube filled with mercury, which he fixed to the cut stem. While observing rising sap through glass tubes, Hales noted how the sap flow varied with the weather and the time of day. He also devised a system of glass tubes to measure how much water the root of a plant absorbed. To show "the great force" with which plants absorb moisture, Hales filled an iron pot nearly to the top with peas and water and then weighted the lid with 180 pounds. As the peas absorbed water, they swelled, lifting off the heavy lid.

In perhaps his most brilliant series of experiments, Hales measured how much water a sunflower transpired, or "breathed" out. He then carefully measured each of its leaves and was thus able to calculate how much water was lost in relation to the surface area of the leaves. In other experiments Hales sliced off sections of tree bark to observe the direction of the sap flow, which was always upward and never downward. Plants, he determined, did not have a true circulation like the bloodstream of animals—the flow was always in one direction.

Beginning in 1724, Hales presented the results of his plant experiments to the Royal Society. In 1727 he published his findings in *Vegetable Staticks,* which launched the science of plant physiology.

The Analysis of Air. His studies of plants had convinced Hales that plants release air—that they perform a kind of breathing. Although scientists of Hales's time did not yet understand that "air" is comprised of many gases, they were aware that various materials either absorb or release "airs" under certain circumstances. *Vegetable Staticks* includes a chapter, titled "The Analysis of Air," that deals with the experiments Hales had performed to discover the amount of air or gas given off or absorbed by substances, such as hog's blood, powdered oyster shell, amber, honey, and various plant materials, when he heated them in a glass or iron vessel. Although Hales did not explore the different chemical properties of air produced from different substances, he suspected that physical differences existed. His analysis of air was a starting point for the study of gases by later investigators, including the Englishman Joseph PRIESTLEY.

An ingenious and persistent experimenter, Hales devised several instruments to help him study air. One of them, a bladder equipped with valves and a breathing tube, let him breathe his own exhaled air. He could do so for only about a minute, but he discovered that if he passed his exhaled air through a chemical solution, he could rebreathe it for more than

Disagreeable Dissections

Perhaps one reason Hales liked studying plants is that he disliked dissecting animals to study their anatomy. Around 1713 he abandoned animal experiments because of "the disagreeableness of anatomical Dissections." However, because such experiments were vital to biological research, Hales resumed the practice of dissection in the late 1720s. In his most dramatic experiment, a bold and bloody one, he tied a live mare on her back and attached one of her veins to a glass tube nine feet high. The mare's blood pressure drove the blood eight feet up the tube. Detaching the tube at intervals, Hales allowed a measured quantity of blood to flow out, noting how the pressure changed during the draining of blood. Hales also studied the blood pressure of oxen, sheep, and dogs.

eight minutes. Scientists now know that the chemical Hales used, salt of tartar, absorbs carbon dioxide from exhaled air.

Animal Circulation. After publishing *Vegetable Staticks,* Hales turned his attention to completing and publishing his experiments on blood circulation in animals. This work appeared in 1733 under the title *Haemastaticks;* later Hales combined the two as *Statical Essays.*

Hales's study of animal physiology was influenced by the ideas of the iatrophysicists, physicians who believed that the best way to understand living organisms was by applying the principles of mechanics*. At Cambridge, Hales had read a book by James Keill, a Scottish iatrophysicist, who gave quantitative estimates of the amount of blood in the human body, the velocity of the blood as it left the heart, the amounts of various animal secretions, and similar functions. Hales wanted to use what he called "the statical way of inquiry" to arrive at accurate information about such aspects of animal bodies.

Focusing on blood pressure and the mechanics of circulation, Hales conducted dissections and vivisections* to study the amount and force of blood in the systems of horses, dogs, and other animals. He also studied their heartbeat and pulse, noting that the pulse was faster in small animals than in larger ones. He injected the animals with various chemical substances—brandy, saline solutions, and extract of Peruvian bark—and noted that these chemicals changed the rate at which blood flows through an organ. Hales correctly concluded that the chemicals caused the blood vessels in the animals to shrink or expand, although he did not observe these phenomena directly.

Practical Uses of Scientific Knowledge. For Hales science was more than the hobby of a country minister—it was a natural outgrowth of religious faith. Although he believed that living organisms and nature were complex machines, he considered them evidence of the wisdom, power, and goodness of their creator.

Hales also believed that science should be useful, and he was always alert to the practical possibilities of his discoveries. After studying the effects of alcohol on animal circulation, he warned people of the medical consequences of heavy drinking and even joined the campaign to reduce alcohol consumption in Great Britain. Applying his knowledge of chemistry, he suggested methods of keeping stored water fresh during long sea voyages, and he studied the difficult problem of making fresh water from seawater.

One of Hales's medical concerns was the formation of stones in the bladder and kidneys. He hoped to find a solvent that would dissolve the stones without surgery. Although he failed to find such a solvent, he did invent a surgical tool that surgeons used successfully to remove stones from the human urinary tract.

Hales's experiments on air and breathing led to the invention that made him famous in his own time—ventilators that removed foul, stale air from enclosed places, such as hospitals, prisons, naval vessels, and slave ships. Although the ventilators did not eliminate diseases caused by

* **mechanics** science that studies how energy and force affect objects

* **vivisection** practice of dissecting or cutting into the body of a living animal

bacteria and viruses carried in the air, they helped reduce the incidence of some illnesses. As one of the first to call attention to the importance of fresh air, Hales deserves recognition as a pioneer in public health.

Edmond
HALLEY

1656–1743

ASTRONOMY, GEOPHYSICS

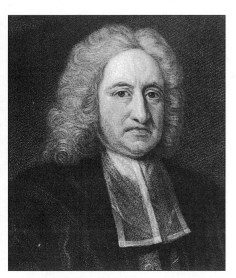

The British mathematician and astronomer Edmond Halley cataloged the positions of many stars and constellations. Halley was also the first to determine that the motion and appearance of comets could be predicted.

---

* **geophysics** scientific study of the physics of the earth, including weather, magnetism, volcanoes, earthquakes, and ocean structure

* **diving bell** dome-shaped machine that can be lowered into water, carrying air down inside it for divers to use

The British scientist Edmond Halley, like many other learned people of his time, had widely varied interests. In addition to being a skilled mathematician, he conducted research on subjects ranging from archaeology to the fortification of seaports to magnetism. Halley's most important achievements, however, were in the field of astronomy and in geophysics*, a science that he founded. He is best remembered for his theory about comets, including the comet that bears his name.

The Young Astronomer. Halley was born in London, England, into a prosperous merchant family. He received an expensive education and developed an interest in the heavens at an early age. His father bought a valuable collection of astronomical instruments, which Halley took with him when he entered Queen's College at Oxford University at the age of 17.

At Oxford, Halley met John FLAMSTEED, whom the king named Britain's first astronomer royal. Although Flamsteed initially encouraged Halley in his scientific career, he later turned against Halley, and his active disapproval delayed recognition of Halley's work. In 1720, however, Halley followed Flamsteed as astronomer royal, becoming head of the royal observatory at Greenwich. Halley would live in Greenwich until his death.

After leaving college, Halley served for a time as Flamsteed's assistant at Greenwich. Inspired by Flamsteed's use of a telescope to map the stars of the Northern Hemisphere, Halley decided to do the same for the Southern Hemisphere. In 1676, with financial support from his father, Halley sailed to the southernmost British-held territory, the island of St. Helena in the South Atlantic Ocean. During the next year he cataloged the positions of 341 stars, made other astronomical observations, and discovered a star cluster in the constellation Centaurus.

After his return to London, Halley published the first catalog of southern stars based on his telescopic observations. He also prepared a star map of the Southern Hemisphere, presenting a copy of it to King Charles II. On the strength of the catalog and star map, the Royal Society, Britain's leading association of scholars and scientists, elected Halley to membership.

Scientist and Diplomat. In 1685 Halley accepted a job as an assistant to the officials of the Royal Society. During the 14 years that he held that post, he edited the society's journal and corresponded with many leading scientific researchers, including Antoni van LEEUWENHOEK, inventor of the microscope. Halley also carried out numerous experiments in various fields, often publishing his results.

Turning his attention to underwater diving, Halley designed a diving bell* and diver's helmet that were more advanced than anything in use at the time. His underwater observations had a scientific purpose—he noted

* **optics** scientific study of the properties of light

how the colors of sunlight changed at different depths and sent his reports to mathematician and physicist Isaac NEWTON, who used them in his work on optics*. Halley also tried to take practical advantage of his inventions by launching a company for salvaging wrecked ships.

Another of Halley's researches with a practical application was a pioneering example of social statistics. Halley gathered information about the ages at which people had died in a single European city, and in 1693 he published one of the first tables relating age and death rate. He suggested that such tables might be used to calculate average life spans within a population. Life insurance companies later continued Halley's work in this area.

A skilled mathematician, Halley published seven papers on pure mathematics. He applied mathematics to practical questions, such as focusing thick lenses and determining the angle of flight of missiles fired from artillery weapons. Halley translated and published the writings of the ancient Greek mathematicians Apollonius and Menelaus. Oxford University recognized this achievement by granting Halley a doctoral degree.

One of Halley's most significant contributions to the advancement of science was his role in the publication of Newton's *Principia*. Halley, Newton, and Robert HOOKE were among the scientists who were seeking an explanation of the forces that kept the planets orbiting around the sun. Halley visited Newton, encouraged him in his work, smoothed over a quarrel between Newton and Hooke ". . . over who had first reasoned that the orbits of the planets must be elliptical if the force from the sun to the planets varies in the inverse square proportion," saw Newton's manuscript through the press, and paid for its publication. Halley even contributed some Latin verses in honor of Newton.

Investigating the Past

Human history as well as physical science attracted the attention of Edmond Halley, who took a lively interest in archaeology. In 1691 he published a paper on the time and place of Julius Caesar's first landing in Britain, basing his ideas not just on other histories but also on ancient accounts of an eclipse of the moon, which helped him fix a date. In 1695 Halley published an article about the ruins of the ancient city of Palmyra, in Syria. Halley's paper aroused much interest and led British historians to make a detailed study of the site in the 1700s.

Major Achievements in Astronomy. Halley's best-known scientific achievement was his method for determining the motion of comets. Since ancient times history had recorded the appearances of these heavenly bodies, which seemed to blaze through the solar system at random intervals. After Newton's *Principia* was published in 1687, Halley began an intensive study of comets and decided to investigate the possibility that they traveled around the sun in elliptical, or oval-shaped, orbits.

Using historical records of comets and mathematical calculations based on Newton's laws of celestial motion, Halley concluded that the bright comets that had appeared in 1531, 1607, and 1682 were the same comet, traveling around the sun in an orbit that caused it to appear every 75 years or so. He later added the bright comets recorded in 1305, 1380, and 1456 to the list of this single comet's appearances. He also predicted that it would appear again in 1758.

Halley published his comet theory in 1705. Although astronomers were interested, Europe's intellectual community did not take notice until the comet reappeared in 1758, just as Halley had predicted. By then Halley had been dead for 15 years, but the comet was named after Halley in his honor. Halley had been the first to demonstrate that comets travel on set paths and that their appearances can often be predicted. His successful prediction of the reappearance of Halley's comet confirmed Newton's work on gravitation.

* **nova** star that explodes, suddenly increasing in brightness

* **nebula** cloud of gas or dust inside the galaxy; also used to refer to patches of light now known to be distant galaxies; *pl.* nebulae

Halley also contributed to stellar astronomy, the study of the stars. In addition to his catalog of the southern stars, he published papers on novas*, nebulae*, and the size of the universe (which he believed to be infinite). His most notable achievement in stellar astronomy was his discovery that the stars, which had always been regarded as fixed, are actually moving. After comparing his observations with the star positions recorded 1,500 years earlier by the Greek astronomer Ptolemy, Halley rightly concluded that at least some of the differences in position were due to the proper motion of stars, not merely to errors in observation.

After his appointment to Greenwich, Halley embarked on an ambitious 18-year plan to observe and carefully map the motion of the moon throughout a complete cycle of its positions relative to the sun. He completed this task and suggested ways in which precise knowledge of the moon's orbit might be used to solve one the most challenging navigational problems of the time, determining longitude at sea. As astronomer royal, Halley lent his support to the researches of instrument maker John HARRISON, who eventually developed the most successful solution to the longitude problem. Halley was known for his encouragement of other young astronomers as well.

The Beginning of Geophysics. Halley was the founder of a field of study now known as geophysics, the study of the physics operating in various phenomena of the earth. His first major work in this field was a paper on trade winds and monsoons, published in 1686. Along with the article Halley published the first known meteorological* map, a chart of the winds that showed the direction of the prevailing winds over each ocean. Halley also studied the tides—the twice-daily risings and fallings of the oceans—and published a tidal survey of the English Channel.

* **meteorological** pertaining to weather

Halley's most important contribution to geophysics concerned magnetism, the force that draws a compass needle toward the magnetic pole. Between 1698 and 1700 Halley commanded the small ship *Paramore* across the Atlantic Ocean, despite a mutiny aboard ship, to chart magnetic patterns in the ocean. Halley later published the first charts on which curving lines connected points of equal magnetic variation. Modern mapmakers use such lines to convey many kinds of information—one common example is the lines that connect points of equal temperature on daily weather maps. Once called Halleyan lines and known today as isograms or isolines, those useful lines were Halley's legacy to geophysical mapmaking.

John HARRISON
1693–1776
HOROLOGY

John Harrison was the son of a carpenter and joiner who designed and built a number of unique and important early clocks. He is best known for inventing the first timepiece (the chronometer) that enabled sailors to determine longitude accurately at sea.

In 1714 the English Parliament offered a prize of £20,000 for a reliable and accurate method to measure longitude. Sixteen years later Harrison published a paper that included a design for such a device. He built an early model and successfully tested it in 1737 on a voyage to Portugal. The Board of Longitude gave him £500 to continue his work, and over the next 25 years, Harrison produced smaller and better designs. Finally, he designed a timekeeper in the form of a large watch that was both extremely accurate and much smaller than his earlier efforts. The timepiece passed rigorous tests, but the Board of Longitude awarded Harrison only half the prize money, stipulating many new conditions that had not been part of the original competition. King George III was made aware of the unfairness of the process, and he sided with Harrison. Harrison finally received the full award in 1773.

William
HARVEY

1578–1657

PHYSIOLOGY, ANATOMY

Best known for discovering the circulation of blood, English physician William Harvey also made major advances in the understanding of generation, sensation, and locomotion. His methods stimulated a fundamental change in the study of anatomy and the functioning of the body, marking the end of the brand of medicine established by the ancient Greek physician Galen. His accomplishments helped fuel the popular enthusiasm for science that was a hallmark of the late 1600s. Harvey played a major role in the birth of the scientific revolution that marked the beginning of the modern world.

Life and Public Career

Harvey was the oldest of seven sons and the only one who did not pursue a career in business. His father took up commerce after many years as a farmer and landowner, and his brothers achieved success in the same field. William, however, studied arts and medicine at Cambridge. He finished his education at the University of Padua in Italy, the leading medical school in Europe, where he studied under some of the most prominent medical scholars of his day. He graduated at the age of 24 and returned to England to practice medicine. In 1607 he was elected to the Royal College of Physicians, and he rapidly rose to a position of great importance in that organization. In 1616 he performed a series of anatomical demonstrations at the college. The notes from these lectures contain the first insights into his later theories. Two years later Harvey was named as a physician to King James I on a part-time basis. He retained that position when Charles I succeeded James seven years later.

In 1628 Harvey published *Exercitatio anatomica de motu cordis et sanguinis in animalibus* (On the Motion of the Heart and Blood in Animals), in which he announced his discovery of the circulation of the blood. Three years later he became a full-time physician at the royal court, and in 1639 he was named the king's senior physician. He developed a close relationship with Charles and traveled with him on several military expeditions into Scotland. Harvey also took part in a special embassy that Charles sent to the Holy Roman Emperor Ferdinand II. Charles took an interest in Harvey's work, providing him with deer from the royal parks to dissect as part of his anatomical investigations. Harvey stayed with the

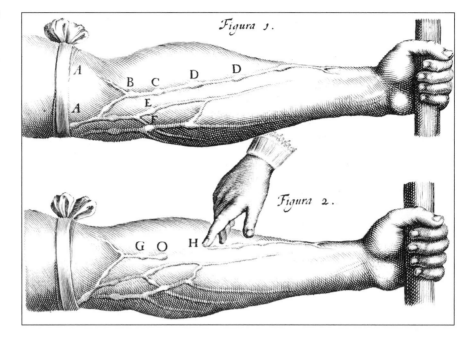

In 1628 William Harvey published a book in which he explained the circulation of blood. These drawings illustrate an experiment in which he showed how blood flows through arteries and veins.

king during the English Civil War from 1642 to 1646. However, after Parliament defeated the royal forces and beheaded Charles, Harvey returned to his private practice in London.

Five years later Harvey published his other major work, *De generatione* (On Generation). He continued to lecture at the Royal College until a year before his death, and late in life he donated money to the college for the construction of a library. In old age Harvey was plagued by gout* and kidney stones, and he often relieved his pain with large doses of a powerful drug called laudanum. He survived one overdose in 1652, but another one five years later led to a stroke that took his life.

* **gout** disease marked by painful inflammation of the joints

Scientific Accomplishments

As with many scientists of the time, Harvey's discoveries stemmed from his close observation of animals of all types. What set Harvey apart was his ability to grasp the importance of what he saw, formulate theories based on his observations, and test his theories through experimentation. He was also not afraid to challenge accepted theories that did not adequately account for the phenomena he observed.

* **physiology** science that deals with the functions of living organisms and their parts

Philosophical Roots of Harvey's Work. When Harvey began his scientific career, knowledge of anatomy and physiology* was based on the works of the ancient Greek philosopher Aristotle and the physician Galen. Harvey studied under teachers who supported both men, but his own views were more influenced by Aristotle. One of the basic ideas he shared with Aristotle was the belief that the soul and the body are inseparable. By contrast, most scholars of the day believed that the body was merely a passive object that was animated by the addition of a separate substance known as the soul. As a result, most physicians felt that separate forces or

79

spirits directed the activities of different parts of the body. These forces supposedly flowed to the various parts from a central source in the body. Like Aristotle, Harvey contended that the same life force resided simultaneously in all parts of the body. However, Harvey was not single-mindedly devoted to Aristotle's ideas. Although they served as a starting point for his studies, he was more than willing to criticize and modify Aristotle's theories when his own observations led him to different conclusions. Harvey drew on the writings of other authors as well. But he was always independent in his judgments and did not uncritically accept traditional views of medicine, anatomy, or physiology. At the same time, he never completely rejected the philosophical foundations on which much of Renaissance* medicine was based.

Circulation. Harvey's research on circulation was stimulated by his belief that blood was the most important substance in the body, that the soul resided in the blood, and that the blood was the only part of the body that was truly alive. Harvey believed that an embryo began as a single drop of blood and created the rest of the body from itself. The blood used the body to ensure its own growth and survival. In addition to creating the organs and other bodily structures, the blood supplied them with the heat and nutrition they needed to live and function properly. In this manner, he proved that the body existed to serve the needs of the blood.

To understand the significance of his discovery, it is necessary to discuss the beliefs of his day concerning the heart and blood vessels (veins and arteries). The prevailing medical view was that the veins and arteries comprised two separate systems that performed different tasks. The venous system was involved in nutrition. Nutrients from the intestines were soaked up by blood and carried by veins to the liver. This nutrient-rich blood then flowed into a large vein near the heart, called the vena cava, that distributed it to the other veins in the body. The right ventricle* of the heart pumped some of this blood to the pulmonary artery that supplied blood to the lungs. The arteries, along with the lungs, left ventricle, and pulmonary vein, formed a separate system that provided the body with heat and oxygen. The left ventricle and arteries were believed to supply oxygen to the body's heat by inhaling and exhaling. This caused the heart and arteries to contract and dilate (expand), producing pulse. At no point did the arteries and veins connect with or interact with each other.

In 1559 Realdo COLOMBO challenged the existing view of the role of the heart and arteries. His investigation of circulation in the lungs showed that the primary function of the heart and the arteries is to supply the body with blood. However, Colombo still believed that arterial and venous blood served different purposes. Harvey adopted Colombo's ideas and set out to investigate whether the arteries pulsated on their own or because the heart pumped blood. Colombo had identified both a passive phase of the heartbeat (dilation), when the heart relaxes and receives blood, and an active stage (constriction), in which it squeezes out the blood it contains. The previously accepted view was that both phases were active and that dilation was the stronger of the two. Harvey proved that the active phase of the heartbeat involved the contraction of the ventricles, not their dilation.

* **Renaissance** period that marked the beginnings of modern science and the rebirth of interest in classical art and literature that occurred in Europe from the late 1300s through the 1500s

* **ventricle** chamber of the heart

He proved this by showing that a punctured heart expels blood powerfully during contraction. He also noted that the walls of the heart become thicker during contraction, which meant that the cavities in the heart that receive the blood must become smaller at the same time. Turning to the arteries, Harvey demonstrated that their pulse results from blood being forced into them by the contraction of the heart. To support this theory he noted that a cut artery expels blood much more forcefully when the heart contracts. He also observed that animals with a more vigorous pulse have thicker arteries.

This new view of the heartbeat suggested that the amount of blood that flowed into the arteries had to be quite large. It was so large that unless the blood somehow returned to the heart, all of it would be emptied into the arteries in just a few beats. How then did the heart and veins replenish themselves with blood? Harvey concluded that blood pumped from the heart into the arteries must pass into the veins at some point before returning to the heart. To prove this, he tied a cord tightly around a subject's arm, cutting off the arterial pulse. The arteries above the cord swelled with blood. When he loosened the cord, the swelling in the arteries went down, and the veins in the arm below the cord swelled with blood. The blood from the arteries had clearly flowed into the veins.

Another critical factor in Harvey's debates was the discovery in 1603 of the valves in the veins by Harvey's teacher, the anatomist Girolamo FABRICI. Fabrici argued that the purpose of the valves was to slow the blood flow, enabling the tissues to absorb nutrients. However, Harvey believed that the valves were positioned so that the blood could move freely to the heart but not away from it. Such an arrangement made sense, Harvey argued, if the blood were pumped to the limbs through the arteries and returned to the heart through the veins.

Harvey's theory of the circulation of the blood was well received, but his critics pointed out that it failed to specify a precise connection between the arterial and venous systems. Harvey insisted, without empirical evidence, that the arteries and veins were connected, but with only a magnifying glass at his disposal, he made no progress on this problem. Later, in 1661, Marcello MALPIGHI observed the connection between the two systems (anastomoses) through a microscope.

Although he discovered circulation, Harvey failed to grasp its true purpose—to replenish the supply of oxygen in the blood by cycling it through the lungs. He fell back on his earlier idea that the blood supplied the body with heat, and he argued that the purpose of circulation was to distribute heat throughout the body. He continued to explore this topic to find a better explanation for circulation, but he never arrived at the correct answer. Nevertheless, his discovery revolutionized physiology, which had been based on accepted notions of the functions of the heart and blood vessels.

Generation. Harvey's investigations led him to challenge the accepted view of the formation of new life, or generation. The old view was that semen combined with menstrual blood in the uterus to form the heart of a fetus. The heart then used additional menstrual blood to create the rest

New Buildings, Old Foundations

Harvey's work on circulation illustrates his sympathy for some of the basic philosophical concepts of his day. Traditional philosophy considered circular motion to have a special preservative character that set it apart from regular motion. Harvey's familiarity with and support of this idea might have provided a spark of insight that helped him recognize the circular nature of the blood's movement and shaped his theory. In fact, his essay on circulation compares the movement of blood to other circular processes—in the atmosphere—noted by earlier natural philosophers.

of the fetus. All of the organs and structures of the fetus were assumed to be present at the moment of conception. During pregnancy they grew until they assumed their final form. The same process supposedly occurred in animals that laid eggs, except that the fetus grew inside an egg rather than in the uterus. Harvey, however, carefully observed developing chick embryos and found no evidence that semen ever enters or even touches eggs while they are forming within a hen. He also dissected the uteri of female deer at various stages of mating and pregnancy and observed no menstrual blood before mating. He noted that the fetus does not appear until quite some time after the male's semen has disappeared from the female's body.

Harvey concluded that the purpose of semen was simply to make the female fertile. In egg-laying animals, the fertile female produces an egg that has the ability to nourish itself and to generate a fetus from material contained within itself. This material begins as a homogenous substance but eventually differentiates itself into different organs and structures that become a new individual. Harvey called this gradual emergence of the fetus epigenesis. He based his conclusions about generation of live-bearing animals on his ideas about egg-bearing ones. The semen fertilizes the female, enabling her uterus to produce a fertilized conceptus, which is similar to the egg. The conceptus then grows within, and is nourished by, the uterus. Although much of Harvey's thinking on this topic has since been disproved, he was the first to realize that it was a new entity, the egg, which develops into the new being.

Sensation and Locomotion. In an unfinished paper, Harvey outlined his ideas about sensation and locomotion, again overturning existing wisdom. Earlier physicians believed that the brain created both sensation and movement. Consequently, cutting a nerve to one part of the body destroyed that part's mobility and sensibility. This belief also implied that the muscles involved in voluntary movement were fundamentally different from organs of involuntary movement, such as the heart. Harvey argued that the brain does not actually create sensation or movement, but that the organs and muscles contain these powers as long as they receive blood, heat, and spirits. The nerves transmit sensations from the organs to the brain, which then analyzes and makes sense of them. Similarly, he argued, the brain does not supply the power to move muscles, it simply coordinates the movements they make. The nerves supply the external sensations upon which the brain acts. Cutting a nerve thus does not destroy a muscle's mobility but its ability to take part in coordinated activity.

Other Works. From his writings it appears that Harvey planned to conduct a comprehensive program of research into the many fields he studied and that he hoped to publish the results. Unfortunately, little of his work was ever printed. He lost many notes and manuscripts when his room was looted in 1642. The rest were probably consumed in the Great Fire that destroyed much of London 24 years later. All that survives of his work are his lecture notes, drafts of his papers on muscles and movement in animals, and a few letters. However, his published essays represent breakthroughs that established Harvey as one of the most brilliant minds of his time.

Johannes Baptista van
HELMONT

1579–1644

CHEMISTRY, MEDICINE

* **analogy** form of reasoning based on the assumption that if two things are alike in some respects, then they are alike in all other respects as well

Johannes Baptista van Helmont is best known for his discovery of gases, but during his career as a physician, he also made many advances in medical theory and in the treatment of disease. His achievements were largely a result of his rejection of traditional learning based on analogy* and of his passion for precise observation, experimentation, and measurement. In turning away from the accepted doctrines of medicine and natural science, Helmont opened new frontiers of science for exploration by future generations of investigators.

Born into a Flemish aristocratic family, Helmont received a traditional education, earning his M.D. degree at the age of 20. Even at that young age, he had already come to consider much of his learning to be "dung" and "senseless prattle." He spent the next six years traveling through Europe to gather knowledge and later devoted another seven years to private research in Belgium. When he was about 42, a treatise citing his youthful support of a "magical" cure for wounds was published against his will. This resulted in a confrontation with church authorities, who accused him of promoting "monstrous superstitions" and placed him briefly under house arrest. The church conducted proceedings against him until 1642, two years before his death. However, these difficulties did not deter Helmont from his scientific investigations.

Helmont believed that water was the chief constituent of matter. To support his theory he grew a willow tree for five years in a measured amount of soil. He found that the tree increased its weight by 164 pounds, while the soil had decreased in weight by only a few ounces. The water added to the tree over the years accounted for the difference.

Helmont was also intrigued by the smoke produced by the combustion (burning) of solids and liquids. He burned a variety of substances and closely analyzed the smoke, which he found to be different from air or water vapor. Helmont observed that smoke exhibits properties that are specific to the substance that produced it, and he called this "specific smoke" *gas*. The name derived either from the word *chaos* (since the smoke could not be contained in a vessel or reduced to another substance) or the word *gaesen*, meaning "to ferment." Helmont believed that gas was not only matter but also the essence, or "spirit," of a substance. He felt that in gas he had discovered the solution to the theological problem of the relation of matter to spirit, or "soul." To Helmont gas represented divine truth that could be seen by the experimenter. He ultimately identified a number of gases, including carbon dioxide, carbon monoxide, chlorine gas, and sulfur dioxide. Although he did not name these gases or identify them as separate elements, he was the first to recognize gas as a distinct chemical entity.

Helmont was also a pioneer in the development of modern disease theory and medical practice. During his day the prevailing theory of disease was the humoural theory. Proposed by the ancient Greeks, the theory claimed that the body contains four vital fluids, or humours, and that disease was the result of an imbalance of the humours within the body. The preferred treatment for diseases was to restore the body's balance by removing excess humours through such procedures as bleeding the patient or administering laxatives. Helmont argued that disease was caused by external agents that invaded the body and acted on specific organs. He identified the causes of certain diseases, such as asthma, and was the first to argue that fever was not caused by problems with the humours but was the body's reaction to irritation. Thus he identified it as a natural healing process rather than a disease in itself. In 1642 Helmont obtained permission from the church to publish his essay on fever.

A follower of PARACELSUS, Helmont improved and widely used chemical medicines prescribed by the Swiss scientist. Following hints provided by Paracelsus, Helmont identified stomach acid as the main agent of digestion and came very close to identifying the digestive acid with hydrochloric acid. He also discovered that the lungs expel "volatile salts" (now identified as carbon dioxide) when a person exhales. By refusing to accept traditional scientific methods and theories, Helmont broke through barriers in the fields of medicine and chemistry. His legacy of empirical investigation was as important as the discoveries he made by employing the technique.

William HERSCHEL

1738–1822

ASTRONOMY

* **optics** scientific study of the properties of light

William Herschel was the most famous British astronomer of the 1780s. A self-taught amateur, using a telescope he had made himself, Herschel discovered Uranus. Later, established as a professional scientist, Herschel made other important contributions to stellar astronomy, the study of the stars. Chief among these were his theories that some patches of light in the night sky were really clusters of stars at immense distances and that star systems change and age according to the universal laws of physics.

The Amateur Stargazer. The discoverer of Uranus was born Friedrich Wilhelm Herschel in Hannover, Germany. His father, an army musician, trained the boy for a career in music. In 1756 young Herschel visited England with his father and learned the English language. The following year, when French troops occupied Hannover, Herschel and one of his brothers fled to England. Herschel worked as a performer and music teacher and became known by the English version of his name.

By 1766 Herschel had begun working as an organist for a chapel at Bath, a popular resort town near London. In his spare time he studied musical theory. Around this time he also turned his attention to a book on optics*, which contained fascinating descriptions of telescopes and astronomy. In 1772 Herschel brought his sister Caroline to England, and she became his assistant and companion in astronomical research. Preparing telescopes and observing the sky through them took up more and more of Herschel's time, sometimes interfering with his musical responsibilities. The following year he began renting telescopes, building them from parts, and making his own mirrors for use in telescopes.

Eventually Herschel's telescopes were recognized as the finest and most powerful of his time. He ground and polished ever larger mirrors, believing that the larger the mirror, the more light the reflecting telescope can gather. Herschel believed that light-gathering power was "the power of penetrating into space." Herschel's favorite telescope, completed in 1783, had a mirror 18 inches in diameter. Around the same time he tried twice to create larger mirrors, but these efforts failed. On one such occasion Herschel and his brother were lucky to escape with their lives when molten metal flowed across a stone floor.

In the late 1770s Herschel began a series of detailed surveys of the heavens. In 1781 he spotted an object that he knew was neither a star nor one of the familiar five planets—Mercury, Venus, Mars, Jupiter, and Saturn—known since ancient times. Herschel thought the new object was a comet. News of his discovery reached the Royal Society, Britain's leading association of scientists and scholars. Soon the object was recognized as the first planet discovered since ancient times—and Herschel as its discoverer. Although Herschel tried to name the planet Georgium Sidus, meaning "George's Star," after King George III, it became known as Uranus, a name, like those of the other planets, drawn from Roman mythology.

The Professional Astronomer. Almost overnight Herschel was world famous. The Royal Society made him a member, and the king granted him a pension. In exchange for an annual salary, Herschel was to live near Windsor Castle and occasionally demonstrate the heavens to the royal family. The pension enabled him to give up teaching music and become a full-time scientist. He and Caroline settled in Slough in what became known as Observatory House, where Herschel lived for the rest of his life. He married in 1788. His son, John Frederick William Herschel, attended Cambridge University, and in 1816 he became Herschel's assistant. That same year Herschel received a knighthood in recognition of his services to British science.

Early in his professional career, Herschel convinced the king to pay for a new telescope that contained mirrors measuring 48 inches in diameter. Completed in 1789, this monster telescope, considered one of the wonders of the scientific world, was never fully satisfactory, although almost immediately it enabled Herschel to discover a sixth satellite of Saturn.

Herschel's detailed sweeps, or surveys of the night sky, continued until 1802. He used his hundreds of hours of observation, as well as the published observations of other astronomers, as the basis for new ideas about the universe. His most important single achievement in astronomy was his development of far-reaching theories about cosmology*.

After surveying the glowing patches of light called nebulae*—and increasing the number of known nebulae from about 100 to 2,500—Herschel concluded that they were distant star clusters, soon to be called island universes and today known as galaxies. Later, however, he acknowledged that some nebulae were closer to the solar system and were shells of matter, not clouds of stars. Herschel also realized that the Milky Way, the dense band of stars that crosses the sky, is a flattened star system or cluster that includes the solar system. Although Herschel was not the first to speculate on the structure of the Milky Way, he was the first to try to count its stars and to measure it.

Astronomers of the time were eager to establish the distance of the stars and the size of the universe. Herschel could not correctly answer these questions, mainly because he believed that all stars were of the same

* **cosmology** set of ideas about the origin, history, and structure of the universe

* **nebula** cloud of gas or dust inside the galaxy; also used to refer to patches of light now known to be distant galaxies; *pl.* nebulae

brightness as the earth's sun and that distance alone caused the observable differences in their brightness. Because he did not realize that stars are of many sizes and varying brightness, his calculations of their distances were wrong. Herschel did, however, contribute an important theory of stellar evolution. He believed that the universe began with stars scattered through infinite space and that over time, gravitational forces drew them together into loose associations and, eventually, into tight clusters. The notion that the entire universe was involved in a grand process of evolution shaped many later cosmological theories.

In addition to his studies of the stars, Herschel observed and published papers about the bodies of the solar system. Besides the discovery of Uranus, his accomplishments in solar astronomy included the discovery of invisible, infrared heat waves in light emitted by the sun; the conclusion that white spots on the poles of Mars are frozen regions; the suggestion of the term *asteroid* for the small bodies that orbit the sun beyond the orbit of Mars; and discovering the sixth and seventh satellites of Saturn and two satellites of Uranus.

Johannes HEVELIUS

1611–1687

ASTRONOMY

* **mechanics** science that studies how energy and force affect objects

* **optics** scientific study of the properties of light

The German astronomer Johannes Hevelius is perhaps best known for his work in compiling an atlas of the earth's moon that contains one of the earliest detailed maps of the lunar surface. Some of the names that Hevelius gave to lunar features remain in use, and a crater on the moon is named in his honor. Hevelius also compiled an important star catalog and a celestial atlas showing, for the first time, several constellations.

Early Life and Career. Hevelius was born in Danzig (present-day Gdansk), Poland. The son of a prosperous brewer and property owner of German ancestry, he received his early education at local schools. In 1627 he began taking private lessons in astronomy from Peter Krüger, a teacher of mathematics and astronomy, who also taught Hevelius the practical arts of making scientific instruments and engraving.

Three years later Hevelius entered the University of Leiden in the Netherlands to study law as well as mathematics and its applications to mechanics* and optics*. Hevelius left Leiden in 1631 and visited London and Paris. After his return to Danzig, he worked in his father's brewery and began preparing to enter public service. In 1639 Hevelius began systematic astronomical observations, and soon the course of his life turned to astronomy. He began to construct his own astronomical instruments and corresponded with foreign astronomers.

Meanwhile, he also held public office in Danzig. Although his father's death in 1649 meant that he was responsible for running the family brewery, it also gave Hevelius the funds to pursue his interest in astronomy. At his home he built one of the world's leading astronomical observatories. In 1679 the observatory was destroyed by fire, but Hevelius quickly rebuilt and reequipped the space, although with fewer and inferior instruments. The shock of losing many of his books and papers in the fire took a toll on Hevelius's health, and he died several years later.

Accomplishments. Hevelius published several important works. The first was *Selenographia* (Pictures of the Moon), published in 1647, which recounts his observations of the planets, sunspots, and eclipses. It also contains a map of the moon that he engraved. Hevelius gave new names to the lunar mountains, craters, and other formations shown on the map. Astronomers rejected his system, which he based on names taken from the earth. The book also has descriptions of lunar motion based on his observations.

His second great work, *Cometographia* (Pictures of Comets), was published in 1668. This work contains his observations and thoughts on comets, which he believed were composed of condensed planetary matter and were linked with the material responsible for sunspots. Although his ideas on the motion of comets were quite vague, he believed that comets travel in a curved path around a fixed point—an idea proven true by later scientists.

Hevelius owed much of the success of his observations to his skill in designing and making scientific instruments. He described the techniques he used to build telescopes and other instruments in *Machina coelestis* (Celestial Machines), published in 1673 and 1679. Hevelius also evaluated the accuracy of the observations of astronomers from ancient times to his era.

His final work, *Prodromus Astronomiae* (Guide to Astronomy), was published in 1690, after his death. This work is a catalog of 1,564 stars—the most comprehensive of its time—arranged alphabetically by constellation and according to the brightness of the stars. Accompanying the text were 56 engravings of constellations, some done by Hevelius himself.

Although Hevelius does not rank among the greatest astronomers of all time, he was respected by his colleagues. He also corresponded with all the leading astronomers of the era, including Edmond HALLEY, Robert HOOKE, and Johannes KEPLER.

Robert HOOKE

1635–1702

PHYSICS

Robert Hooke was one of the most unlikely of all great scientists. His physical appearance was so sickly that a contemporary said that he "is the most, and promises the least, of any man in the world that I ever saw." He never completed a college degree and constantly quarreled with his colleagues. Nevertheless, he left a legacy of scientific and mechanical achievement that rivals the greatest scientists of his day.

Early Life. Few people who knew Hooke as a boy would have guessed that he was destined for great things. The son of a minister in Freshwater, England, he was so sickly in his early years that his parents had little hope that he would survive to adulthood. His father had planned for Robert to pursue a career in the church, but severe headaches prevented Hooke from concentrating on his studies. He did, however, show a keen talent for mechanics. He built a working wooden replica of a clock based solely on his observation of the dismantling of the original clock. Among the many toys he created for himself was a model sailing ship that could actually fire its

Hooke, Robert

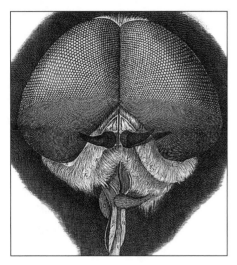

In 1665 Robert Hooke published his famous work *Micrographia,* which contained descriptions and drawings of the minerals, plants, and animals that he studied under a microscope. This illustration from his book shows the eye of a gray drone fly.

* **curator** person in charge of a place of exhibit, such as a museum

cannon. His fascination with and understanding of mechanical devices served him well in later life.

When Hooke was 13, his father died, and his family sent him to London to work as an artist's apprentice. Hooke, however, had no desire to pursue a career in art. Fortunately, the master of a London school saw that Hooke had intellectual potential and took him on as a pupil. Hooke learned rapidly, picking up several languages and, more important, mathematics, including geometry. Five years later he moved to Oxford, where he joined a group of scholars who later formed the core of London's Royal Society. One of these men, physicist Robert BOYLE, took him on as an assistant. This marked the beginning of Hooke's professional career.

Early Career. Hooke's first great triumph came when Boyle instructed him to design an improved version of the air pump built by German engineer Otto von GUERICKE. Hooke responded by creating the first modern air pump. With Hooke's pump and assistance, Boyle performed experiments that led to Boyle's Law, published in 1662. Although Boyle did not cite Hooke's participation in his achievement, most modern scholars believe that he played a significant role, and some feel that the credit should rightfully go to him. This was the first instance of a dispute involving Hooke's contributions to major discoveries. The second, which occurred around the same time, concerned Hooke's design for a clock driven by a coiled spring instead of a pendulum. Unlike a pendulum clock, a spring-driven watch can keep accurate time even on a tossing ship. This was an important consideration, since having an accurate clock on board was the only way to determine the ship's longitude. Hooke patented the device but never produced it. When the Dutch scientist Christiaan HUYGENS later built a watch using the principle of the coiled spring, Hooke accused Huygens of stealing his idea.

In 1662 Hooke's academic circle officially formed the Royal Society and chose Hooke as its curator* of experiments. Although he was given the difficult task of coming up with several experiments for each meeting, he was more than up to the challenge, and his experiments were probably the driving force behind the society in its early years. Four years later, London city officials asked Hooke to supervise the rebuilding of the city after it was destroyed in the Great Fire. Hooke not only drew up plans for rebuilding the city; he also designed many of the new buildings himself.

Micrographia and Newton. In 1665, the year before the fire, Hooke published the work for which he is most famous, *Micrographia.* The book featured descriptions and drawings of observations he had made through a microscope. His detailed diagrams of minerals, plants, and insects fascinated both scientists and nonprofessionals and established his reputation with the public. Besides drawings and observations, *Micrographia* contains the outlines of many of Hooke's theories. The theory of light that he sets forth in the book is one of the earliest statements of the wave theory of light. The work also presents a theory of optics on which Isaac NEWTON based the second volume of his famous work, *Opticks.*

Hooke and Newton crossed paths on other occasions. The first incident involved a paper on color theory that a young Newton submitted to the Royal Society. Hooke dismissed the theory, which he did not understand, in a rude manner. When Newton sent in a second paper on color theory, Hooke claimed that the ideas it contained could be found in the *Micrographia*.

Later, in a series of lectures he published in the 1670s, Hooke proposed several ideas that anticipated Newton's work on the law of universal gravitation. Although Hooke's work was mistaken in several of its arguments, it did provide one important key to Newton's theory. Hooke rejected the notion that the orbits of planets were the result of a balance between centrifugal* and centripetal* forces. Instead, he said that a body continues to travel in a straight line unless it is diverted from its course by some force directed toward a center (such as the gravitational pull of a larger body). He also said that gravity decreases in proportion to the square of the distance from the object exerting the force. Hooke later claimed that Newton stole his idea of the inverse square relation when formulating the law of universal gravitation.

Other Accomplishments. Hooke made two other major contributions to physics. One is Hooke's law, which states that the stress placed on an object is proportional to the amount of strain the object experiences. His other contribution was on the topic of respiration, in which he proved that the purpose of breathing is to maintain a constant supply of fresh air to the lungs and that air is essential to life. The existing wisdom was that the purpose of breathing was merely to cool and pump air though the body.

In addition to physics, Hooke was a pioneer in the field of geology. In an era when people accepted the biblical view of creation, animal fossils remained a mystery. Hooke argued that the fossils were the remains of organic creatures, a position that was irrefutably proved many years after his death. He also refused to accept the biblical flood as an explanation for the presence of marine fossils in inland regions. He contended instead that the presence of fossils there was evidence that the earth had undergone dramatic changes in the past. He was also willing to consider the possibility that the discovery of fossils unlike living creatures suggested that species mutated, or evolved, over time.

Perhaps his greatest contributions were the instruments he devised. Hooke had a hand in the design of every important instrument of his time, from the air pump to clocks to the telescope. He constructed the first reflecting telescope and the compound microscope. He created the first barometer that used needles to record air pressure, and he developed a weather clock that measured air pressure, temperature, humidity, rainfall, and wind speed. He also invented a device to calibrate* thermometers. One contemporary called him "the Newton of mechanics."

Later Life and Assessment of His Work. In 1677 Hooke became secretary of the Royal Society, but by this time his creative genius had begun to decline. Although he lived another 25 years, he produced nothing of note during this time. He died in his room at the age of 67. Hooke's legacy to science is the subject of debate. His strength lay in his keen insight into many difficult problems of physics. He had an incredible ability to grasp

* **centrifugal** force on a body moving in a curved line that is directed away from its center of rotation

* **centripetal** force on a body moving in a curved line that is directed toward its center of rotation

* **calibrate** to adjust or standardize the markings on a measuring device

Genius at Work, but not at Rest

Hooke thrived on daunting challenges and a hectic work schedule. His task of providing experiments for every meeting of the Royal Society was incredibly difficult and time-consuming, yet it was one of the most productive times of his life. He also spent countless hours on his plan to rebuild London after the city had been destroyed by the Great Fire of 1666. After he took over as secretary of the Royal Society, however, he had far fewer demands on his time. Lacking challenges, he lost his drive and produced no significant work thereafter.

the solution to many such problems, but he lacked the analytical and mathematical abilities he needed to prove scientifically the validity of his insights. He also lacked the discipline to do the dirty work of following up the many ideas he generated. Most of the ideas he introduced during his lifetime were developed by other scientists, such as Newton, who possessed the technical abilities Hooke did not. Nevertheless, this does not diminish the importance of his accomplishments. Hooke made invaluable contributions to groundbreaking work by Boyle, Newton, and others and was undoubtedly one of the foremost scientific minds of his time.

James HUTTON

1726–1797

GEOLOGY, AGRICULTURE

* **geology** science that studies rocks and the earth

James Hutton is widely regarded as the founder of modern geology*. He was the first prominent scientist to reject the popular idea, based on church teachings, that the earth was only a few thousand years old. Through his extensive and careful observation of rocks, soil, and fossils, he concluded that the earth was actually much older than most people had imagined. Moreover, at a time when most scholars believed that the earth had remained unaltered since its creation, Hutton's studies convinced him that the structure of the earth had changed radically over the course of time. Hutton's ideas, set forth in his masterwork, *Theory of the Earth,* changed the course of geology and revolutionized popular conceptions about the physical evolution of the planet.

Life and Career

Hutton was the son of a wealthy Scottish merchant who died when James was three years old. He left a fortune large enough to provide for all his children, so James was never under pressure to work for a living. As a student at Edinburgh University in Scotland, Hutton attended lectures that introduced him to chemistry, a subject that proved valuable in his later work in geology. In 1743 he became a lawyer's apprentice, but soon left the law firm to study medicine. This discipline allowed him to learn more about chemistry, and for five years he attended courses in Scotland and France.

In 1750 Hutton returned to Edinburgh, but not to practice medicine. He decided instead to pursue farming. For the next four years, he traveled through England, Holland, Belgium, and France to learn more about methods of scientific agriculture. It was during these travels that he first became interested in geology. After returning to Scotland, he settled on a small farm inherited from his father and applied the agricultural knowledge he had gained. After 18 years he leased the farm to a tenant and moved to Edinburgh. He spent most of the rest of his life there, studying his twin passions of chemistry and geology. He took field trips around England and became familiar with the geology of England, gathering the knowledge that later led him to formulate his theory of the earth.

Hutton was one of the founding members of the Royal Society of Edinburgh and he was later elected a member of the French Society of Agriculture. Two years before his death, he published *Theory of the Earth,* a work he had been preparing for more than ten years. In his later years, Hutton suffered from problems related to stones in the bladder that apparently led to his death in 1797.

Scientific Accomplishments

Hutton's claim to fame lies in his revolutionary ideas about geology. However, he was also an avid student of agriculture, and he made important contributions in that field as well.

Geology. During Hutton's day, theories of the earth were based on interpretation of the biblical book of Genesis. By tracing the generations of Adam listed in Genesis, scholars concluded that the earth was only about 6,000 years old. Marine fossils found on land were explained as products of the great flood from the story of Noah and the ark. Although a few scholars had gathered some information that led them to challenge these ideas, no one had brought all of the evidence together into a coherent theory about the history of the earth. In 1788, the Royal Society of Edinburgh published a paper authored by Hutton, in which he argued that the world was older than previously thought. This was the first rough statement of the theory of the earth that he published ten years later.

Hutton observed that most sedimentary* rocks were composed of marine fossils and other materials similar to those found on the seashore (products of erosion). Consequently, these rocks could not have formed part of the original crust of the earth, but were formed by some "second cause" and deposited on the ocean floor. Hutton explained the formation of the present land as a two-step process—the consolidation of the loose material at the ocean floor into solid rock and the elevation of that seafloor.

Hutton offered explanations for both of these events that differed sharply from the accepted theories. He argued that, over long periods of time, great heat from the mineral region just below the earth's crust had fused the loose materials together to form rocks. To support his argument, he pointed out that rock formations made of these former marine deposits were often broken and folded. This indicated that they had been exposed to violent expansion caused by exposure to extreme heat. He also claimed that because similar rocks occur in different countries, the same processes that created them in England must have operated throughout the world.

The most important part of Hutton's theory was his argument that these processes occur in cycles. According to Hutton, the action of wind and water erodes the land and transports the eroded material to the sea. There it is washed into the water and deposited as sediment on the seafloor. As the sediments build up over many years, they are subjected to great heat that fuses them together. The same heat causes the seafloor to expand and pushes it up to form new land. This is a never-ending process that, as far as Hutton could tell, would continue to operate indefinitely into the future. Because of the extremely slow rate at which this process occurs, and because it obviously occurred in the past, the earth must be much older than previously believed. Hutton's theory stirred a great deal

* **sedimentary** referring to soils, rock particles, and other materials that are deposited over time and make up the ground, whether on dry land or at the bottom of a body of water

No Water, Just Ice

Hutton's innovative approach to geological processes is apparent in his explanation of the presence of granite boulders in some areas of Switzerland. The accepted explanation was that the biblical flood had deposited them there. Hutton argued that glaciers had eroded the boulders and carried them down from the mountains several thousands of years ago. Although Hutton had never been to Switzerland, his explanation was closer to the truth—that the boulders were moved by the great ice sheets that covered Europe during the last Ice Age.

of controversy and did not gain widespread acceptance until more than 30 years after his death. It is now recognized as the foundation on which modern geology is based.

Hutton made another significant contribution to geology by realizing that many rocks were produced by volcanic activity. At the time, most scholars believed that all rocks not deposited by the biblical flood were created at the beginning of time and remained unchanged since then. Hutton argued that some rocks, such as granite, are formed in the mineral region when different substances melt together and cool into a solid form—Hutton had thereby discovered the true origin of igneous rocks.

Agriculture and Animal Husbandry. Just before his death, Hutton was working on a manuscript titled *Principles of Agriculture.* Among other topics, this work included an early theory of animal evolution. At the time, the popular notion was that all species of animals on earth had existed in their present form since the beginning of creation. Hutton, however, rejected this belief, using the dog as an example to prove his position.

If the existing theory were correct, he argued, then over time the different types of dogs would have bred with each other. The result would be a single type of dog that contained a mix of all the traits of the various species. There were obviously many very different types of dogs, so the theory must be wrong. Hutton said that the evidence suggested that there had originally been only one type of dog. However, under "the influence of external causes," different types of dogs developed in different ways. Those best adapted to their particular environment would survive; the others would die out. As Hutton wrote, "for example, where dogs are to live by the swiftness of their feet and the sharpness of their sight, the form best adapted to that end will be the most certain of remaining while the forms least adapted . . . will be the first to perish." His notion that there is a natural mechanism for the variation of species bears a close resemblance to the theory of evolution by natural selection later proposed by Charles Darwin.

Despite promoting ideas that challenged accepted church doctrine, Hutton was no atheist*. He believed that there was an intelligent design in nature that suggested the existence of divine wisdom. However, he rejected the notion that the Bible was a literal account of the history of the earth. He also felt that it was not the purpose of science to prove the truth of religious beliefs, nor the purpose of religion to provide a natural history of the earth. To him the goals of religion and science were, and should remain, separate, and neither one should interfere with the other.

* **atheist** person who believes that no god or supernatural force exists

Christiaan
HUYGENS

1629–1695

PHYSICS, MATHEMATICS,
ASTRONOMY, OPTICS

One of Europe's greatest early mathematicians, Christiaan Huygens also made significant contributions in many other fields. His work in optics* led him to develop superior telescopes with which he discovered Saturn's largest moon, Titan, and identified the true shape of Saturn's rings. This work led to breakthroughs in understanding phenomena such as the refraction* and distortion of light rays passing through a lens. He also proposed the earliest statement of the wave theory of light. Huygens

* **optics** scientific study of the properties of light

* **refraction** deflection of a light ray or energy wave as it passes at different speeds through media of different densities

* **mechanics** science that studies how energy and force affect objects

Huygens and the ETs

Huygens was an early supporter of the possibility of extraterrestrial life. He accepted Copernicus's view that the earth was not at the center of the universe, but was merely one of many planets. He felt that the creation of life was the highest expression of God's wisdom. To Huygens it was inconceivable that God would make countless planets but create life on only one of them. He concluded not only that life existed on other planets, but also that it must be very similar to life on earth. Huygens also believed that the culture on those planets would be similar to that of earth.

achieved many successes in the field of dynamics, which deals with the action of forces on bodies of all types. Late in his life, he speculated on the possibility and nature of life on other planets.

Life and Career

Huygens was a child of privilege who grew up in a wealthy and prominent Dutch family. Both his grandfather and his father held diplomatic positions with the Dutch ruling family, and his brother followed in their footsteps. His father, Constantijn, was widely read in both science and literature. He was also a gifted artist, musician, and composer, and an outstanding poet who is considered one of the most accomplished figures in Dutch literary history. Constantijn was determined that his sons would receive a strong education, and to this end, he schooled them at home until the age of 16 with the help of private tutors. Christiaan proved to be a gifted student with an aptitude for drawing, mathematics, and mechanics*, as well as music and languages. The philosopher and mathematician René DESCARTES occasionally visited the Huygens home, and Descartes's ideas had a great influence on young Christiaan's thinking. When Huygens he was 13, he built a lathe, demonstrating his ability to combine theoretical insights with practical knowledge, a characteristic of his later work.

Huygens studied mathematics and law at the University of Leiden, graduating at age 18. During his time at university, his father wrote to the philosopher Marin MERSENNE about Christiaan's study of falling bodies. Mersenne and Huygens soon began a direct correspondence in which they shared their ideas. After Leiden, Huygens enrolled at the College of Orange at Breda, where he studied law. This was a natural course of action for a young man from a prominent diplomatic family who would likely become a diplomat himself. Christiaan, however, found little fascination with the world of royal courts and diplomacy. Instead, he remained at home to pursue his studies of nature, supported by an allowance from his father. His early investigations of mathematics led to a publication in which he showed that Gregory of St. Vincent had not solved the problem of squaring the circle, as he had claimed. This was the first of many important mathematical works he published dealing with the areas of geometric figures. Huygens later published the first book on the theory of probability, which remained the only book on this topic until the century following his death.

In 1655 Huygens turned his talents to the creation and refinement of several practical devices. He and his brother perfected techniques for lens grinding that dramatically improved the quality of existing telescopes and microscopes. In fact, Christiaan was using one of the telescopes he had built with his brother when he discovered Titan and identified the rings of Saturn. Later the same year, Huygens invented the first pendulum clock during his investigations into the motion of bodies. He later devised a clock driven by a coiled spring, although his claim to have invented the first such mechanism was challenged by the English scientist Robert HOOKE. Huygens also began a series of journeys to Paris and London that put him in touch with some of the leading figures in science. On his first trip to Paris he met with several scientists who later founded the French Académie Royal des Sciences. A journey to Paris in 1663 included a side trip to London, during which time he became a member of England's Royal Society.

* **natural philosopher** person who develops theories to explain the natural world

The following year, the prominent scientist and natural philosopher* Melchisédech Thévenot offered Huygens membership in a scientific academy to be formed in Paris. Jean-Baptiste Colbert, an adviser to King Louis XIV, proposed that the society would sponsor scholarly meetings that had previously been taking place informally, and would support its members with government funds. In 1666 the Académie Royal des Sciences officially opened and Huygens traveled to Paris to become a member. He lived in Paris for much of the next 15 years, returning to Holland just twice for health reasons. Huygens, the star of the academy, encouraged it to undertake a thorough and systematic program for studying natural processes and phenomena. His time in Paris was marked by great activity. There he formulated his theory of gravity and developed the wave theory of light. He investigated the motion of bodies and designed his spring-driven clock. He also pursued both astronomical and microscopical investigations.

In 1672 war erupted between France and Holland, complicating Huygens's life in Paris. As a Dutchman, the war placed him in a delicate relationship with his French hosts, but he continued to pursue his studies there. In 1673 he dedicated the *Horologium oscillatorium,* an essay in which he outlined his ideas for a spring-driven clock, to Louis XIV. This helped secure his position in France but caused displeasure among his countrymen in Holland. In 1681 he left Paris because of ill health and returned home.

He recovered enough to return two years later, but the circumstances in France had changed. Colbert, his great ally and patron, had died. Without his support, Huygens's nationality, his religion (he was a Protestant and France was a Catholic country), and his family's ties to the Dutch ruling family made a return to Paris impossible. He went back to Holland where he continued to study optics and built several clocks in the hope of designing one that would enable sailors to determine longitude. In his final years, he published the *Cosmotheoros,* in which he outlined his ideas on extraterrestrial life. He also visited Isaac NEWTON and carried on a correspondence with Wilhelm LEIBNIZ, the inventors of calculus*. Huygens was never a very healthy person, and in 1694 he contracted an illness from which he failed to recover. He died the following year.

* **calculus** advanced form of mathematics that involves computing quantities that change as functions of different variables

Scientific Achievements

Although Huygens was keenly interested in mathematics, he achieved most of his lasting fame in the areas of mechanics, optics, and astronomy.

Mathematics. Most of Huygens's work in mathematics was theoretical, including the determination of the areas of parabolas and hyperbolas, and the study of logarithms and algebraic problems. He never mastered the new calculus, instead exploring the limits of old methods of calculation. In addition, he developed no new mathematical theories of his own but rather improved existing methods and applied them to problems in the natural sciences. Although Huygens achieved some important mathematical proofs using these techniques, his work in mathematics essentially looked to the past. His work was quickly superseded by the revolutionary principles of contemporaries such as Newton and Leibniz. Ultimately, his work had little influence on later generations of mathematicians.

Optics and Astronomy. Some of Huygens's successes were in optics and his application of his theories to the improvement of lenses and their use in astronomical observation. In 1653 he wrote *Tractatus de refractione et telescopiis,* which discussed the law of refraction, the focusing of lenses and spheres, the structure of the eye, the shape of spectacle lenses, and the construction of telescopes. After reading Newton's work on the distortion of colors passing through a lens, he determined the most advantageous shapes for lenses in telescopes of varying lengths.

Christiaan Huygens developed a telescope to identify Saturn's rings and studied the refracting and reflecting properties of light. He also built the first pendulum and spring-driven clocks.

Using his improved telescopes, Huygens determined that what earlier observers had identified as arms around the planet Saturn were actually rings. During an extended period of observation, he noted that the arms did not change their shape or orientation with respect to Saturn, which meant that they must form a ring around the planet. Huygens also discovered Saturn's largest moon, defined the period of Mars (how long it takes to rotate once on its axis), and explored the nebula* in the constellation Orion. Huygens published his findings on Saturn in a pamphlet titled *De Saturni lunâ observatio nova*.

* **nebula** cloud of gas or dust inside the galaxy; also used to refer to patches of light now known to be distant galaxies; *pl.* nebulae

Wave Theory of Light.

Huygens's work in optics is closely related to his theories about light. According to Huygens, light is an irregular series of shock waves that move at a very fast speed through the ether, an invisible medium that permeates all space and transmits these waves. Light displaces particles in the ether, causing those particles to collide with each other. These collisions form new wave fronts around each particle, which extend outward from the particle in the form of hemispheres. When infinite numbers of these wave fronts overlap each other, they produce light. He used this principle, called Huygens's principle, to explain the phenomena of reflection and refraction. His theory was able to explain that light should travel more slowly through dense media, but it was not able to handle the phenomenon known as polarization.

The Pendulum.

The Italian scientist Galileo GALILEI first noticed that the swing of a pendulum was apparently tautochronous. That is, it always takes the same amount of time, regardless of the length of the pendulum or the heaviness of the weight attached to its end. Galileo attempted to use this insight in the construction of a reliable clock but with no success. Huygens realized that this property of the pendulum made it an ideal device for driving the mechanism of a clock. In 1657 he built the first such clock and spent years thereafter studying the motion of pendulums. He discovered that the pendulum is not exactly tautochronous. Its period (the time it takes to swing back and forth once) depends on its amplitude (the distance it covers in one swing). To produce an equal-timed swing, Huygens realized that the pendulum would need to move in a curve known as a cycloid. He later proposed that one could develop a universal measure of length based on the distance traveled by a pendulum in one second. However, this theory was later proven incorrect when it was discovered that the period of a pendulum differs from place to place. This happens because the centrifugal* force produced by the earth's rotation is not uniform throughout the planet. Interestingly, the subject of centrifugal force was another area in which Huygens made important discoveries.

* **centrifugal** force on a body moving in a curved line that is directed away from its center of rotation

Gravity and Centrifugal Force.

Huygens's theory of gravity built on the work of Descartes. Huygens believed that a vortex* of very tiny particles constantly circled the earth, and that they have a tendency to move away from the earth's center. This centrifugal tendency, or center of gravity, caused ordinary matter in the vortex to move toward the earth's center. Huygens argued that the gravity of an object is equal to the amount of

* **vortex** mass of whirling fluid that tends to form a cavity or vacuum in the center; whirlpool

centrifugal force generated by an equivalent amount of the tiny particles moving very rapidly around the earth.

His explorations of gravity led him to investigate the phenomenon of centrifugal force. These studies confirmed his belief that the centrifugal force was similar to the force of gravity. However, he could never explain exactly how the centrifugal tendency of the tiny particles caused gravity, or a centripetal* tendency, in larger bodies. Huygens rejected Newton's theory of universal gravitation. As a firm believer in mechanical explanations, he interpreted Newton's law of universal gravitation as synonymous with the claim that bodies attract one another across empty space at a distance. Since there could be no possible mechanism for action at a distance, Huygens continued to support Descartes's mechanical model of a fluid vortex, which transports the planets through the heavens. Extending Descartes's model to gravity, Huygens concluded that bodies are heavy because they are pushed by other bodies, not because they are attracted at a distance.

centripetal force on a body moving in a curved line that is directed toward its center of rotation

Mechanistic Philosophy. Much of Huygens's work was based on a mechanistic philosophy that stated that all natural phenomena must ultimately be explained by the motions and interaction of particles of matter. This was essentially the position taken by Descartes. Huygens argued that there were four or five distinct types of particles of varying sizes, and that the movement and collisions of these particles could explain all natural effects, such as gravity, centrifugal force, magnetism, and the transmission of light. This was an area of fundamental disagreement between Huygens and his younger contemporaries, such as Newton. Because Newton did not offer mechanistic explanations for many of his concepts, Huygens rejected them. He might have been justified in some of his criticism, because some of his most important work, such as his discovery of Saturn's rings and his studies of centrifugal force, was based on mechanistic beliefs. However, his insistence on mechanistic explanations for natural phenomena ultimately fell out of favor among the scientific community.

Huygens's adherence to traditional methods and philosophies undermined the influence of many of his studies on later scientists. Nevertheless, he was one of the greatest mathematicians and mechanical theorists of his day, and his achievements in astronomy, time measurement, and light theory are still considered fundamental.

Edward
JENNER
1749–1823
NATURAL HISTORY, IMMUNOLOGY, MEDICINE

natural history systematic study of natural objects, especially in their natural settings

The English physician Edward Jenner was interested in many aspects of natural history*, but he was a pioneer in virology, the study of viruses and their effects. By promoting the practice of inoculation* to immunize people against the deadly disease smallpox, Jenner launched a worldwide revolution in preventive health care.

Born in Berkeley, Gloucestershire, England, Jenner was raised by an older brother after both his parents died when he was five. The young Jenner showed his interest in science by collecting fossils. After a nine-year apprenticeship with a surgeon, Jenner went to London in 1770 to study anatomy and surgery. Three years later he returned to Berkeley and began

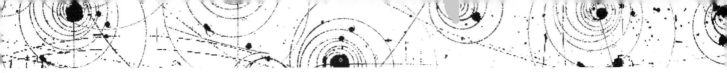

* **inoculation** treatment to protect someone from disease, sometimes by injecting the person with a bacterium or virus to produce a mild version of the disease

to practice medicine. In his leisure time he wrote poetry and observed birds. Jenner married in 1788; he and his wife had four children.

As a physician Jenner was often asked to inoculate people against smallpox, which was responsible for 10 percent of all deaths in London in the 1600s. Inoculation, which began in England in the early 1700s, involved infecting a healthy person with material taken from a smallpox sore. This usually gave the inoculated person a mild case of smallpox that would prevent future, more severe, infections. Sometimes, however, the inoculations were fatal. Unless the inoculated persons were isolated, they would infect others, starting an epidemic. As he performed inoculations, Jenner discovered that some people were completely resistant, or immune, to smallpox. Many had previously been infected with cowpox, a nonfatal disease that affected milk cows and could be transferred to people who handled them. Jenner believed that cowpox inoculations could protect people from smallpox, and in 1796 he inoculated an eight-year-old boy with matter taken from a milkmaid's cowpox sore. When Jenner later inoculated the boy with smallpox, no infection resulted. Jenner had found a safer, more effective way to protect people from smallpox. After he published the results of his researches in 1798, the practice of preventive inoculation, or vaccination, spread with astonishing speed. Jenner discovered that material taken from sores could be dried, stored, and shipped around the world. He sent this vaccine to India and to President Thomas Jefferson of the United States, who vaccinated his family and neighbors.

The rest of Jenner's life was occupied with writing about vaccination, providing vaccines, and supervising what became England's national vaccination program. Among the honors that he received were cash grants from the British government and a gold medal from Napoleon Bonaparte of France. He is recognized as the founder of immunology, the science of preventing illness by strengthening the body's own defense systems.

Immanuel
KANT

1724–1804

PHILOSOPHY OF SCIENCE

Germany's Immanuel Kant was among the greatest philosophers of modern Western civilization. His ideas about morality, knowledge, beauty, and the nature of reality, presented in his thorough and highly organized writings that emphasize the importance of reason and experience, influenced many later thinkers and schools of philosophy.

Kant took a keen interest in science and made important contributions to the philosophy of science. In writings spanning half a century, he discussed such basic concepts as space, time, matter, force, motion, and cause. Kant performed no experiments and did not add to the body of scientific knowledge—instead, he concerned himself with the nature of scientific knowledge. His focus was not facts but rather the grand framework of understanding into which the facts must fit.

Life and Career. Kant was born in the city of Königsberg, Germany (present-day Kaliningrad, Russia). Königsberg and its surroundings were Kant's home for his entire life. He never traveled farther than about 60 miles from his birthplace, although his thoughts ranged across the universe and his reputation eventually spanned the globe.

Kant's father was a saddle maker, and the family was not wealthy. Still, they managed to educate Immanuel, who was the oldest surviving child. The boy became skilled in Latin and enjoyed reading the classics*. At the age of 16 Kant entered the University of Königsberg. He was there as a student of theology*, but he studied mainly mathematics and physics. His interest in the philosophy of science probably began during this period.

After Kant's father died, the young man had to interrupt his studies to care for his younger brothers and sisters. For nine years he served as a private tutor for the children of various local families. In 1755 he resumed his work at the university and received his doctoral degree in philosophy. For the next 15 years, Kant worked at the university as a lecturer on physics and philosophy. Although he was offered higher-ranking positions elsewhere, including a professorship of poetry in Berlin, he chose to stay in his home city and concentrate on his philosophical work. In 1770 he was made Königsberg's professor of logic and metaphysics*, a position he held until his retirement 27 years later.

Kant never married; he lived in a modest but cheerful style. He enjoyed hosting dinner parties for his friends, most of whom were men of great culture and learning. His parties were lively but small because he owned only enough dishes to serve six people. Although the style of his books is dense and dry, Kant was known for his wit and humor, and he used anecdotes drawn from history and his own observations to add interest to his lectures. He was not physically strong but protected his health through regular habits—so regular, in fact, that the townspeople claimed that they could set their clocks by his daily walks. A long illness claimed him in the end, however, and he died after uttering the words, *"Es ist gut"* ("It is good").

Philosophical Background. Kant's fame as a philosopher rests primarily on the three major works of his career: *Critique of Pure Reason,* published in 1781; *Critique of Practical Reason,* published in 1788; and *Critique of Theological Judgment,* published in 1790. Some concepts of his scientific thought appear in these works, especially in the *Critique of Pure Reason,* which discusses mental processes and the nature of the reality that exists outside the mind. Kant also produced many works dealing with science and the scientific enterprise, ranging from early articles on fire, earthquakes, and wind; to books on mechanics* and cosmology*; to notes for a book on metaphysics and physics that Kant did not live to complete.

Over the course of Kant's long career, his scientific thinking evolved and was influenced by prominent scientists, including Isaac NEWTON and Gottfried Wilhelm LEIBNIZ. Kant followed their disputes about the nature of space and time. Leibniz argued that space and time were sets of relationships among things. If nothing existed, there would be no space and no time. Newton, on the other hand, believed that space and time were absolute and that they would exist even if physical bodies did not.

In his early years Kant pondered space and time from both points of view. He eventually found both positions unsatisfactory and set forth his

* **classics** written works from ancient Greece and Rome
* **theology** study of religion

* **metaphysics** branch of philosophy that deals with the fundamental principles or ultimate nature of existence

* **mechanics** science that studies how energy and force affect objects
* **cosmology** set of ideas about the origin, history, and structure of the universe

own conclusions in a paper. Titled *On the Form and Principles of the Sensible and Intelligible World,* it contained ideas similar to those he later presented in the *Critique of Pure Reason.*

Kant argued that space and time are the necessary framework for all human knowledge, which is based on sensations aroused in the mind by physical objects. For Kant space and time were linked with the nature of the mind and how it operates rather than with the nature of external things. He turned from ontology, which is the branch of philosophy that tries to define existence, to epistemology, the branch that deals with what humans can know and how they come to gain this knowledge. This epistemological concept—that our understanding of the universe around us is filtered through and shaped by the operations of the mind—underlies Kant's philosophy of science. Kant believed that there is a fundamental reality behind the appearances of things but that, although humans can have real and detailed knowledge of the appearances, they can only speculate about the reality. He called this position transcendental idealism.

Scientific Thought. Kant also explored Newton's and Leibniz's views on the nature of matter. Newton believed that matter is composed of physical atoms that would exist even if no conscious beings were present to observe them. Leibniz held that physical objects are groups of what he called monads, points of substance that fill the universe.

In a 1786 work titled *Metaphysical Foundations of Natural Science,* Kant defined matter as an appearance in space. Physical objects derived their appearance from the two moving forces—attraction and repulsion—that Kant believed were the basic properties of matter. The force of attraction (gravitation) keeps bodies of matter from flying away into space while the force of repulsion keeps different bodies of matter from colliding with each other. Consequently, the possibility of matter as an entity filling space depends on a balance between attraction and repulsion.

According to Kant, varieties in matter are caused by differences in the force of repulsion. These differences enable space to be filled in varying degrees, from dense to very rare. Kant believed that empty space could not exist, especially because it could not be perceived by any of the senses. He believed that the senses could only recognize full spaces. Because of his belief in this theory, Kant, like many other thinkers of his time, accepted that a highly rare, invisible matter called ether filled every part of space. Matter was a more condensed form of ether.

Motion is another fundamental scientific concept that Kant considered. In *New Conception of Motion and Rest,* he argued that all motion is relative, not absolute. Motion is merely the change in a body's relationship to the space around it. There is no difference in the effect whether a ball rolls across a tabletop or the tabletop moves underneath the ball, which remains at rest.

In 1755 Kant set forth his cosmological ideas in an early work bearing the ambitious title *Universal Natural History and Theory of the Heavens: An Essay on the Constitution and Mechanical Origin of the Whole Universe Treated According to Newtonian Principles.* Using Newton's laws of motion and their application to celestial bodies, Kant made bold

One of the greatest philosophers of science, Immanuel Kant made important contributions to many concepts of science, including space and time, the nature of matter, and the forces of attraction and repulsion.

claims. Later astronomers, using powerful telescopes and new theories, showed some of them to be true. Kant speculated correctly that the solar system is part of a vast system of stars making up a single galaxy. He also suggested that certain luminous objects in the night sky, called nebulous stars at the time, were really separate, distant galaxies—a fact not confirmed until the 1900s.

Like Newton and Leibniz, Kant took the position that God created time, space, and matter and the laws that govern their behavior. He argued, however, that since its creation, the universe has continuously changed. The sun, planets, and moons formed as material that had been spread through the solar system thickened into balls. All through this time the galaxies and stars are born, die, and are reborn in a cosmic cycle. Although developments in cosmological theory have discredited some of Kant's ideas, his sweeping vision did inspire later investigators.

Kant believed that the features of nonliving nature could be explained in terms of mechanics. He also believed that living things (biology) could not be explained solely in terms of physics and chemistry but that biologists could and should investigate their mechanical aspects thoroughly. Some critics have accused Kant of being an "armchair scientist" who merely thought about science without doing any of its real work. Kant, however, knew quite well that understanding the particular aspects of nature required observation and experiments. His role was not to make those observations or conduct those experiments but to arrive at a clearer understanding of where science fits into the realm of human activity and knowledge.

The Wise Man of Königsberg

During Kant's lifetime his work was widely read and taught in the major German universities. His reputation as a wise man led people to bombard him with questions—not just about big philosophical issues but also about practical matters, including scientific issues, such as whether it was right to vaccinate against disease. The philosopher's fame also drew pilgrims and students to Königsberg. So highly prized was Kant as a national resource that the government paid the expenses of some of the young men who were eager to be tutored by him.

Johannes
KEPLER

1571–1630
ASTRONOMY, PHYSICS

* **mercenary** soldier who is hired to fight, often for a foreign country

One of the greatest astronomers of all time, Johannes Kepler is remembered primarily for his three laws of planetary motion, which explained the motion of the planets around the sun. His work provided important evidence and support for the heliocentric (sun-centered) model of the universe developed by Polish astronomer Nicholas COPERNICUS in the early 1500s. In addition to giving scientists more accurate knowledge of the solar system, Kepler also developed concepts in physics that laid the foundation for the groundbreaking work of such later scientists as Isaac NEWTON.

Early Life and Career. Born in Weil der Stadt, Germany, Kepler had a rather unhappy childhood. His family was quite poor, and his father, a mercenary* soldier and quarrelsome individual, was often away from home, fighting in other lands. In 1588 Kepler's father abandoned the family forever. According to Kepler, his mother also was a rather unpleasant woman. Yet it was she who showed her impressionable young son the great comet of 1577, perhaps stimulating his interest in astronomy.

After attending various local schools, Kepler enrolled in the University of Tübingen in 1587 as a scholarship student. While at Tübingen, Kepler met Michael Maestlin, a well-known astronomy professor who introduced him to the ideas of Copernicus. At the time, the Copernican model of a sun-centered universe had not yet been accepted by many scientists, who preferred the geocentric—or earth-centered—model developed by the ancient Greek astronomer Ptolemy.

Kepler received a degree at Tübingen in 1591 and then began to study theology* in preparation for becoming a clergyman. During his third year Kepler was invited to Graz, Austria, to replace a mathematics teacher who had died. Kepler reluctantly abandoned his intention of becoming a clergyman and set out on a new career. Kepler arrived in Graz in 1594, ready to take up his duties as teacher and provincial mathematician. The following year Kepler made his mark in another way. He issued a calendar and list of predictions for 1595 based on astrology. All of his predictions—including ones of bitter cold, peasant uprisings, and invasions by Turks—came true, greatly enhancing his reputation.

Astrology at this time was closely associated with astronomy. Kepler's own attitude toward astrology was mixed. He rejected many commonly accepted astrological rules and often criticized astrological predictions, stating: "If astrologers sometimes do tell the truth, it ought to be attributed to luck." Nevertheless, Kepler had a profound belief in the harmony of the universe, and this included the idea that there was a powerful link between the cosmos and the individual. Moreover, his astrological work provided a welcome supplement to his rather meager income.

A Mystical Astronomy

One of the distinguishing characteristics of Johannes Kepler was his almost mystical belief in a close link between religion and astronomy. Kepler believed in a profound order and harmony, which were derived from God and reflected in the nature and structure of the universe. In his work he continually referred to God and to the fact that geometry was eternal like God. He also believed that humans share in this divine order because they are created in the image of God. Drawing on these principles, Kepler believed that there was a cosmic link between the human soul and the geometrical configurations of the planets. These principles also motivated his search for the mathematical harmonies of the universe.

Beginning Work in Astronomy. Kepler was a religious man who believed that God had created the universe according to a divine plan. He came to believe that this plan was based on mathematical principles, particularly those of geometry, and that each of the major features of the cosmos was based on a geometric principle established by God.

About a year after his arrival in Graz, Kepler hit on an idea that he believed held the key to the secret of the universe. In his 1596 work *Mysterium cosmographicum* (Mystery of the Cosmos), he wrote that the relative sizes of planetary orbits were based on certain geometric relationships. When he calculated the size of the orbits using his theory, he discovered that his figures matched very closely to the orbital sizes proposed by Copernicus. He also argued that the sun had to be at the center of the solar system because it provided the driving force that kept the planets in motion. Like Copernicus, he also noticed that the farther a planet was from the sun, the longer it took to orbit the sun.

With the publication of *Mysterium cosmographicum,* Kepler provided the first strong evidence for the Copernican system. Although the principal idea of the book was later proved to be erroneous, it thrust Kepler into the front rank of astronomers and set the direction of his entire life and work. He became the first scientist, until the French philosopher and mathematician René DESCARTES, to demand physical explanations for celestial phenomena. Following this publication Kepler plunged into various astronomical studies, ranging from the observation of solar and lunar eclipses to further work on planetary motion.

Beginning around 1598, religious conflicts between Catholics and Protestants created problems for Kepler and other Protestants in Graz. In early 1600 he traveled to Prague (in the present-day Czech Republic) to visit Tycho BRAHE, the Danish astronomer. Impressed by Kepler's talents,

Brahe invited him to become his assistant and assigned him to study the planet Mars and its movements. The relationship between Brahe and Kepler was often strained, partly because of Brahe's secrecy regarding his own observations. Kepler also disagreed with Brahe over the great scientist's own model for the universe, which combined the ideas of Ptolemy and Copernicus.

Brahe died suddenly in 1601. However, before his death Brahe urged Kepler to complete the proposed *Rudolphine Tables,* a series of tables that summed up observations about the motions and positions of the stars and motions of the sun, moon, and planets. To complete this work Kepler was given access to all of Brahe's many astronomical observations, the most complete and accurate of the time. Without this data Kepler's later astronomical discoveries probably would not have been possible. Kepler eventually published the *Rudolphine Tables* toward the end of his own life.

Kepler in Prague. Kepler replaced Brahe as imperial mathematician in the court of Emperor Rudolph II, the ruler of the Holy Roman Empire. Kepler also continued his work in astronomy. In 1606 he published *De stella nova* (On the New Star), which contained observations and opinions about a brilliant supernova* that had appeared two year earlier. Kepler also compared the new star—now known as Kepler's Supernova—to the star of the Magi, the star that appeared in the year of the birth of Jesus Christ, which he assumed to be 5 B.C.

One of Kepler's most important works, *Astronomia nova* (New Astronomy), was published in 1609. This work presented a revolutionary new look at the solar system. Using Brahe's observations and his own of Mars, Kepler concluded that the orbits of the planets were not circular—as Ptolemy, Copernicus, Brahe, and other astronomers had all assumed—but elliptical, or oval-shaped. The discovery that the planets travel around the sun in elliptical orbits with the sun as a focal point was the key to a true understanding of the solar system, and it became known as Kepler's first law of planetary motion. *Astronomia nova* also included Kepler's second law, which states that a line connecting the sun to a planet sweeps out equal areas of the planet's elliptical orbit in equal times.

While in Prague Kepler also became interested in the study of optics*, largely from having observed a partial solar eclipse in 1600. To observe the eclipse, Kepler, like other earlier astronomers, constructed a pinhole camera—a darkened, boxlike device with a pinhole opening—through which an image of the sun could be projected onto a surface inside the camera. As a result of his observations and analysis of how the device worked, Kepler clearly defined the concept of the light ray, the foundation of modern geometrical optics. He also applied the idea of the light ray to the workings of the human eye, showing that the human eye works in the same way as a camera, except that the eye has focusing properties.

In 1610 Kepler received a copy of *Sidereus nuncius,* a book by Galileo GALILEI that discussed the Italian scientist's discoveries based on his use of a telescope. Galileo had sent the book to Kepler, asking for Kepler's opinion about his startling new discoveries. Kepler responded with a long letter of approval, to which Galileo wrote: "I thank you because you were the

* **supernova** star that suddenly becomes extremely brilliant because it has exploded

* **optics** scientific study of the properties of light

first one, and practically the only one, to have complete faith in my assertions." The same year, Kepler used a telescope for the first time and made his own observations of Jupiter. In 1611 he published the results of his studies, providing strong additional evidence to support Galileo's discoveries, which were doubted or denied by many scholars.

Kepler wrote another book while in Prague, *Tertius interveniens* (Third Man in the Middle), that discussed his opinions about astrology. He criticized those who blindly accept all astrological predictions and those who deny any purpose or truth in astrology. Kepler believed that while the stars do not compel people to act in certain ways, they do impress on individuals a special character that influences their lives and actions.

Troubles and Harmonies. With Emperor Rudolph II as his patron, Kepler lived a rather secure existence despite the religious conflicts between Catholics and Protestants that raged throughout much of Europe. However, in 1611 Kepler's world suddenly collapsed. Within a short time his wife and favorite son died, Prague became a scene of religious bloodshed, and Rudolph II was forced to abdicate (give up) the throne.

Kepler hoped to return to Tübingen as a professor, but his return was prevented by theologians who questioned his religious views. Instead, Kepler went to Linz, Austria, where he took a position as official mathematician for the surrounding province. Although religious conflict swirled around him, and personal problems still threatened to overwhelm him, Kepler continued to revise and refine his astronomical ideas.

During the initial years of his stay in Linz, Kepler published no astronomical works. The first book he produced concerned mathematics. In that work he abandoned the methods of the ancient Greek mathematician Archimedes and adopted procedures that helped lay the foundation for modern calculus*.

In 1617 Kepler was forced to travel to Germany to help his mother, who was accused of witchcraft. For the next four years he found himself drawn away from his work as he arranged for his mother's defense. She was finally released in 1621 but died later the same year. Although helping his mother had disrupted his work, Kepler later continued working toward his lifelong goal—to discover the harmony of the universe in a way that would answer any of the age-old questions of astronomers.

In progress since 1599, Kepler's book *Harmonice mundi* (Harmonies of the World) was finally published in 1619. The work contained the fullest account of Kepler's astronomical ideas and the results of decades of observations and investigations. Combining the basic principles of geometry, music, astrology, and astronomy, he devised an elaborate mathematical model to explain the structure of the solar system and the movements of the earth, sun, moon, and planets—a system that Kepler believed was based on divine cosmic harmony. During the course of his investigations, Kepler encountered a relationship that is now called Kepler's third law. According to the law, there is a precise ratio between a planet's distance from the sun and the time that planet takes to complete its orbit around the sun. For Kepler the fact that this same ratio applied to all known planets was proof of the divine harmony of the universe.

* **calculus** advanced form of mathematics that involves computing quantities that change as functions of different variables

Johannes Kepler discovered that planets move around the sun in elliptical orbits, and he created tables to predict the future positions of the planets. In this illustration Kepler sits with his patron Rudolph II, ruler of the Holy Roman Empire.

Other Major Works. In 1621 Kepler published a work that explained the Copernican system in light of his own ideas. *Epitome astronomiae Copernicanae* (Epitome of Copernican Astronomy) treated heliocentric astronomy, including Kepler's three laws, systematically. Kepler's longest and most influential work, it became one of the most widely read books on astronomical theory in Europe. Among the many scholars influenced by it were probably Galileo and Descartes. The *Epitome* stressed the theological basis of his ideas. One section, for example, presents the three regions of the universe—the center, the outermost sphere, and the space between the two—as symbols of the Holy Trinity of Father, Son, and Holy Spirit.

After publishing the *Epitome,* Kepler refocused his attention on a project that had been going on for a number of years—completion of the *Rudolphine Tables.* Kepler had promised Tycho Brahe that he would finish these tables. The tables were ready for publication in 1624, but religious struggles erupted in Linz, and the printing house where the work was to be published was destroyed in a fire. Kepler packed up his household, books, and manuscripts and went to the German city of Ulm, where the *Rudolphine Tables* were finally published in 1627.

The *Rudolphine Tables* were an important achievement. The astronomical tables, which were based on Brahe's observations and Kepler's laws, gave planetary positions that were far more accurate than those derived by earlier methods. The tables not only contained positions for planets for specified days but also provided perpetual tables that could be used to calculate planetary positions for any date in the past or future. The tables proved to be remarkably accurate and were recognized as evidence of the correctness of both Kepler's laws and the heliocentric system. Besides the planetary, solar, and lunar tables, the *Rudolphine Tables* also contained Tycho Brahe's catalog of 1,000 fixed stars and their positions.

Last Years. Even before the *Rudolphine Tables* were printed, Kepler had begun to search for a new home. Torn between a desire to find religious toleration and a reluctance to lose his salary as a royal mathematician, Kepler traveled to Prague in late 1627 to seek employment from Ferdinand III, the newly crowned king of Bohemia. Ferdinand received Kepler graciously but made it clear that the astronomer should become a Catholic if he wished to be employed. Instead, Albrecht von Wallenstein, an imperial official, arranged for Kepler to go to Sagan in the region of Silesia and agreed to support the astronomer. Kepler readily accepted the support of his new patron. In return Wallenstein expected Kepler to make astronomical calculations that could be used in obtaining astrological predictions.

Shortly after he settled in Sagan, religious strife erupted there. For political reasons Wallenstein pressured the people of the region to convert to Catholicism. Although Kepler was not personally affected, the religious persecutions that occurred made it difficult to attract printers, forcing Kepler to do most of his printing himself.

While in Sagan, Kepler wrote and printed his most unusual work. This short book—*Somnium seu astronomia lunari* (Dream)—tells the story of a man who journeys to the moon in a dream. *Somnium* is a pioneering work of science fiction—perhaps the first true science fiction novel. The work is also an ingenious argument in favor of the Copernican system, since it describes celestial motions as seen from the surface of the moon.

When Wallenstein lost his position in 1630, Kepler left Sagan and headed to Linz, where he hoped to collect money that was owed him. He stopped in Regensburg, perhaps to consult with the emperor and other friends about a new home. A few days after reaching there, the astronomer became sick with a fever. The illness became worse, and he died on November 15, 1630. Kepler was buried in the Protestant cemetery in Regensburg, but the churchyard and his final resting place were completely destroyed and lost during the great religious struggle known as the Thirty Years War.

Joseph Louis LAGRANGE

1736–1813

MATHEMATICS, MECHANICS

* **mechanics** science that studies how energy and force affect objects

Joseph Louis Lagrange was one of the leading mathematicians of the 1700s. His efforts in this field, especially his discovery of the calculus of variations, paved the way for the new mathematics of the following century. The work for which he is most famous—*Mécanique analytique* (Analytical Mechanics)—summarizes the most important findings in mechanics* since the time of Isaac NEWTON and is based on Lagrange's own calculus* of variations. The book adopts a new approach to mechanics, using mathematical operations without relying on geometric or mechanical arguments. Lagrange applied his mathematical genius to solve a variety of problems, including the mechanics of planets and comets.

Early Life and Career

Although he was Italian by birth, Lagrange's true ability was never appreciated in his home country. He produced his best work only after he moved from Italy to Germany.

Education and Early Works. Lagrange was born in Turin, Italy, as Giuseppe Lodovico Lagrangia. His mother, Teresa Grosso, was Italian, but his father's side of the family was French. His great-grandfather was a French cavalry captain who eventually served the Duke of Savoy (a region in northern Italy) and married into a prominent Italian family. Both his grandfather and his father held the post of Treasurer of the Office of Public Works and Fortifications in Turin. Although this position paid a reasonably comfortable salary, Lagrange's father lost large amounts of money in bad investments, and the family lived very modestly. In fact, Lagrange himself wrote that if he had been rich, he probably would not have studied mathematics. From that standpoint his relative poverty was a stroke of good fortune for the world of science.

Throughout his life Lagrange identified more with his French heritage than with his home country. From the time he was a boy, he adopted a French spelling of his last name, signing his name as either Lodovico La-Grange or Luigi Lagrange. In his first published work he used the name Luigi de la Grange Tournier, and the scientists with whom he corresponded referred to him simply as "de la Grange," a common mode of address in France at the time. The conditions that Lagrange endured during his early life ensured that he developed no greater love for Italy, and he never returned to that country after leaving for Berlin at the age of 30. Most of his regular academic correspondents were French, including his most enthusiastic supporters, Pierre-Simon LAPLACE and Antoine LAVOISIER. Lagrange also spent the last 25 years of his life living and teaching in France.

Following his father's expectations, Lagrange studied for a career in law. Ironically, the future mathematical genius did not find mathematics a particularly interesting subject and was bored by Greek geometry. It was not until he read a work at age 18 by the English astronomer Edmond HALLEY on the application of algebra to optics* that Lagrange's interest in mathematics was stimulated. This enthusiasm further developed after he took courses in physics and geometry, and he decided to pursue a career in mathematics. His earliest published effort in this field was a short letter he wrote to the Italian geometer* Giulio da Fagnano, in which he developed a formal calculus that he believed to be original. Shortly thereafter Lagrange was looking through scientific correspondence between the mathematicians Wilhelm LEIBNIZ and Daniel BERNOULLI and discovered a discussion of the technique he thought he had invented himself. Although he was worried that he would be seen as a cheat and impostor, Lagrange suffered no ill consequences from his mistake. Nor was he discouraged from continuing his correspondence with Fagnano, to whom he wrote several more times over the course of a year. One of these letters contains Lagrange's earliest statement of the calculus of variations.

The French mathematician Joseph Lagrange solved a variety of problems, including many related to the mechanics of celestial bodies. He studied the motion of the moon and the gravitational effects of planets on the orbits of comets, and he developed the calculus of variations.

* **analytic geometry** field of mathematics that uses algebra to study the properties and relations of points, lines, and shapes on a coordinate grid

Gaining Wider Recognition. Lagrange also corresponded with the great German mathematician Leonhard EULER, who showed a great interest in the young man's ideas. Euler shared Lagrange's letters with Pierre MAUPERTUIS, the president of the Berlin Academy. Maupertuis, recognizing the importance of the work and Lagrange's potential, offered Lagrange a position at the academy. However, Lagrange was too shy to accept the offer and instead accepted a teaching position at Turin's Royal Artillery School.

In 1757 Lagrange and several other scientists formed a scientific society that later became the Royal Academy of Sciences of Turin. The society published a journal to which Lagrange contributed many papers on calculus and mechanics. He applied some of his work to problems concerning irregularities in the orbits of Saturn and Jupiter. He also employed his findings to answer the question of why the moon always presents the same face to the earth, and whether it wobbles on its axis just as the earth does. Both these problems were the subjects of a prize competition held every two years by the Paris Academy of Sciences. During his time in Turin, Lagrange became a regular entrant and a frequent winner of the contest.

Later Life and Career

The royal court of Turin repeatedly promised to reward Lagrange for his services but never honored that pledge. In late 1765 he was again invited to take a position in Berlin, but he refused to do so as long as Euler remained at the academy. When Lagrange learned that Euler was leaving for Russia, he accepted the offer and left for Berlin the following summer. He was soon named director of the academy's mathematics section and received a salary so generous that he did not ask for a raise for the next 20 years.

In Berlin Lagrange made significant contributions to mathematics and mechanics, including the understanding of the mechanics of celestial bodies. Many of his papers on celestial mechanics were stimulated by the Paris competition. He submitted winning entries on problems concerning the motion of the moon and the gravitational effects of planets on the orbits of comets. In addition, he prepared papers on the stability of the solar system and the orbit of the planet Venus. In the latter work he introduced a method of solving astronomical problems by using the methods of analytic geometry*. In mathematics he tackled problems dealing with number theory and probability. His work in mechanics led him to consider a way to unify all the principles of that field and present them from a single viewpoint. Four years before leaving Berlin, Lagrange wrote to tell Laplace that he had almost finished such a work, but that he did not know when he would be able to publish it. That work, the *Méchanique analytique,* would assure his place in the history of science.

Shortly before, Lagrange had been offered a post in Italy, a country that had finally come to realize his genius and the value of his knowledge. However, the earlier broken promises and Lagrange's satisfaction with his position in Berlin ruled out a return to Turin. It appeared as if he would spend the rest of his life in Berlin, but that soon changed. In 1783 his wife died after a long illness, and three years later Emperor Frederick II,

Lagrange's strongest supporter in Berlin, passed away as well. Many Italian princes competed to lure Lagrange into their employ, but he instead accepted an invitation by the French government to live and work in Paris. The agreement included a large government pension and the promise that Lagrange would not have to teach. In 1787 Lagrange moved to Paris.

Life and Work in France. Lagrange seemed to lose much of his momentum after he moved to Paris. He did not immediately resume his research, and soon after his arrival he began to experience firsthand the difficult times of the French Revolution. However, he weathered the storm with an open-minded attitude about the different ways things were handled in different countries. As he wrote, "I believe, in general, that one of the first principles of any wise man is to conform strictly to the laws of the country in which he is living, even when they are unreasonable." Those "unreasonable" laws would eventually take the lives of some of his closest and most distinguished colleagues.

One year after his arrival in Paris, Lagrange published *Méchanique analytique,* which presented for the first time a unified theory of dynamics*. In this work he aimed to reduce the theory of mechanics, as well as the solution of mechanical problems, to a series of general formulas. He believed that developing these formulas would produce all of the equations needed to solve any problem in mechanics. The work is divided into two parts, one on statics* and one on dynamics, each dealing with the actions of both solid bodies and fluids. Remarkably, the work contains no diagrams at all, merely analytic operations. Before his death Lagrange prepared a second edition of the work that applied his theory to celestial mechanics, but this manuscript was not published during his lifetime.

Lagrange settled comfortably into Parisian life, and four years after his arrival there, he married the daughter of one of his colleagues at the academy. As a member of the Paris Academy of Sciences, Lagrange also established himself as a fixture in the world of French learning. He was appointed to a committee to establish a new standard of weights and measures that developed the metric system. Although the revolutionary government of France later eliminated the commission, Lagrange kept his position as chairman. In 1793 all foreigners born within the borders of France's enemies were arrested and their property seized by the state. However, Lavoisier stepped in and successfully obtained an exemption for Lagrange. For his efforts a French court later condemned Lavoisier to death. It was a graphic reminder to Lagrange of the unpredictability and the ugly excesses of the revolution.

The following year the French government set up a national school to train teachers and standardize education. Although promised that he would not have to teach, Lagrange served as an instructor of elementary mathematics at the school until it was disbanded three months later. Shortly thereafter a new school, the École Polytechnique (technical school), was founded, and Lagrange taught there for another five years. Letters written by his students reveal that although they had a high degree of respect for Lagrange's abilities, they found his lecture style poor and his ideas too advanced for most of his audience.

* **dynamics** study of the relationship between motion and the forces affecting motion

* **statics** study of how energy and force affect stationary bodies

Politics and Memory

Lagrange's funeral was an occasion to commemorate his life and accomplishments. In addition to the impressive funeral he received in France, Lagrange was also honored with memorial ceremonies throughout his home country of Italy. Prussia (former kingdom and state of Germany), however, had previously joined several other countries that had united to oppose the French dictator Napoleon. Consequently, Berlin, where Lagrange had been the most content and had done his most important work, held no services in his memory.

In 1799 Napoleon Bonaparte overthrew the revolutionary government and became emperor of France. Napoleon created a government organization to promote science and academics and named Lagrange as one of its original members. Five years before his death, Lagrange was made a count of the empire, and just a week before he died, he was named *grand croix* of the Ordre Impérial de la Réunion. His funeral was a grand occasion, attended by the most important figures in France.

Johann Heinrich
LAMBERT

1728–1777

MATHEMATICS, PHYSICS,
ASTRONOMY

* **metaphysical** relating to a reality that is beyond sensory perception; abstract

Although forced to end his formal education at age 12 because of his family's impoverished circumstances, Johann Lambert nevertheless made important contributions in many scientific disciplines. Lambert, who was largely self-taught, received his first academic position at age 20 as tutor to the children of a Swiss nobleman. In this position he had access to his employer's library and was able to travel about Europe, meeting with a number of notable scientists. During this time he made his first astronomical observations and constructed various scientific instruments.

After 10 years as a tutor, Lambert left his position and led a wandering life in search of a university position. Although this hope was frustrated, he was elected a member of many scientific societies and helped found the Bavarian Academy. In 1765, after a long wait, Lambert was appointed to the Prussian Academy at Berlin. During the next 12 years, until his death in 1777, Lambert published more than 150 works.

Lambert's main goal was to establish a set of rules by which metaphysical* problems could be solved as surely as mathematical ones. To this end he stressed the importance of building scientific knowledge based on careful observation and experimentation. This striving for precision marked all his scientific efforts.

Some of Lambert's most interesting work was in the field of astronomy. By observing the Milky Way in the night sky, he concluded that its appearance suggested that the universe might be shaped like a lens. He also proposed that the solar system was only one part of a much larger system of stars, anticipating the discovery that the universe contains many such large systems, now known as galaxies. He also concluded that humanlike creatures must inhabit the entire universe. Lambert was also interested in the paths of comets, perhaps stimulated by the appearance of a comet in 1744. While studying the paths of these heavenly bodies, he discovered interesting geometrical theorems, many of which bear his name. He also developed an easy method to determine the distances between the earth and the sun and that between the earth and a given comet.

* **meteorology** science that deals with the atmosphere, especially the weather and weather predictions; also known as atmospheric science

His other contributions to the physical sciences include investigations into light and meteorology*. He formulated a law (Lambert's law of absorption) to explain the exponential decrease in the intensity of light passing through an absorbing medium of uniform transparency. He developed an instrument to measure atmospheric humidity and published his meteorological findings in *Essai d'hygrométrie*. Lambert also studied the physical and psychological effects of heat and sound on humans. These studies included an examination of reflected heat, although at the time, the existence of such heat could not be demonstrated.

Lambert's other major efforts were in mathematics and mapmaking. He was the first to prove that pi is an irrational number*, and he developed a method to calculate the prime factors of a given large number. Lambert was also the first to offer a proof for the axiom (established principle) of parallels, proposed by the Greek mathematician Euclid, which states that parallel lines will never touch or cross. This proof, which had applications in perspective drawing, was unknown until the late 1800s.

In mapmaking, Lambert was the first to state the mathematical conditions for creating map projections that preserved the true angles and areas of items pictured on a map. He also showed how to determine the true distance between two places on a map drawn according to one of his projections. His projections remain a basic part of modern map theory.

Lambert was a somewhat odd and unrefined man who was once called a blockhead by the Prussian ruler Frederick the Great. However, neither this nor his lack of formal schooling prevented him from making significant contributions to science.

* **irrational number** number that cannot be expressed as an integer or as the quotient of two integers

Pierre-Simon
LAPLACE

1749–1827

CELESTIAL MECHANICS,
PROBABILITY, APPLIED
MATHEMATICS, PHYSICS

Pierre-Simon, Marquis de Laplace, was one of history's true scientific giants. He not only made many important contributions in several fields but also played a major role in establishing a number of modern scientific disciplines. However, Laplace was more than an experimental scientist and theoretician. He was active in efforts to reorganize the French educational system and give it a foundation in the exact sciences. He also published a number of works that helped popularize knowledge of scientific fields, such as celestial mechanics and probability. Laplace also developed a philosophical approach to science that had a profound influence on the conduct of scientific research and experimentation.

Life and Career

Laplace's career can be roughly divided into four stages, corresponding to the various areas of scientific inquiry on which he focused. Until about age 30 he laid the foundations of his later work in the areas of mathematics, probability, and mathematical astronomy. During the 10 years following that period, he achieved his most important results in the latter two fields and published the famous treatises that outline his ideas and accomplishments. He also took on new challenges in the field of physics that allowed him to work directly with other leading French scientists. At this time he also began to serve on government commissions and to apply his findings to improve society. Between the ages of 40 and 55, he was at the peak of his influence, playing a major role in reforming the French educational system and training the new generation of scientists. During the final 20 years of his life, he surrounded himself with academics with whom he pioneered the mathematical approach to physics. Laplace also returned to his studies of probability, applying his ideas to different areas such as judicial procedures and the analysis of scientific data.

* **theology** study of religion

Early Life and Career. Laplace was born into a comfortable family in Normandy, France, and attended a secondary school run by the Benedictine monks. His father hoped that Laplace would pursue a career in the clergy, and when Laplace entered the University of Caen, he studied theology*. However, during this time he discovered his gift for mathematics and gave up his theological studies. One of his teachers wrote him a letter of introduction to the great French mathematician Jean d'ALEMBERT, and at age 19 Laplace traveled to Paris to meet the famous man.

D'Alembert gave Laplace a problem to solve and gave him a week to work on it. However, Laplace returned the next day with the solution and solved a second problem just as quickly. Impressed by the youth's abilities, d'Alembert became his patron and landed him a position as professor of mathematics at the French national military school. Although the job was not a great challenge, it allowed Laplace to remain in Paris, where he immediately set about writing scientific papers on a variety of topics. Between 1770 and 1773 he composed and submitted to the French Académie des Sciences 13 scientific papers on topics that later became his life's work. In 1773 he was admitted as a member of the academy. Over the next several

Pierre-Simon, Marquis de Laplace made significant contributions to the fields of calculus, celestial mechanics, probability, and mathematical astronomy. He also developed the metric system and organized a technical school in France.

years, his work in calculus, celestial mechanics, and probability earned him a reputation among the scientific and mathematical community.

Laplace in His Prime. By the time he was 40, Laplace was recognized as one of the leading figures in the academy. During this time he pressed forward with investigations into the topics he had explored in his earlier years and achieved the results for which he became best known. He also extended his efforts to government work and was appointed examiner of cadets for the royal artillery school. In this post he introduced the practice of recruiting top students based on their merit rather than solely on their social or political connections. He later employed the same system during his efforts to reorganize the educational system. Laplace served on a number of other government commissions, including one that investigated hospital care. In this work he applied his findings in probability to calculate absolute mortality rates for individual hospitals as well as comparative mortality rates between different hospitals.

The French Revolution of 1789 changed the face of French society and with it, the academic community. The new government set out to change or abolish institutions closely identified with the monarchy, including the academy. Laplace continued to serve on public commissions, perhaps the most important of which, scientifically, was one to develop a standard system of weights and measures that eventually became the metric system. In 1793 the government suppressed the academy, and Laplace was removed from the commission on weights and measures. Shortly before this time he decided to leave Paris, not returning until the most radical members of the government were removed from service in 1794.

Later Life and Career. The new regime adopted the philosophy that science should be used to educate citizens about nature and applied to public welfare. It organized a new system of secondary schools, founded several specialized scientific colleges, and established a successor to the academy, the Institut de France. One important result was that scientific activity moved from private academies to places of higher education. Universities began to emphasize research and filled the ranks of professors with practicing scientists. Laplace continued his activity on government panels, but his work with the schools was of even greater significance.

At the national technical school, he introduced physics as a mathematical discipline taught to the most qualified students, and he established the content and standards for technical education in the universities. He taught classes in the École Normale, an institution intended to train citizens to become teachers who would, in theory, return home and found secondary schools to pass along what they had learned to others. Laplace also contributed to the popularization of science with the publication of his books *Description du système du monde* (Description of the System of the World) and *Méchanique céleste* (Celestial Mechanics). These works presented nonmathematical accounts of his efforts in astronomy and celestial mechanics.

In 1799 Napoleon Bonaparte seized power in France and appointed Laplace minister of the interior, a position in which he was responsible for most aspects of domestic policy, except finance and the police. Napoleon also elected Laplace to the senate and showered him with a number of titles and honors. Laplace's main work at this time was the reorganization of the national technical school. He overhauled the curriculum and standards, cut the length of the course from three years to two, and made the school a preparation for specialist graduate schools of mining, engineering, and artillery. During this time Laplace assembled a group of young scientists devoted to the study of physics. The group was named the Société d'Arcueil after the town in which one of its members had set up a laboratory. This marked the beginning of a period in which Laplace was centrally concerned with problems in physics. His great public standing enabled him to decide the course of research at the Institut de France and shape the work of the leading young scientists of the day. Despite much important work in physics, many of Laplace's theories were ultimately overturned, and his influence in the field diminished greatly. However, he continued to make discoveries in mathematics and probability, and toward the end of his life, he published a series of scientific histories that he had planned earlier in his career. By this time his greatest work was behind him, and he died in Paris at the age of 78.

Scientific Accomplishments

Laplace's most important early contributions were in mathematics and its application to the fields of probability and celestial mechanics. His later work on physics also owed a great deal to these early works. Throughout his life he championed a mathematical approach to science, a preoccupation that stemmed from his work in probability. Laplace felt that most errors in science were attributable to an ignorance of the causes that produced the events that scientists observed, and on which they based their conclusions. He hoped that a mathematical understanding of the rules of probability could be applied to the physical sciences to increase the accuracy of observations and provide a better foundation for discovering scientific truths. His work in all fields demonstrated a concern for precision based on these principles.

Probability. Before Laplace the science of probability was mainly concerned with analyzing the outcomes of games of chance. The typical question asked: "Given a particular cause, what are the chances on a particular result or results?" This form of the study of chance was largely used to determine the outcome of dice throws or lotteries. Laplace turned around the basic question to ask: "If a particular event can result from a number of different causes, what is the probability that any one of those causes actually produced the event?" He considered this a more useful approach to the study of probability because it could be used to study the origins of problems and yield practical solutions to those problems, based on a firm knowledge of their causes.

Laplace set out to accomplish two main tasks. First, to devise a method to calculate the probability of an event whose outcome is based on several other events whose probability is unknown. Second, to determine the probability of the outcomes of future events, based on the result of past events. In other words, he was concerned with using probability to determine causes, draw conclusions from statistics, estimate the likelihood of error, and assess the credibility of evidence using mathematics.

However, there were two main obstacles to Laplace's method. The first was that it required a large number of observations to draw any conclusions about the causes of an event. The second was that to arrive at numerical solutions to questions of probability, Laplace had to use mathematical equations containing terms raised to very high powers, and these were extremely cumbersome to work with. To solve the first problem, Laplace went to a known source of significant data—population records for France that had been collected for a number of decades. The records of hundreds of thousands of births, deaths, and marriages provided him with a huge pool of accurate data collected under controlled circumstances. To overcome the second obstacle, he applied a mathematical technique he had developed for dealing with problems using very high powers. The technique enabled him to transform formulas into a series of numbers that converged (approached a limit) so rapidly that he only had to consider the first few terms of the series. He could then solve the problem for those lower terms and project the outcome for the higher terms without having to work with extremely large numbers.

Using his methods Laplace was able to project the likely ratio of male to female births for many years into the future. He also arrived at a constant, which, when multiplied by the annual births, gave an accurate determination of the total population of France. Laplace also showed that the more data one had to draw on, the more accurate the figures would be. Laplace considered this extremely important information since population was an indicator of national prosperity, and because the results of population surveys could be used to develop and guide social policy. He demonstrated that information crucial to social welfare could be analyzed mathematically, marking the beginning of social sciences as a mathematical subject. The mathematical techniques Laplace pioneered in his study of probability later proved invaluable when applied to his explorations in celestial mechanics and physics.

Celestial Mechanics. Like many other scientists of his day, Laplace was very interested in the motions of heavenly bodies and the laws that govern their movement. He believed that the law of universal gravitation stated by Isaac NEWTON could explain all such motions. However, he also thought it necessary to modify the law and proposed several changes to the existing theory. These included abandoning Newton's assumption that gravity is propagated instantaneously and replacing it with the idea of propagation over time. He also argued that gravitational attraction operates between all particles of matter individually. Many scientists still held that it operated only between the centers of mass of large bodies.

Laplace pursued the implications of his ideas to make many important discoveries in celestial mechanics. Studying the motions of Jupiter and Saturn led him to propose theories about how gravitation affects the shape and nature of their orbits and their movements through space. He examined the gravitational effects operating between the earth, moon, and sun

At the Center of his own Universe

Although a brilliant scientist, Laplace was not known for his cordial relations with others. There is no record of congeniality between Laplace and his colleagues; d'Alembert apparently resented the fact that Laplace's work was making his own obsolete. One historian at the Académie des Sciences wrote that Laplace believed himself to be the best mathematician in France and that he insisted on making pronouncements about scientific fields other than those in which he did most of his work. Another writer portrayed him as the typical arrogant mathematician who showed contempt for the new generation of physicists.

Laying Odds on the Comets

An example of how Laplace applied his work on probability to other sciences is his work with comets. The orbits and movements of the known comets were so similar to those of the planets that some scientists wondered if the same cause that produced planetary motion also produced the phenomena of comets. Laplace determined that this would be the case only if the odds were very great that the angle of the comet's orbit around the sun varied significantly from those of the planets. However, he found that the odds were very slim, confirming that the motions of planets and comets did not share a common cause.

to explain several phenomena concerning the height and nature of ocean tides. Laplace also applied his findings to explain why the moon appears to slow down during its motion around the earth and why it always presents the same face to earth. His work also showed that both the earth and Jupiter were slightly flattened at the poles. Applying this finding to the effect of Jupiter's gravity on its satellites also helped prove his theory that all the particles of Jupiter exert an attractive force, and that the force is not centered in one location. Laplace published his findings in a series of notes to the Académie des Sciences, and he later published them as books. These works helped introduce celestial mechanics to an educated, but not scientifically or mathematically sophisticated, audience.

Laplace published a popular account of his thoughts on celestial mechanics in 1796. Titled *Exposition du système du monde* (Exposition of the System of the World), this work proposed that the solar system had evolved from a rotating mass of gas that had condensed to form the sun. The planets and then their various satellites were thrown off from this original mass of rotating gas. This nebular hypothesis, as it became known, had been proposed earlier by Immanuel KANT.

Laplace's inquiries into celestial mechanics offer a prime example of his place in the development of scientific thought. Instead of working to develop laws based on his observations, he studied the laws developed by other scientists and the data on which those laws were based. He then analyzed the data to determine if the existing laws adequately explained them. If not, he developed his own analyses to find better explanations. One of his criticisms of contemporary celestial mechanics was that although the data collected were accurate, theories based on the data often failed to explain them correctly. Analyses of these data often gave correct results even when they should not have done so. This was the starting point of much of Laplace's work; trying to find out why an analysis was incorrect led him to discover new relationships between theories that yielded new discoveries. Ultimately, Laplace felt that it was possible to explain the motions of celestial bodies using mathematical formulas. In his view, all scientific laws should be based on such formulas. Moreover, because observations are subject to error, and because scientists are unaware of all the possible sources of such error, he maintained that observations should serve to confirm theory and should not be the starting point from which theories are formulated.

Physics. Laplace's most noteworthy work in physics was concentrated in three main areas—the chemical physics of heat, short-range forces of attraction, and the velocity of sound. In his early 30s Laplace teamed up with Antoine LAVOISIER to investigate the vaporization of water and cooling caused by evaporation. As part of this work, Laplace wrote a memoir discussing the nature of heat and how to quantify it. Two of the most important principles outlined in the memoir were the conservation of heat and the reversibility of heat exchange within a system of bodies.

He stated that every body contains heat that may pass to another body during heating or chemical reactions. Laplace called this "free heat" (it is now called specific heat) and devised a unit of measurement called the calorie to quantify it. A calorie is the amount of heat required to raise the temperature of one pound of water by one degree. Lavoisier and Laplace then developed a device called an ice calorimeter, a kind of hollow sphere lined with ice, in which they placed warm substances. The heat of the substance would melt the inner ice, which was then collected and weighed to determine the free heat of many materials as well as the heat given off during different chemical reactions and the body heat of animals.

Laplace hoped to form a general theory of heat based on this work, which led him to consider how changes in state affect the relationship between absolute heat and specific heat. He proposed that the relationship might depend on the physical arrangement of molecules in a substance. He noted that heat tends to separate molecules in a substance, whereas chemical affinity between similar molecules draws them together. By studying the equilibrium between heat and affinity, he believed that he might be able to compare the chemical affinities of certain substances. This was the first time anyone had considered chemical affinities as a source of attraction between molecules, and it revealed that Laplace was beginning to pay attention to forces and structures at the molecular level.

He then went on to study these "short-range forces," so called because they operate at the molecular level. He believed that the refraction of light, capillary action*, the cohesion of solids, and chemical reactions could be explained as the results of attractive forces between molecules. He saw this as a manifestation of the same gravitational force that worked at extremely long ranges between planets and other celestial bodies. Other scientists followed Laplace's initial work with experiments of their own, and Laplace himself tried to refine and correct errors in his theory.

Laplace's work on the velocity of sound was another effort that grew out of his desire to correct the theories of other scientists by studying those cases where their theories did not adequately explain the data they gathered. In this case, Newton had proposed a formula for determining the velocity of sound that disagreed with the experimentally observed speed by around 10 percent. Drawing on his earlier work with heat, Laplace suggested that Newton had ignored changes in temperature that occur when sound waves alternately compress and rarify (make thin or less dense) the air in which they travel. This causes an alternate heating and cooling of the air that causes the velocity of sound to vary. Based on his studies, Laplace calculated a constant to determine the effect of temperature and used it to determine the correct velocity of sound.

Laplace's contributions in physics, mathematics, mechanics, and other subjects were not valuable merely for the many discoveries he made. As important, if not more so, is his philosophical contribution to science. He stressed not only what science knew, but also what it did not know. He attempted to show how that lack of knowledge led to error that affected the practice and progress of science, and he developed techniques to help researchers identify and take into consideration the sources of possible error in their work. His relentless drive to reach agreements between experimentally obtained data and the theories developed to explain the same inspired a new age of scientists and set the tone for the scientific investigations of those who followed in his footsteps.

* **capillary action** interaction between a liquid and the solid surface of a vertical container, such as a thin glass tube, occupied by the liquid

Antoine-Laurent
LAVOISIER

1743–1794

CHEMISTRY

Antoine-Laurent Lavoisier's achievements encompassed many fields, including chemistry, geology, agriculture, and finance. A champion of the common people and of liberal causes, he participated in the French Revolution and used his position as a prominent scientist to address the injustices of society. Best known as the scientist who laid the foundations of modern chemistry, he introduced the modern definitions for element and compound, explained burning and rusting as a chemical combination with oxygen, and included emission and absorption of heat in his chemical system. His *Traité élémentaire de chimie* (Essays on Elementary Chemistry) is a landmark in the history of science, changing the direction and content of chemistry.

Life and Career

Lavoisier was born in Paris, the oldest child of a lawyer who married into a wealthy Parisian family. His mother died when he was five, and his father sent the children to live with their aunt. Lavoisier lived in this household until he married, receiving unlimited love from his aunt and ample money from his mother's estate. Financial security provided Lavoisier the freedom to pursue his studies, and later his scientific career, without having to worry about taking on a full-time job to earn a living.

Education and Early Career. Lavoisier attended the Collège des Quatre Nations, where he studied literature, language, and philosophy as well as mathematics and sciences. He studied under the famed astronomer Lacaille, from whom he acquired a passion for precise measurement that was a hallmark of his later career. Lavoisier then transferred to the law school and received a legal degree at the age of 20. He continued informal studies in science, attending lectures by Lacaille and pursuing his interest in botany. The geologist Jean-Étienne Guettard, a friend of the family, urged Lavoisier to study chemistry. During his final year in college, Lavoisier further developed his interest in and knowledge of the chemistry of minerals.

After graduation Lavoisier joined Guettard on expeditions to study the geology of France. Their efforts resulted in the publication of a geologic atlas of the country. The two men also traveled throughout France, examining rock formations, collecting mineral samples, and taking measurements. Observations made on these trips formed the basis for the theory of earth that Lavoisier later developed. They also stoked his enthusiasm for the chemical investigation of minerals that eventually led to his important discoveries. During breaks between his trips with Guettard, Lavoisier pursued varied scientific activities. He entered a contest to determine the best method for lighting the streets of Paris. Although he did not win the competition (no one did), he was awarded a special gold medal by the king. He also performed experiments in chemical analysis that resulted in his election to France's Académie des Sciences at age 24. Just before his election he joined the Ferme Générale, a group involved in the collection of state taxes; this required extensive travel throughout France. He continued his studies while performing his duties, and the additional income he made from the post further assured his financial independence.

Later Career and Death. In 1771 Lavoisier married the daughter of a colleague in the Ferme Générale. His wife became his collaborator and assistant in his experiments. A skilled artist, she executed the illustrations in *Traité élémentaire de chimie.* She learned English and translated papers for Lavoisier, who did not speak the language. This was the most productive period of Lavoisier's scientific career. A tireless worker, he rose at six in the morning to pursue his scientific studies for two hours. He then tackled his duties with various government and scientific agencies until seven in the evening, at which time he returned to his science.

During the early stages of the French Revolution, Lavoisier served as a member of the assembly in his home province, and he was later elected to the national assembly. His political activities included writing proposals for old-age pensions, charity workshops to employ the poor, and tax reform. He also studied and reported on the problem of issuing paper money and served in several high positions in which he dealt with national finances. One of the scientific committees he served on during this time was responsible for the development of the metric system. However, as radical elements took control of the revolution, Lavoisier and the institutions of which he was a member became the target of political attacks. In

Antoine-Laurent Lavoisier laid the foundations of modern chemistry. He introduced the terms *element* and *compound,* explained the processes of burning and rusting, and described how materials emit and absorb heat.

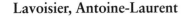

1793 all the members of the Ferme Générale, including Lavoisier, were arrested. They were all convicted and sentenced to death the following year. Lavoisier's execution prompted one colleague to remark: "It took them only an instant to cut off that head, and a hundred years may not produce another like it."

Scientific Accomplishments

Lavoisier's fame stems mainly from his discovery of the role of oxygen in combustion (burning). However, the investigations that led to that discovery had much more far-reaching consequences. His work led to a new way of looking not only at oxygen but also at air and water. Lavoisier's work disproved ideas accepted for hundreds of years and ushered in a new age of scientific chemical analysis that changed the field forever.

Oxygen and Combustion. In Lavoisier's day combustible matter was thought to contain phlogiston (from the Greek *phlogistos,* meaning "burnt"), an imponderable* substance that was released during combustion. Considered the "principle of fire," phlogiston was supposedly a very subtle material that could be detected only when it left a material containing it, and under such circumstances it appeared as fire, light, and heat. Some substances (charcoal) had phlogiston; others (air) had none.

Phlogiston was used to explain the reactions of combustion and calcination*. During combustion, phlogiston flowed from a substance in which it was contained to a substance that contained none. For example, when wood is burned, it gives off smoke and flame and is reduced to ash, proving that it had given off phlogiston. In contrast, because charcoal only leaves ash when burned, scientists believed that it was composed almost purely of phlogiston. Sulfur and phosphorus were also believed to be high in phlogiston. When charcoal was used to extract metals from their ores, it combined with the ore to yield metal. In this reaction the metal absorbed the phlogiston from the charcoal and separated from the ore.

Calcination was also explained similarly. Metals such as lead, when heated until molten, leave an impurity on the surface called a calx. In this process the metal is believed to have released phlogiston, yielding calx. For the first time combustion and calcination, the major categories of chemical reactions, were united by one explanation—both involved the release of phlogiston. Chemists also extended the phlogiston theory to explain the respiration of animals, putrefaction*, fermentation, exothermic processes (releasing or giving off heat), rusting of metals, and oxidation.

Lavoisier was interested in experiments with air, including the findings of the English scientist Stephen HALES, according to whom air could be fixed (trapped) in substances. When a lighted candle was exposed to this fixed air (now known as carbon dioxide), it extinguished itself instead of burning. Around the same time, many French scientists and the English scientist Joseph PRIESTLEY conducted experiments in which they partially burned the red calx of mercury. This produced a type of air that caused a candle to burn more brightly than when burned in normal air. Priestley believed that this air caused better combustion because it contained only

* **imponderable** incapable of being weighed or evaluated exactly

* **calcination** process of heating solids to high temperatures (but not to their fusion point) to remove volatile substances or to effect such changes as oxidation

* **putrefaction** decay of organic matter

very small amounts of phlogiston. According to prevailing beliefs, this enabled the air to draw more phlogiston out of the burning matter than could normal air. He called it dephlogisticated air.

Building on Priestley's work, Lavoisier burned regular mercury (not the oxide) for a prolonged period. This produced a type of air (nitrogen) that did not support combustion. When Lavoisier combined this air with dephlogisticated air, the mixture supported combustion about as well as normal air. A series of later experiments led him to believe that dephlogisticated air, when combined with other substances, produced acid. He named this type of air *principe oxigine,* a French term meaning "begetter of acids." However, he did not yet connect *oxigine* with combustion.

Lavoisier then studied the inflammable air produced when iron or copper is treated with a weak acid. He designed a device to mix *oxigine* with inflammable air, believing that it would produce acid. Instead, it produced water. He reversed the process, passing water through a superheated tube to separate it into *oxigine* and inflammable air. This demonstration proved that water was not a true element but a compound consisting of two gases. He named the inflammable air *principe hydrogine,* or the "begetter of water," better known as hydrogen. A series of later investigations confirmed Lavoisier's suspicion that the oxygen in which candles burned so well must be the agent that produces combustion. Shortly thereafter, he published his results in a paper, permanently discrediting the theory of phlogiston.

Respiration. Lavoisier's studies led him to consider the role of oxygen in respiration. He suggested that oxygen might enter the bloodstream in the lungs, where it was exchanged for carbon dioxide. However, experiments conducted on animals showed that the amount of carbon dioxide an animal exhaled was less than the amount of oxygen inhaled. Because he believed that no matter was ever lost in a chemical reaction, he concluded that the amount of oxygen not converted into carbon dioxide either unites with the blood or combines with hydrogen in the body to form water. His experiments convinced him that both processes occur. Lavoisier also discovered that an animal consumes more oxygen as its temperature rises, as well as when it is exerting itself or digesting food. He concluded that the burning of oxygen in the body is what produces body heat, and he said that this combustion takes place in tiny tubes in the lungs.

Important Publications. Lavoisier's work with oxygen formed the basis of the *Méthode de nomenclature chimique,* a book in which he and several collaborators introduced a new lexicon (dictionary) for the field. The book includes a table of 55 substances that the authors considered elements. None of the elements identified as such in ancient times—air, earth, fire, and water—appears on the list, which contains such substances as oxygen, hydrogen, carbon, sulfur, and various metals and bases. Compounds were now identified by the substances they contained, calxes were renamed oxides, and salts were named from the acid from which they are formed. The book was extremely influential, and in the words of one scientist, to accept the new naming scheme was basically to accept the new French theories.

Radical Rock Bands

Lavoisier's theories about the earth were as radical as his ideas in chemistry. During his expeditions with Guettard, Lavoisier noted that bands of rocky sediments, obviously deposited when the sea covered the continent many years ago, actually appeared in several layers. Bands of sediments similar to those formed at the bottom of the sea alternated with bands of sediments similar to those that formed on the seashore. He concluded correctly that the sea had advanced across the land and retreated again many times, not just one time as most people believed.

Two years later Lavoisier published the *Traité élémentaire de chimie,* a summary of his discoveries and an introduction to the new chemistry, based on the concept of the chemical element (substance not susceptible to decomposition). The book contains a list of 33 elements and an explanation for the phlogiston theory. One of the elements in his list is the matter of heat, or *"calorique"*—a weightless substance that he said could combine chemically with substances that did have weight. These names were as new as the concept of the element, representing a new naming system that hinged on the properties of the elements and chemicals. The known facts about the characteristics of chemical reactions became the basis for the new chemistry. The term *oxygen* meant "acid former," and *hydrogen,* "water former." These properties were determined by experimentation and observation, eliminating speculations such as those prevalent in the chemistry of PARACELSUS.

Lavoisier's *Traité* also contains the law of the conservation of mass, which is implicit in the use of a balance for chemical reactions. According to the law, matter is neither created nor destroyed. Lavoisier states that matter does not alter its chemical properties unless it is broken down into simpler forms or combined with other forms to make new substances. Moreover, changes in the properties of matter are caused by definite chemical reactions, not because of a gain or loss of phlogiston.

Lavoisier also remarked that elements might well be made of smaller particles, but scientists at the time lacked the knowledge to break them down. He hoped and believed that by applying the principles in the book, scientists could eventually learn even more about the basic structure of all matter. In fact, it was not long before all chemists adopted and applied his principles. In so doing, they built the modern age of chemistry on the foundation laid down by Lavoisier.

Antoni van
LEEUWENHOEK

1632–1723

NATURAL SCIENCES, MICROSCOPY

* **microorganism** tiny living things that generally can be seen clearly only through a microscope

Antoni van Leeuwenhoek discovered a world of tiny microorganisms* that he called "animalcules," meaning "little animals," by observing parts of plants and animals through magnifying lenses, or microscopes. Grinding lenses began as a hobby of his but soon developed into a lifelong pursuit of microscopic investigation. Leeuwenhoek became a legend in his own time, receiving awards from societies and visits from foreign scholars.

Born in Delft in the Netherlands, Leeuwenhoek was the son of a basketmaker, who died when Leeuwenhoek was six. After attending grammar school, Leeuwenhoek became an apprentice to a cloth merchant in Amsterdam. Later he opened a shop of his own. Then, in 1660, he began a new career as a civil servant in the service of the city of Delft, becoming chief warden of the city in 1677. The pension he received from his civil service positions gave him financial security for life.

Leeuwenhoek's scientific work began in about 1671. Already familiar with the special glasses used by drapers to inspect the quality of cloth, Leeuwenhoek took the idea further and constructed his first simple microscope. It consisted of a tiny lens, ground by hand from a small piece of glass and clamped between two metal plates. A special holder attached to this apparatus enabled Leeuwenhoek to view specimens through the lens.

Antoni van Leeuwenhoek constructed an early microscope and discovered a world of tiny microorganisms. He observed anatomy of insects; particles of skin, hair, and bone; and parts of plants. This illustration shows different types of insects.

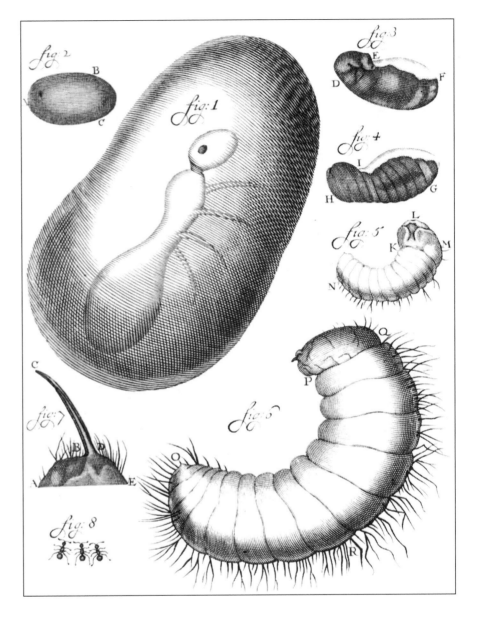

During his lifetime Leeuwenhoek made about 550 lenses. The quality of his lenses improved over time, making greater magnification possible. Moreover, because he was always secretive about his technique and refused to take on apprentices who might become proficient in his craft, his instruments were unsurpassed until the 1800s. Through his lenses Leeuwenhoek observed particles of skin, hair, and bone; insects; parts of plants; and many other objects. Carefully, he recorded his observations, always in Dutch, for he knew no other language.

Leeuwenhoek made his most important discovery in 1674, when he observed tiny moving objects—the one-celled animals known as protozoa. He recorded his observations and two years later communicated them to the Royal Society in London. The findings caused a sensation, and Leeuwenhoek felt obliged to obtain written testimony about his findings from ministers, judges, and medical professionals. Leeuwenhoek's observation was considered sensational because of his claim that these little animals were a naturally occurring phenomenon and not the by-product (as contemporary wisdom would have it) of the decomposition of organic material.

In the years that followed, Leeuwenhoek observed and described many kinds of microorganisms, including bacteria. He also became interested in the process of reproduction in animals and humans. He observed spermatozoa* and suggested that for reproduction to take place, the sperm would have to penetrate the ovary. He was unable to detect the human egg with his microscope and so mistakenly took the ovary to be the egg. Because the ovary could not pass through the fallopian tubes of the female, and the spermatozoa swam rapidly through the male's semen, Leeuwenhoek concluded that the spermatozoa were the principal agent in animal reproduction. The scientists who adopted Leeuwenhoek's view became known as "animalculists," and their view was strongly opposed by followers of William HARVEY, who believed that the ovary was the principal agent in animal generation. Harvey's idea went against the accepted wisdom of the day, which held that the egg was the source of all new life.

Leeuwenhoek took particular interest in the blood and blood vessels. He observed corpuscles and capillaries and investigated the walls of blood vessels. Because he spoke and read only Dutch, he was unaware of the work of another microscopist, the Italian Marcello MALPIGHI, who had made similar observations of the blood earlier.

Leeuwenhoek continued to share his findings with the Royal Society, and as the importance of his work became apparent, the society prepared English translations of his letters and encouraged him to investigate new fields. From 1684 onward Leeuwenhoek published his own works, first in Dutch and then in Latin. In recognition of his achievements, he was elected a fellow of the Royal Society in 1680 and a correspondent of the Académie des Sciences in Paris in 1699. As his fame spread, scholars and eminent people from around the world, including kings and princes, came to visit him.

* **spermatozoon** male reproductive cell; *pl.* spermatozoa

Gottfried Wilhelm LEIBNIZ

1646–1716

MATHEMATICS, PHYSICS

Gottfried Wilhelm Leibniz pursued one of the most varied careers of any great scientist. The nature of his education, the scope of his interests, and the demands of his career as an adviser to German noblemen ensured that he would apply his intellectual gifts across a great number of fields. His overriding desire was to create a unified system of knowledge that would reconcile the ideas of modern thinkers, such as Francis BACON and René DESCARTES, with those of the ancients, such as the Greek philosopher Aristotle. He also wanted to create a method that would enable scholars to determine "truths of reason in any field whatever . . . through a calculus, as in arithmetic or algebra." His efforts in this area led to his invention of calculus—an advanced form of mathematics that involves computing quantities that change as functions of different variables. This invention is especially important because mathematics was never his primary field of interest.

Life and Career

Leibniz spent most of his adult life in the employ of various German noblemen. His duties included diplomatic missions, legal studies, and the design and implementation of practical scientific projects. Consequently, he undertook his scientific work in a largely piecemeal fashion. He was the only major philosopher of his time who had to earn a living, which makes his accomplishments even more impressive.

Early Life and Career. Leibniz's intellectual curiosity was in part a reflection of his upbringing—his father was a professor of moral philosophy at the University of Leipzig, and his mother came from an academic family. When Leibniz was just a boy, a relative recognized that he possessed great intellectual skills and a remarkable ability for teaching. He recommended that Wilhelm be given free access to his father's library. Leibniz was an eager reader who devoured books on all sorts of subjects, a habit that led to his extensive knowledge and varied interests.

At age 15 he entered the University of Leipzig, which at the time placed very little emphasis on science. Consequently, his studies focused on philosophy and law. He finished his legal studies at the university when he was 20 but was refused a doctorate, possibly because he was too young. Leibniz then moved to Altdorf and received his doctorate at the university there, which then invited him to accept a teaching position. However, he declined the offer. Instead, he worked in the city of Mainz for a nobleman named Johann Philipp von Schönborn.

During his service with Schönborn, Leibniz worked on the legal reform of the Holy Roman Empire (which included the German states) and undertook diplomatic missions on behalf of the archbishop. On one of these trips, he traveled to Paris to forestall an attack on Germany by the French king, Louis XIV. Leibniz hoped to convince Louis to attack Egypt instead and create an empire in North Africa. He also hoped that such a project would help promote a reunion between the Catholic Church (which was dominant in France) and the Protestant religions that had broken away from it (which were prominent in Germany). This was only one of many efforts by Leibniz to realize his lifelong goal of reuniting the two churches.

Although Leibniz never met the king, and the plan failed, he met many prominent scientists during his time in Paris. In early 1673 Leibniz left Paris for London to arrange a peace treaty between England and Holland. There he was elected to the Royal Society, to which he presented a calculating machine that he had designed some years earlier. Around this time Schönborn died, and his successor showed little interest in Leibniz's work. Although this left Leibniz searching for financial support, it freed him to pursue his scientific studies. He spent several years in Paris before accepting a position in the court of Johann Friedrich, the Duke of Brunswick-Lüneburg.

Later Life and Career. Leibniz was very active in many areas during his service with the duke and later with the duke's brother and successor,

The German physicist and mathematician Gottfried Wilhelm Leibniz invented an advanced form of mathematics called calculus. With this math, he calculated the area and volume of geometric figures and the values for velocity and acceleration.

* **dynamics** study of the relationship between motion and the forces affecting motion

Ernst August. Among the scientific and technical projects he worked on were plans for a variety of mechanical devices, such as windmills, clocks, and a submarine. He also designed a windmill-powered pump to help increase the yield of the silver mines in the Harz Mountains and served as an engineer in the mines. His observations during the course of this work led him to propose the theory that the earth was originally molten and not a solid body. He also perfected the binary (base-two) number system, outlined a process to remove salt from seawater, and continued his studies in the fields of philosophy and dynamics. In 1679, after Johann Friedrich died, Ernst August commissioned Leibniz to undertake a genealogy of the family. This work required extensive travel through Germany, Austria, and Italy, bringing Leibniz into contact with some of Europe's renowned scientists.

August died in 1698, and the dukedom passed to his son, an uneducated man who had little interest in or use for Leibniz's talents. Neglected by his employer, Leibniz took the opportunity to leave the court and pursue his interests. Two years later he traveled to Berlin, where the Berlin Academy was founded on his recommendation. That same year he was elected to the Académie des Sciences in Paris. He continued to develop his philosophical and mathematical theories and pursued efforts to reunite the two Christian churches. In 1712 Leibniz visited Peter the Great, czar of Russia, and served as his councillor in Vienna. Two years later Leibniz returned to Hanover, where he spent the rest of his life working on the genealogy he had begun 30 years earlier. He never finished the work and died in 1716, neglected by the noble families he had served during his lifetime.

Scientific Accomplishments

Leibniz's outstanding contribution to science was undoubtedly his invention of calculus. However, he also made important strides in analyzing the motion of bodies and has been called the founder of the field of dynamics*.

Calculus. For years, certain problems had eluded solution by even the best mathematicians. These included accurately determining the area enclosed by circles—a process called quadrature—and various types of curves, as well as calculating the exact volume of solid objects, such as a cone. The classic approach to solving such problems relied on a concept known as limit. For example, to determine the area of a circle, one inscribed a square in the circle. In those portions of the circle not occupied by the square, one inscribed other squares until a limit was reached at which any additional squares would be infinitely small. Before the invention of calculus, it was necessary to undergo this painstaking process, known as the use of infinitesimals, to calculate the area of a circle, the area under a curve, or the volume of a curved solid.

Between 1673 and 1676, Leibniz was in Paris, where he began to study infinitesimals and investigate the method of quadrature used by the Italian mathematician Cavalieri. In the process, he discovered a method to express the process of limiting using a standard set of symbols, known today as integral calculus. Using this method, Leibniz could quickly and accurately solve problems of length, area, and volume of geometric figures that had previously taken a great deal of time and effort and many separate calculations.

Leibniz also developed differential calculus, by which he could calculate the slope of a line tangent to a curve. Differential calculus offered mathematicians a tool to calculate accurately values for velocity and acceleration. Together, integral and differential calculus revolutionized mathematics and the physical sciences. For the first time scientists could calculate planetary motion, the effects of gravity, and a host of other phenomena that described the workings of the physical universe.

During the time that Leibniz was developing calculus, he received a letter in which the English scientist Isaac NEWTON reported the results of his work, which were very similar to his own. However, Newton did not report the methods he had used to obtain his results. Quickly realizing the similarities between their work, Leibniz rushed to publish his results in 1684, three years earlier than Newton. This led to a bitter dispute over who had first conceived the idea of calculus. At the time the Royal Academy in London declared in favor of Newton. However, the committee that decided the issue consisted of Newton's supporters, and in fact, the final report was written by Newton himself. Leibniz had the final say because it is his notation and differentiation and integration, rather than the clumsy methods of Newton, that are in use in modern texts. Only many years after Leibniz's death was he given credit for his independent role in inventing calculus.

Dynamics. Leibniz was critical of the accepted laws of motion and impact of bodies presented by the French philosopher René Descartes. According to Descartes, all physical phenomena must have a mechanical explanation. Descartes believed that the motion of a body is caused by forces external to the body. Consequently, motion can occur only through contact. Descartes rejected the notion that the moon orbited the earth because of the effect of an unseen force called gravity, acting from a distance. Instead, Descartes proposed that a vortex (whirlpool) of tiny particles carried the moon in its orbit and caused the planets and comets to orbit the sun. Leibniz rejected this mechanical explanation for planetary motion. He instead argued that the motion of all bodies was caused by an internal force called *vis viva* that did not depend on impact or an external force. Leibniz's system of motion, called dynamics, provided a better explanation for the movement of bodies than did Descartes's mechanical theory. However, Leibniz did accept a modified version of Descartes's vortex theory to explain planetary motion.

Leibniz's adaptation of Descartes's ideas was characteristic of his work. He eagerly studied the ideas of other scientists and scholars, accepting ideas with which he agreed but not hesitating to change or reject those with which he did not. He strongly believed that all science was interdependent and that progress came about through the sharing of ideas across disciplines. His faithfulness to this philosophy is apparent in the breadth of his scientific interests and activities.

Seeking Unity, but not with Descartes

Leibniz was overwhelmingly concerned with uniting disciplines torn by controversy, including science and religion. Consequently, he rejected Descartes's ideas, which separated the body and mind (soul). Instead, Leibniz's notions on the relationship of the body to the soul formed part of his theory of dynamic motion. Leibniz also attempted to prove that God was the ultimate origin or cause of everything. His ideas about motion and philosophical outlook directly opposed those of Descartes. Leibniz believed that Descartes's notions posed a danger to religious faith.

LEONARDO DA VINCI

1452–1519

ANATOMY, TECHNOLOGY, MECHANICS, MATHEMATICS, GEOLOGY

* **mechanics** science that studies how energy and force affect objects

* **optics** scientific study of the properties of light

Leonardo da Vinci was one of the towering figures of the Renaissance, the era of new ideas in scholarship, art, science, and technology that began in Europe in the 1300s. He also won lasting fame as an artist, the painter of such well-known masterpieces as the Mona Lisa and *The Last Supper.* Throughout his life Leonardo was interested in scientific theory and the practical uses of science. For instance, his thorough study of human anatomy may have reflected his desire to portray the body accurately in painting and sculpture. He had many scientific concerns, ranging from pure mathematics to military engineering and problems in mechanics*, such as the question of how birds fly—and how humans might be able to do the same.

Although Leonardo has been recognized as one of the most extraordinary minds of all time, his place in the history of science is unusual because he did not contribute directly to the development of scientific thought. For three centuries after Leonardo's death, his scientific work lay buried in notes that were overlooked or lost in museums, libraries, and archives throughout Europe. Except for some aspects of his mechanical and engineering activities and the tradition that he knew much about anatomy, Leonardo was not well known as a scientist. For this reason some modern historians of science, rather than regarding Leonardo as the discoverer of a principle or the inventor of a device, focus instead on what he knew and how he knew it. In Leonardo's work they find a window into the possibilities of scientific knowledge during the Renaissance.

Leonardo as a Scientist

Leonardo da Vinci's life and scientific work illustrate what some scholars have seen as the spirit of the Renaissance—curiosity about the world, interest in a wide range of matters, and knowledge or expertise in more than one subject.

Life and Career. The illegitimate son of a peasant girl and a citizen of the Italian city of Florence, Leonardo was born in Vinci, near Empolia, Italy. He received an ordinary education in reading and writing, but his gifts for music and art led his father to apprentice him to a sculptor in Florence. In the artist's workshop the young Leonardo studied painting, sculpture, and mechanics.

Leonardo had already produced impressive paintings when, at the age of 30, he left Florence to enter the service of Ludovico Sforza, the duke of Milan, a city in northern Italy. For 17 years Leonardo was part of the duke's household. During these years he painted, produced a clay model for a statue of one of the Sforzas on horseback, and planned books on painting, architecture, mechanics, and the human figure. He also advised the duke on engineering and technical matters and became increasingly interested in mathematics and optics* and in solving mechanical problems.

After the French captured Milan in 1499, Leonardo moved to Venice and then back to Florence. For about a year he served as military engineer and chief inspector of fortifications in the northern Italian region called the Romagna. While living in Florence, Leonardo began his systematic

* **hydrology** study of the movement of water

* **meteorology** science that deals with the atmosphere, especially the weather and weather predictions; also known as atmospheric science

study of human anatomy and spent time studying mathematics and mechanics. He also pursued his lifelong interest in hydrology* and approached the question of flight in two ways—by intensively researching weather and bird flight and by considering the problem of human flight.

In 1506 Leonardo returned to Milan, where the city's French governor befriended him. There he produced most of his brilliant anatomical drawings. By this time Leonardo had come to believe that mathematics held the key to understanding nature. His work in hydrology, geology, meteorology*, and biology was devoted to a search for the geometrical rules that he believed underlay the physical world.

Leonardo moved again in 1513, this time going to Rome in the hope that Pope Leo X would offer him encouragement, a good working environment, and large commissions for artworks. Disappointed in this hope, three years later Leonardo and one of his pupils, Francesco Melzi, left Italy for Amboise, France. There Leonardo spent the final years of his life as the honored guest of King Francis I.

The Notes. Throughout his life Leonardo recorded his thoughts, observations, experiments, and designs in notes. In these notes he frequently mentions books that he had completed on various subjects, including anatomy, water, and mechanics, but the manuscripts of these books have been lost. The only books published under Leonardo's name are *Treatise on Painting* and *Treatise on the Movement and Measurement of Water,* both of which were compiled from his notes by two of his followers after his death.

Masses of other notes remain—some 6,000 sheets of them, although scholars believe that many more sheets have been lost or destroyed. The surviving pages are laid out in great confusion. Leonardo made no attempt to organize them, and after his death they were disarranged, spread out among various owners, and even cut up and pasted together in new ways. They are like mixed-up pieces of a jigsaw puzzle, with a large part of the puzzle lost. As the notes have become known in recent times, they have been published and studied, but the full scope of Leonardo's genius is still unfolding. As recently as 1967 two large collections of his notes were found in Madrid, Spain. Others may await discovery.

Leonardo's notes have several distinctive features. One is his "mirror writing." Leonardo, who was left-handed, wrote normally on many occasions, but in his notes he wrote backward, from right to left, in a script that can easily be read when a mirror is held to the page. A more significant feature of the notes is Leonardo's creative but sometimes confusing way of expressing himself. He often presented his thoughts visually, in the form of drawings or designs. A single page, for example, might contain many examples of aspects of the study of curves—grass curling around a flower, an old man with curly hair, billowing clouds, rippling waves in a pool, geometrical exercises, and notes developing each image in detail. It is dangerous to dismiss any drawing as a mere doodle. Some of Leonardo's most interesting scientific concepts appear in the form of casual, small sketches.

Leonardo's habit of returning to subjects after long absences is another source of confusion. A note made in 1500 or 1510 may disagree with one made in 1490. Leonardo himself recognized that his ideas had grown and changed over the years. In 1508 he called his notes "a collection without order taken from many papers . . . blame not me because the subjects are many, and memory cannot retain them . . . because of the long intervals of time between one writing and another."

Scientific Philosophy and Methods. Leonardo saw no opposition between art and science. Both, he claimed, followed universal laws, and the key to both lay in the careful observation of the physical world.

Leonardo believed that the natural world was created by God to obey laws. Human senses could perceive these laws, and human intelligence could understand them through mathematics and logic. Understanding entered the mind through the senses, especially vision—Leonardo called the eye "the window of the soul," through which a person could best see and appreciate "the infinite works of Nature." Humans could then interpret what they observed about the natural world by using mathematics, particularly geometry. Leonardo used geometrical figures, chiefly pyramids and circles, to illustrate what he thought were the laws that governed phenomena such as light spreading out from a source or the intersecting ripples formed by two stones dropped into a pond.

In Leonardo's view all phenomena in the physical world could be explained through a proper understanding of what he thought were the four basic powers of nature—force, energy, weight, and percussion. (Leonardo included light and sound in this last category, which refers to a force striking a surface). Leonardo tried to apply this simplified view of nature to all fields of scientific research and practical invention. The system was best fitted to mechanics, which he called "the paradise of mathematical science." Mathematical rules, however, had to fit what Leonardo called experience, the raw material of knowledge. A researcher could acquire experience by observing the world and conducting experiments. Leonardo's three main methods of observing and experimenting involved measurement, models, and markers.

Measurement became important after about 1490, when Leonardo decided that the powers of nature operated in geometrical relationships. In an effort to introduce numerical quantities into all his scientific work, he measured weights, distances, and speeds. He also described instruments of measurement, such as anemometers, to measure wind speed and balances for weighing things. Leonardo's favorite form of experiment used models, especially to study the flow of water or blood. Among the models he constructed were a small glass cast of a blood vessel with its valves and a large model of the Mediterranean Sea that he built to show the effects of rivers entering the sea.

To study the flow of water, Leonardo frequently used markers, such as seeds, bits of paper, or colored inks, either in tanks or in rivers. These experiments and observations gave him a wealth of information about the directions and speeds of water movements, the movements of sand and stones in water, and the action of water on surrounding surfaces, such as a riverbank. He also used markers, such as dust and small objects, to study the movement of solid bodies in air.

Decoding the Secrets of Trees

Leonardo studied plants as well as animals. In his early years he took great trouble to reproduce the outward forms of flowering plants accurately. Later he explored growth processes of plants. Experimenting on a gourd plant, he discovered that a single root, if well supplied with water, could nourish 60 fruits. Studying tree growth, Leonardo discovered that the rings in branches and trunks indicate how many years a tree has lived and whether each year was wet or dry. He originated the science of dendrochronology, or dating trees by their rings.

Leonardo believed that a scientific investigator should repeat each experiment to be certain of the results. He also performed the same experiment repeatedly in a series, with slight variations in one element each time. For example, he made a model resembling a bird and twisted its tail at a series of different angles, noting each time how the twist affected the flight of the model. Remarkable patience, thoroughness, and innovation characterized his experiments.

Interests and Achievements

Leonardo's achievements in science, as in art, depended mainly on three factors—his extremely sharp vision, his awareness of the geometrical relationships among the things he saw, and his creative power. These gifts led him to insights and inventions in several scientific fields.

Anatomy. Leonardo was interested in both the anatomy and the physiology, or functioning, of the human body. During the 1490s he investigated vision, attempting to discover how light affects the eye. He also studied the movement of the human body in activities such as sitting, running, digging, and pushing. He turned these simple movements into more complex studies of how the body behaves as a mechanical device (an arrangement of levers and weights) during work. These studies, in turn, led to studies of how levers, pulleys, and other devices allow people to transform human energy into the work of machines.

Later Leonardo turned his attention to the internal structure and function of the human body. Again, he regarded the body as a kind of machine that obeyed the mechanical laws of motion and force, with bones as levers and muscles as lines of force acting on them. Leonardo's anatomical studies required many dissections, and he wrote of how he disliked "passing the night hours in the company of corpses, quartered and flayed and horrible to behold."

In the set of drawings now known as *Anatomical Folio A,* Leonardo systematically illustrated all the main bones and muscles of the body, often adding diagrams to show them in action. While dissecting the body of an old man in a hospital in Florence, Leonardo became interested in the digestive system and made drawings of the esophagus, stomach, liver, gallbladder, and intestines. He also made the first known illustration of the appendix.

Leonardo's studies of the heart and its action fill more notes than those he made of any other organ. In one of his experiments, aimed at finding out how the heart and blood vessels work, he made a glass model of the large blood vessel called the aorta. To this he attached a bag to represent the heart. Squeezing the bag forced water through the model, just as the heart pushes blood into the aorta. The water contained grass seeds as markers so that Leonardo could observe the direction of the blood flow through the valves in the aorta model. In this characteristic manner he labored to examine the smallest details of the body in action.

Humans were not the only subjects of Leonardo's anatomical work. Scattered through his notes are studies of oxen, pigs, dogs, monkeys, lions, and frogs. As a painter and sculptor, Leonardo was very much interested in the anatomy of horses. His concern with the question of flight led to a close study of the anatomy of birds and bats.

Technology and Engineering. All of Leonardo's employers and patrons recognized him as an engineer and as an artist. At the court of Ludovico Sforza, for example, he was called *ingenarius et pinctor,* or "engineer and painter." In his own lifetime he was known as a military engineer, designer of technology, mechanic, and architect, and he was admired as a painter.

Leonardo's skill in the technical arts may have originated in Florence, where he served as an apprentice, but it reached full flower in Milan, Italy's industrial center. There he had close contact with architects, engineers of dams and canals, stonemasons, textile workers, casters of bronze and iron, locksmiths, clockmakers, and jewelers. Many of his technical drawings were of industrial equipment, such as pumps, spinning wheels, and grinding machines. Others were of original inventions, although even here Leonardo drew on the work of engineers who had come before him.

Leonardo was the first engineer to try systematically to overcome the shortcomings, such as excessive friction and wear, in the machines of his time. He was also the first to recognize that every machine is a collection of universal mechanisms, such as wedges, gears, levers, cranks, pistons, valves, and springs. Although many engineers of the day spent immense effort trying to create perpetual motion machines—mechanical devices that would produce more energy than was needed to run them— Leonardo eventually realized that such machines could not exist. He understood that machines do not produce work or energy but only modify the way in which it is applied. Leonardo hated waste, whether of time,

Leonardo da Vinci is recognized not only for his talent as an artist but also for his skill as an engineer. His notebooks contain sketches and designs for various mechanical devices and models. This drawing shows a machine for removing earth from a canal bed.

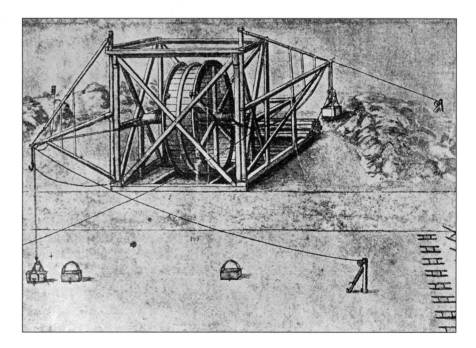

power, or money, and his goal as a designer was to produce efficient, practical, economical machines.

Among the many devices that Leonardo designed—and sometimes built—were treadmills, waterwheels, gear systems, and a few windmills. He experimented with steam as an energy source and designed a steam cannon and the first turbine moved by a jet of steam. He also designed a thermal engine "to lift a great weight by means of fire."

Many of Leonardo's projects involved hydraulics, or water engineering. In addition to waterwheels, he designed a water pump and several highly original canal-building machines. He also improved structures for managing the water flow in canals. Although he built canals in the Romagna and was involved in hydraulic projects along France's Loire River during his last years, one of his most ambitious hydraulic projects, changing the course of the Arno River near the city of Pisa, was never carried out.

Leonardo left plans for many machines and industrial techniques that were unequaled until the 1700s and 1800s. Among these were improved pile drivers, spinning machines for textile factories, a rope-making machine, a mechanized printing press, a water-cooled barrel for a rapid-fire gun, and a simplified method of making etchings, a type of illustration printed from a metal plate. He also designed chemistry equipment, such as a distilling device, and carried out chemical experiments. Some of his original experiments were concerned with producing decorative items of imitation stone. In his directions for making this material from proteins and pigments and shaping it into forms that "will be like glass and resist humidity," he outlined the basic operations of modern plastic technology.

Flight and flying machines were also of great interest to Leonardo. His studies of bird flight were the most productive aspect of this research. Some mechanical aspects of the flying machines he designed are interesting, but the machines, which used muscle power and attempted to mimic the flight of birds with flapping wings, were unsuccessful. Later Leonardo turned his attention to gliders, a more promising avenue of research. He also designed a parachute and a machine resembling a helicopter, although earlier engineers may have had similar ideas.

Mechanics. The science of mechanics studies movement, energy, and force as they relate to physical objects. It is the basis of mechanical design and engineering, but it is concerned with theories and universal principles rather than with specific applications or machines. Although Leonardo was interested in mechanics for most of his adult life, he turned increasing attention to the subject after 1508.

One aspect of mechanics is statics, the study of the weight (an effect of gravity) and balance of bodies. Another is dynamics, the study of forces—such as speed, weight, and resistance—on moving bodies. Leonardo absorbed the work of ancient and medieval* writers on these subjects and then extended it through experimentation. He discovered a method to analyze the relationship between the tension in a segment of cord, the weight supported by the cord, and the position of the point supporting the cord. He also made advances in determining the center of gravity in a solid body

Science in a Sacred Scene

One of Leonardo's most famous paintings is the *Virgin of the Rocks,* which depicts a meeting in the wilderness between the young Jesus and another youth. It reveals that the artist carefully observed and portrayed the natural world. The picture shows complex rock formations—layers of sandstone weathered in different degrees, volcanic lava that has cooled into columns, jagged rocks left by erosion—in accurate detail. Its botany is also accurate. No plants grow out of the volcanic rock, for example, because such rock is too hard for roots to take hold.

* **medieval** relating to the Middle Ages in Europe, a period from about 500 to 1500

and proved that a quantity of water will never lift another quantity of water to a level higher than its own.

In dynamics, Leonardo framed an early version of Isaac NEWTON's third law of motion. He stated: "An object offers as much resistance to the air as the air does to the object," adding that the same is true of an object in water. He also studied gravity and the velocity of falling objects, and he invented percussion as a branch of mechanics concerned with the laws of impact.

Mathematics. Leonardo admired mathematics and considered it the key to unlocking the mysteries of nature and science. However, he was not primarily a mathematician, and his work had no influence on the subject. Leonardo was proud of what he believed were his mathematical discoveries, but some were incorrect. Understanding his mathematical and geometrical work is particularly difficult because of the scattered nature of his notes. Some contain incomplete discussions, geometrical drawings without accompanying explanations, or bare statements of solutions without the accompanying proofs to show how Leonardo solved the problems.

* **geometer** specialist in geometry

Manuscripts from Leonardo's first stay in Milan show that he had studied the work of Euclid, an ancient Greek geometer*, and that geometry was the branch of mathematics that interested him most. One of his main concerns was proportionality, the relationship of parts to each other and to wholes. Another concern was the relationship between straight and curved lines and surfaces. Leonardo attempted to solve many complicated problems, such as the challenge of squaring a circle, or finding a formula that would produce a square equal in area to a circle. He thought that he had solved this puzzle, but his solution was incomplete.

Geology. Leonardo's study of the earth was based on the philosophical notion that the study of the great world was related to the study of man. Man was a microcosm, or smaller version, of the world, "composed like the earth itself, of earth, water, air, and fire." He also believed that the human skeleton corresponded to the earth's rocky structure, the "lake of blood" in a human body corresponded to the sea, and so on.

In a more practical sense, Leonardo's geology, like so much of his work, was based on keen observation. As an engineer and canal builder as well as a painter, he was very aware of the differences in rock types and formations, and he strove to understand how they had arrived at their present shapes and appearances.

Leonardo claimed that the earth's crust had reached its present appearance because of natural processes, especially floods, river flows, and rainfall, over immense periods of time. He estimated that it had taken 200,000 years, for example, for Italy's Po River to form the plain through which it flows. Leonardo had clearly abandoned the biblical timescale of a mere few thousand years for much greater expanse of geological time.

Leonardo saw the world as caught up in the process of slow but ceaseless change. The highest mountain peaks are former islands in an ancient sea. As wind and rain slowly wear down the mountains, the land becomes lighter and rises slowly, bringing up layers of soil and fossils that were once sea bottoms. One modern scholar has called Leonardo's system of geology "perhaps his most complete and lasting invention."

Carl
LINNAEUS
1707–1778
BOTANY, ZOOLOGY

* **naturalist** student of natural history, the systematic study of natural objects, especially in their natural settings

The Swedish naturalist* Carl Linnaeus is perhaps most famous as the inventor of modern systems of classification for plants, animals, and minerals. Linnaeus is also considered the founder of binomial nomenclature—a system of naming plants and animals by using two names. His achievements in classifying, ranking, and naming organisms earned Linnaeus the title "father of taxonomy." Because he wrote many of his works in Latin, he is sometimes referred to by the Latin form of his name—Carolus Linnaeus.

Life and Career. Carl Linnaeus was born in Råshult, a small town in southern Sweden. His father, Nils, was a Lutheran priest who had a great love of flowers and introduced Carl to the mysteries of botany at an early age. By age eight Carl had acquired the nickname "the little botanist."

In 1716 Linnaeus was sent to school in the nearby city of Växjö, where he pursued his interest in botany and natural history. An average student, he spent much of his time studying and learning about plants. Linnaeus's father hoped that Carl would become a clergyman like himself, but Carl's interest in science drew him away from that career path. In 1727 Linnaeus entered the University of Lund to study medicine. At the time botany was part of the curriculum for medical students. Because the medical instruction at Lund was mediocre, Linnaeus made many trips to surrounding areas to study and collect plants on his own. After only a year he left Lund and enrolled at the University of Uppsala, near the city of Stockholm, the most prestigious university in Sweden.

Linnaeus spent his time at Uppsala collecting and studying plants. He found the school's botanical garden especially interesting because of the many rare foreign plants it contained. He met Olof Celsius, a veteran botanist with whom he studied the plants of the surrounding region. Soon Linnaeus began to formulate the basic features of a new classification system for plants, based on plant sexuality. He classified plants according to their stamens (male structures) and pistils (female structures).

In 1735 Linnaeus enrolled at the University of Harderwijk in Holland, where he received a degree in medicine. He also met some of Europe's best-known botanists and gained wealthy patrons. Linnaeus's reputation as a botanist was firmly established after he published much of his research while in Holland. The most important of these was *Systema naturae* (The System of Nature), which contains a detailed explanation of his system of classification for plants, animals, and minerals.

Returning to Sweden in 1738, Linnaeus worked as a physician in Stockholm and became one of the founders of the Swedish Academy of Science. Three years later he accepted a position as professor of medicine at Uppsala, and the following year he became professor of botany at that school. In 1747 Linnaeus was appointed official physician to the royal

Carl Linnaeus is best known as the inventor of the modern system for classifying plants, animals, and minerals. He also introduced a method for naming organisms by using two names, in either Latin or Greek, for the genus and species. This system simplified their identification and classification.

* **genus** sixth broadest classification of organisms into related groups according to their characteristics

court, and he was granted a title of nobility as Carl von Linné 15 years later. Linnaeus remained at Uppsala for the rest of his life, but his fame as a botanist spread throughout the world. Forced to retire from teaching in 1774 because of illness, he died of a stroke four years later.

Work and Accomplishments. A successful teacher, Linnaeus gave lectures filled with humor and unusual ideas. The excursions he led to collect plants were popular among his students. Many foreign students came to Sweden to study with Linnaeus, and they helped spread his ideas. His students also enriched Linnaeus's studies by sending him specimens that they collected during their own travels. He also maintained contact with many botanists and naturalists, sharing his ideas with them. These scholars sent Linnaeus specimens from around the globe, helping him in his work.

Linnaeus's mission during his years at Uppsala was to complete his reform of botany. Although his early work had established the basic principles, they still had to be developed and put into practice. In 1751 he published his most influential work, *Philosophia botanica* (Philosophy of Botany), which dealt with the theory of botany. The work also discussed the laws and rules that a botanist must follow to describe and name plants correctly and to organize them into their proper categories.

Linnaeus also struggled with the enormous goal of cataloging all the world's plant and animal species and giving each its correct place in his system of classification. This was especially important since a steady stream of new and unknown plants was arriving in Europe in the 1700s from Africa, Asia, and the Americas. Linnaeus began with his native Sweden, publishing *Flora suecica* (Swedish Plants) and *Fauna suecica* (Swedish Animals) in 1745 and 1747. By 1753 he had cataloged about 8,000 plant species from around the world and described them in *Species plantarum* (Plant Species). He also continued to update and revise his *Systema naturae,* which became the bible of natural history.

Linnaeus cataloged every plant and animal specimen he came across, and he sorted and classified them into groups and subgroups. His need for order contributed to another major accomplishment—fixed rules regarding the distinction between genus* and species and a system of binomial nomenclature based on these two classifications.

Although Linnaeus was not the first to use a two-name system for classifying organisms, earlier systems were not applied uniformly. For instance, the name of a particular organism might differ from one source to another, resulting in confusion. Linnaeus's system, on the other hand, was simple, uniform, and easy to use. According to his system of binomial nomenclature, first introduced in 1747, every plant or animal received two names (in Latin or Greek)—one for the genus and the other for the species. The consistent use of this system made it easy for scientists to recognize a particular plant or animal, no matter what common name it might have. For example, *Canis familiaris* is the scientific name for dog, while *Canis lupus* is the name for wolf. Linnaeus recognized three other levels of scientific classification—order, class, and kingdom. (Later scientists added two more: family and phylum). Each of these could be divided into subgroups, providing a very specific system by which to classify all organisms.

Linnaeus's classification system for plants was much better than those for animals and minerals. Nevertheless, his work marked a considerable advance over earlier classifications. The first to recognize whales as mammals, he also noted the link between humans and apes. He also made important contributions to paleontology* and historical geology, describing many fossils and accurately classifying various fossil species.

His work was accepted by scientists throughout the world, and his ideas influenced generations of future biologists. Although modern scientists have devised more accurate systems of classification, Linnaeus's accomplishments laid the foundation for their work.

* **paleontology** science that deals with prehistoric plants and animals through the study of fossils and other remains

Colin
MACLAURIN

1698–1746
MATHEMATICS

* **calculus** advanced form of mathematics that involves computing quantities that change as functions of different variables

* **conics** branch of geometry that deals with the curves formed by the intersection of a plane, or flat surface, with a circular cone, ellipse, parabola, or hyperbola

A disciple of the English physicist Isaac NEWTON, the Scottish mathematician Colin Maclaurin helped develop and extend Newton's work in calculus*, geometry, and the laws of gravitation. Perhaps one of his best-known accomplishments was the introduction of the Maclaurin series to solve problems in conics*.

Born in Kilmodan, Scotland, Maclaurin was the son of a Protestant minister. At the age of 11 Maclaurin entered the University of Glasgow, where he became very much interested in mathematics, showing a remarkable aptitude for the subject. Awarded a master's degree in 1715, Maclaurin was appointed professor of mathematics at Marischal College in Aberdeen, Scotland, two years later. This appointment, made when Maclaurin was still only a teenager, marked the beginning of a brilliant mathematical career.

In 1719 Maclaurin traveled to London, where he met many scientists—including Newton—and was elected to England's Royal Society. The following year, he published *Geometrica organica* (Organic Geometry). Maclaurin's most important work, the book deals with the general properties of conics and of certain types of curves. It contains proofs of many important theorems, some of which were found in Newton's famous work *Principia* (but without proofs) and others discovered by Maclaurin himself.

In 1722 Maclaurin left Scotland to serve as companion and tutor to the son of a nobleman in Cambrai, France. They visited Paris, where Maclaurin engaged in a period of intense mathematical activity. His efforts resulted in the publication of *On the Percussion of Bodies,* for which he won a prize from France's Académie des Sciences. In 1724 the sudden death of Maclaurin's pupil caused him to return to Aberdeen, where he discovered that his position at Marischal College was no longer available. He then accepted a professorship of mathematics at the University of Edinburgh, a position for which he was recommended by Newton. There Maclaurin lectured on a wide range of topics including geometry, trigonometry, and astronomy.

In 1742 Maclaurin published *Treatise of Fluxions,* the earliest logical and systematic publication of Newton's methods. Written partly to silence criticism of Newton's ideas, it contains a geometrical framework for Newton's doctrine of fluid motion and his use of calculus in support of his ideas. The *Treatise* also contains solutions to several problems in geometry, an elaborate discussion of infinite series, and a remarkable investigation of the series of curves that bears his name—Maclaurin series. The work also contains the correct theory for distinguishing between maximum and minimum values of a mathematical function.

Maclaurin was also a skilled experimenter; he constructed valuable astronomical observations and devised several mechanical devices. He also took part in improving maps of the Orkney and Shetland Islands, north of Scotland. Maclaurin also became involved in political matters. When an army from the Scottish Highlands marched to Edinburgh during an uprising in 1745, Maclaurin organized the city's defenses, planning and supervising the construction of fortifications. When the city fell to the rebels, he fled to England. Although he returned soon after, his health had been undermined by his efforts during the crisis, and he died shortly after his return.

Marcello MALPIGHI

1628–1694

MEDICINE, ANATOMY

* **vivisection** practice of dissecting or cutting into the body of a living animal

* **naturalist** student of natural history, the systematic study of natural objects, especially in their natural settings

The Italian physician and biologist Marcello Malpighi, considered one of the founders of the science of plant anatomy, made many valuable observations on the structure of animals and plants. Using different types of lighting and degrees of magnification, he developed techniques in microscopic observation that revolutionized the field of anatomy. Malpighi also pioneered the study of abnormal tissues to gather information about normal tissues.

Early Life and Career. Born in Crevalcore, Italy, Malpighi entered the University of Bologna in 1646. On the advice of his tutor, the philosopher Francesco Natali, he began to study medicine. He attended various private schools in pursuit of his medical education and was one of a select group of students allowed to attend dissections and vivisections*.

Malpighi received doctoral degrees in both medicine and philosophy in 1653. Three years later he began teaching as a lecturer in logic at the University of Bologna. At the end of the first year, however, he accepted a position as professor of medicine at the University of Pisa. The three years that Malpighi spent in Pisa were crucial to the formation of his scientific pursuits. Influenced by the mathematician and naturalist* Giovanni BORELLI and the ideas of Galileo GALILEI, he began to question many of the traditional medical and scientific teachings at the university.

In 1659 Malpighi left Pisa and returned to Bologna to teach medicine and continue his research. At this time Malpighi made one of the major discoveries in the history of medicine. While studying frogs under a microscope, he identified a network of tiny tubes in the lungs that connected the arteries and veins. Malpighi published his findings in *De pulmonibus* (On the Lung), which became one of his most important works. His discovery not only added to current knowledge of the lungs but also confirmed the theory first proposed by the English scientist William HARVEY concerning the circulation of blood through the body.

Further Discoveries. Malpighi's discoveries and growing fame led to jealousy on the part of many of his colleagues. Frustrated at the increasingly

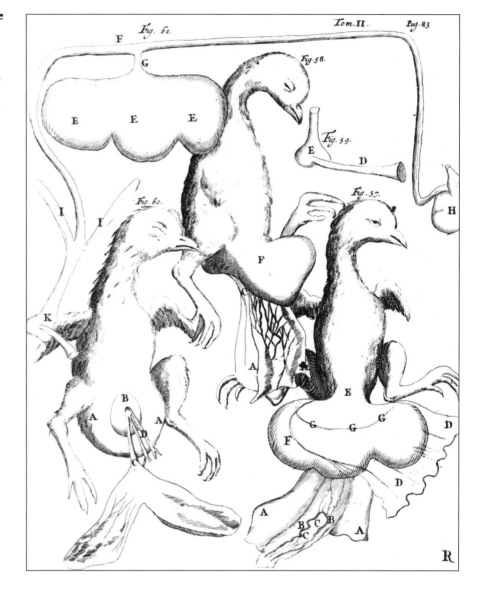

Marcello Malpighi revolutionized the field of anatomy with his observations on the microscopic structure of plants and animals. Also interested in animal embryology, he studied the development of chickens, silkworms, and other organisms. This drawing shows the early developmental stages of a chicken.

hostile environment at Bologna, he left there in 1662 and took a position as professor of medicine at the University of Messina, Sicily. There he enthusiastically continued his researches on anatomical structures, including studies of various marine animals.

Some of his most important studies during this period focused on the nervous system and the blood. Malpighi discovered that the central nervous system and the nerves are composed of the same type of fibers. He pictured these fibers as long, fine channels filled with a liquid—the nerve fluid—produced by glands in the brain. From his observations, Malpighi described the entire mechanism of the central nervous system, from the brain to the outer nerve endings.

In his study of blood, Malpighi discovered that it contains tiny red cells, known today as red corpuscles. The first to see these cells, Malpighi also correctly attributed the red color of blood to them. Another of his discoveries at Bologna involved the tongue and the sense of taste. While closely examining the surface of the tongue, he noticed that it has many small bumps. He speculated that these were sensory receptors that were stimulated by particles in saliva and produced the various sensations of taste. Today these receptors are known as the taste buds.

Later Life and Career. Malpighi returned to Bologna in 1667 and spent most of his remaining career there, continuing to make important discoveries. He discovered microscopic subdivisions in the liver, spleen, kidneys, and other organs and concluded that all organs are composed of tiny glands that separate or mix different types of bodily juices.

Around this time Malpighi also began to study plants. He concluded that plants have anatomical structures similar to those of animals. He published his findings in a work titled *Anatome plantarum* (Anatomy of Plants), which earned him acclaim as one of the founders of plant anatomy.

Malpighi also became interested in animal embryology*. He studied the development of chickens in eggs and observed the stages through which a silkworm is formed. He helped to clarify the structural development of higher life forms. In later studies Malpighi observed abnormal tissues, such as warts. His investigation of the breakdown of these tissues showed the effect of such disturbances on the organism as a whole.

In his final years Malpighi struggled with declining health and personal problems. Many of his colleagues still refused to accept his work, and the climax to this opposition came in 1684, when his home was burned and all his books, manuscripts, and other possessions were destroyed. In 1691 Pope Innocent XII invited Malpighi to Rome to become his personal physician. Malpighi died there three years later.

* **embryology** science that deals with the formation, development, structure, and function of embryos, or organisms in the early stages of their development

---

Edmé
MARIOTTE

d. 1684

EXPERIMENTAL PHYSICS

* **optics** scientific study of the properties of light

Edmé Mariotte was a pioneer of experimental physics in France. His career consisted not of new breakthroughs in theory but of devising and carrying out careful experiments to investigate and confirm the properties of matter and energy. Although Mariotte's work generally built on the discoveries of other scientists, his contribution lay in recognizing the importance of those discoveries and what they might mean in practical terms. Mariotte turned his attention to a wide range of subjects, including vision, plant growth, optics*, air, weather, and hydraulics.

Entering the Academy. For most of his life Mariotte was an active member of the Académie des Sciences, which was founded by French scientists in 1666. In fact, his academy-related activities are almost all that is known about him, for no documentary evidence about his family, birth, or education survives. Indirect evidence suggests that he might have been born in the Burgundy region of France and become a member of the clergy of the Roman Catholic Church.

Mariotte left no biographical information about the dawn of his interest in science or about how he received his scientific training, although it seems likely that he was self-taught. All that is known is that in the mid-1660s, when he began corresponding with the academy, he was living in

Dijon, France. By the 1670s he had moved to Paris, where he spent the rest of his life.

Members of the academy apparently knew that Mariotte had developed a distinctive theory about the structure of plants. Consequently, soon after the academy was formed, its founders invited Mariotte to present his idea that sap circulated through plants in the same way as blood through animals. Around the same time, the academy made Mariotte a member, and in 1667 Mariotte presented the first part of his theory of plant structure, which was widely accepted during the 1670s.

In 1668 Mariotte wrote to the academy announcing his discovery of a blind spot in the eye at the place where light strikes the base of the optic nerve. This discovery caused Mariotte to abandon the traditional (and correct) view that images in the eye are formed on the layer of tissue known as the retina. Instead, Mariotte thought that they were formed on a coat of tissue behind the retina, through which the optic nerve passes. Other scientists of the time, while admitting that the blind spot was an important discovery, disagreed with his conclusion and continued to regard the retina as the seat of vision. The question was not reconciled during Mariotte's lifetime.

Soon after his study of the eye, Mariotte experimented with freezing and invented a new form of level* that used the surface of standing water as a horizontal reference point. He also made astronomical observations that confirmed astronomer Gian Domenico CASSINI's discovery of a spot on Jupiter and of a new satellite, Rhea, orbiting Saturn.

Major Works. In 1673 Mariotte published the first comprehensive work on the laws that govern the behavior of bodies on impact, titled *Traité de la percussion ou choc des corps* (Essay on Percussion or the Collision of Bodies). This work remained the standard treatment of this subject for many years. It illustrated Mariotte's ingenuity in creating experiments to test ideas. For example, he wanted to show that even seemingly hard materials, such as ivory, change their shape slightly under the pressure of an impact with a hard surface. In one experiment he covered a steel anvil with dust and dropped ivory balls onto it from varying heights. The circles that the balls made in the dust differed in width. The balls had temporarily flattened slightly on impact, and the differing circle sizes showed that the degree of flattening was proportional to the speed of impact, which in turn was relative to the height from which the balls were dropped.

Mariotte next began experimenting with the properties of air. His 1679 work, *De la nature de l'air* (On the Nature of Air), like the earlier work on impact, reviewed and confirmed much of what was already known but added some original contributions. One section of the book discussed the principle of physics and chemistry that is sometimes called the volume-pressure law. Also discovered by Robert BOYLE in England, this principle is widely called Boyle's law, but in France it is Mariotte's law. The principle states that as the pressure on air increases, the volume occupied by the air shrinks, and that air expands as pressure decreases. Knowing that a gas expands and contracts when the temperature increases and decreases, Mariotte noted that this principle holds only if there is no change in temperature.

* **level** tool used to determine whether something is horizontally balanced

Color and light formed the next area of investigation for Mariotte, who believed that air was blue, not colorless. Experimenting with rays of light focused through prisms and glass spheres filled with water, Mariotte sought to explain the physics behind the appearance of rainbows. Although some of his conclusions were incorrect, Mariotte demonstrated an understanding of how heat and light interact with water vapor in air to create rainbows and other phenomena, including the coronas, or glowing rings, that sometimes appear to surround the sun and moon.

Diverse though it was, Mariotte's research reflected an overall interest in how bodies or fluids move and how they react to resistance. Even his minor works, such as a study of the behavior of cannonballs striking water, pursue this theme. Mariotte's final work, published two years after his death, united all of his research. It is *Mouvement des eaux* (Movement of Waters), a study of natural springs, artificial fountains, and the movement of water through pipes. The work begins with a review of the properties of air and water, including an account of the world's major winds and how they are produced by heating, cooling, and the rotation of the earth. This part of the *Mouvement* is notable for the large amount of meteorological* and geographical information that Mariotte gathered from around the world.

* **meteorological** pertaining to weather

One section of the *Mouvement* is based on Mariotte's study of fountains at Chantilly in northern France. Another section of the work deals with practical considerations for builders of reservoirs and fountains, such as the determination of the proper size of pipes for reservoirs of various heights. The only one of Mariotte's major works to be translated into English, the *Mouvement* remained for many years a standard practical guide to fountain construction.

Pierre Louis Moreau de MAUPERTUIS

1698–1759

MATHEMATICS, BIOLOGY, PHYSICS

* **mechanics** science that studies how energy and force affect objects

The French mathematician and scientist Pierre Louis Moreau de Maupertuis played an important role in popularizing the ideas of the English physicist Isaac NEWTON in France. He also made significant contributions of his own, including his formulation of the "principle of least action."

Born in Saint-Malo, France, Maupertuis was homeschooled until age 16. He later studied in Paris, where he developed an interest in mathematics. In 1728 Maupertuis traveled to London, where he discovered Newton's works and ideas and became a supporter of Newton's mechanics*. From this point Maupertuis became the foremost proponent of Newton's ideas in France.

In the late 1720s Maupertuis published his first work on Newtonian principles, *Discours sur les différentes figures des astres* (Discourse on Different Types of Heavenly Bodies). Around the same time he led a scientific expedition to northern Scandinavia to measure a degree of longitude near the North Pole. Another expedition set out from France to southern Peru to take similar measurements near the South Pole. Newton had surmised that the earth is flatter at the poles, and the measurements made on these expeditions helped verify that Newton was correct.

In the early 1740s Maupertuis was elected to scientific societies in Berlin and in France. Around this time he was engaged in research in biology. In a work published in 1745, he presented an argument against the then dominant biological theory of preformation, which stated that eggs and sperm contained "preformed" living organisms that simply enlarged into an embryo. Maupertuis argued that the embryo could not be "preformed" because hereditary characteristics can be equally passed down through either the male or the female parent. He also rejected the idea that some "essence" of one of the parents could affect the preformed embryo in the other parent.

The same year, Maupertuis accepted an invitation by King Frederick the Great of Prussia (in present-day Germany) to move to Berlin. There he was elected president of the Berlin Academy of Sciences, a position he held until 1753. His first contribution to the academy was a paper in which he set forth the famous "principle of least action," which states that all moving bodies in nature move along the most economical paths. A similar, more precisely formatted version of this principle had been advanced by Leonhard EULER.

In 1751 he published *Système de la nature* (System of Nature), which contains theories about heredity and the first careful analysis of the transmission of dominant traits in humans. Maupertuis founded a theory of the formation of the fetus and the nature of heredity that was at least a century ahead of its time. He theorized the existence of tiny hereditary particles, present in males and females, which come together by chemical attraction and account for the formation of hereditary traits.

Despite his achievements, his time at the Berlin academy was marred by recurring controversies. His friends turned against him and wrote savage attacks, mocking his work. Maupertuis left Berlin in 1753 and returned to France. Crushed by the insults, depressed by the outbreak of the Seven Years War in Europe, and suffering from poor health, Maupertuis died in 1759.

Gerardus MERCATOR

1512–1594
GEOGRAPHY, CARTOGRAPHY

* **theology** study of religion

Gerardus Mercator studied several scientific disciplines but gained fame for his achievements as a geographer and mapmaker. In making a map for seafarers, he set a new standard in cartography (mapmaking), and his technique became one of the most widely used in the world. The map projection that Mercator pioneered remains in use in modern cartography and navigation.

Becoming a Geographer. Named Gerhard Kremer, Mercator was born to a German family living in Rupelmonde, Flanders, in present-day Belgium. In 1530 he began attending the University of Louvain, Belgium, where he studied philosophy and theology*. At this time he began using the Latin version of his name, Gerardus, a common practice among students and learned people of the day.

After graduating from the university in 1532, Mercator spent time traveling before he returned to Louvain. He continued to study there, concentrating on geography, mathematics, and astronomy. Mercator received guidance in these subjects from a noted scholar named Gemma Frisius, and both he and Frisius spent time in the workshop of a jeweler and engraver. Mercator became skilled at engraving, the principal method then used for making illustrations and maps.

Mercator's earliest known cartographic work was a globe made in 1536. The following year he published his first printed map, which was of Palestine. His reputation as a cartographer was established in 1544, when he published a map of Europe. A world map and a map of Flanders followed. In addition to engraving, Mercator had mastered calligraphy, the art of elegant handwriting. After he published an influential handbook on the subject in 1540, other mapmakers adopted his style.

In 1544 Mercator was one of 43 citizens of Louvain charged with heresy*. His frequent absences from the city to gather information for his maps and his propensity for Protestantism had aroused suspicion. He spent seven months in prison until, eventually, the charges were dropped, and the authorities allowed him to resume his scientific and cartographic work. By this time Mercator was well known as a mapmaker, a maker of scientific instruments, and a surveyor*.

Contributions to Cartography. In 1552 Mercator moved to the city of Duisburg in present-day Germany, where he spent the rest of his life in high regard as a man of science and learning. Twelve years later the local ruler, the duke of Cleves, named Mercator his court cosmographer*. At Duisburg, Mercator continued to produce some of the finest maps of his time. Among them were the first modern maps of France, Germany, the

* **heresy** beliefs contrary to the doctrine of the established church

* **surveyor** one who measures land area and boundary lines

* **cosmographer** one concerned with cosmography, the science that describes the world or the universe

Gerardus Mercator became famous as a geographer, surveyor, and mapmaker. He developed the Mercator projection, which despite its polar distortion, is extremely useful for navigation at sea. This illustration shows Mercator (at left) conversing with another cartographer.

Netherlands, the Balkan region, Greece, and Britain. His most significant contributions to cartography were the Mercator projection and his atlas.

The projection was a technique Mercator first used in a map of the world that he published in 1569. His goal was to produce a map that could easily be used for navigation at sea, but like other cartographers before him, Mercator had to wrestle with the fact that the curved surface of the earth cannot be translated to a flat sheet of paper with complete accuracy. His solution was to project, or depict, the world on a rectangular map, with straight horizontal and vertical lines representing latitude and longitude, instead of the curved lines that earlier mapmakers had used. However, Mercator's projection is entirely accurate only at the equator—the greater the distance north or south of the equator, the more inaccurate the map becomes. The distortion is greatest near the poles: On a world map using the Mercator projection, Greenland looks far larger than it really is. The Mercator map was extremely useful at sea despite the distortion. Because its lines of latitude and longitude were straight, a navigator could use the map to plot a long course—across an entire ocean, if necessary—using a straight-line compass bearing, or line of travel, instead of making the frequent adjustments to the compass demanded by other maps. The Mercator projection remains an important navigational tool today.

Mercator's second major contribution was his grand atlas, or bound collection of maps. In 1578 he published a set of 27 maps based on the maps of Ptolemy, the ancient Greek astronomer. Several volumes of new European maps followed, and Mercator's son, Rumold, published the final volume the year after Mercator's death. Although Mercator was not the first cartographer to publish a set of maps in book form, he introduced the term *atlas* for such collections by using an illustration of the giant Atlas, a Greek mythological figure who bore the world on his shoulders, on the opening page of the book.

Marin MERSENNE

1588–1648

ACOUSTICS, OPTICS, PHILOSOPHY OF SCIENCE

* **optics** scientific study of the properties of light

* **theology** study of religion

Marin Mersenne was one of the most prominent early philosophical leaders of the scientific revolution. A champion of careful observation and precise experimentation, he also firmly believed that humans could only hope to understand the external effects of the natural phenomena they studied. He believed that it was impossible to uncover the causes of natural phenomena simply by studying their effects and that only God knew the true "nature of things." However, with careful observation and precise experimentation, one could hope to obtain enough knowledge about nature to guide one's actions. Knowledge thus obtained was the only true knowledge available to humans. He believed that if investigators throughout the ages had pursued such a philosophy, the "truth would not be so deeply sunken; nature would have taken off most of her envelopes." Mersenne not only devoted his energies to promoting this view of science but also made important scientific contributions of his own in music, acoustics, and optics*.

Mersenne began his studies at the Jesuit school in La Flèche, France, and later studied theology* at the Sorbonne in Paris. At the age of 23 he left the Sorbonne to join the order of monks known as the Minims. Eight years later he returned to Paris and took up residence at the Minim Convent de l'Annonciade, where he spent the rest of his life. His earliest scientific publications featured discussions of ancient and modern science in which he defended orthodox religion against "atheists, magicians, deists, and suchlike." In his writings he supported the ideas of the ancient Greek philosopher Aristotle, who believed that nature was rational (based on reason) and understandable. However, unlike Aristotle, he felt that nature was a mechanism that operated according to quantitative laws that could be understood only through careful observation. Nevertheless, knowing how nature operated did not explain why it operated as it did. Mersenne's response to the controversy over the system of the universe proposed by Nicholas COPERNICUS provides an example of his philosophy. At first he rejected Copernicus's ideas on the earth's motion because he did not think that Copernicus had offered enough evidence to support his theory. Although Mersenne later supported Copernicus's theory as the most probable explanation, he denied that one could generalize from the motions that Copernicus observed to build an entire theory of how the universe was structured. He did not say that Copernicus's theory was wrong, just that it could not be proved from the information Copernicus had gathered.

Mersenne's own scientific research was concentrated in the areas of music, acoustics, and optics. He did not accept any of the current theories of light and sound but agreed with René DESCARTES that these phenomena must be produced by physical motions. He was interested in the effects of sound and vision on the senses and their impact on the soul. He argued that an animal's experience of sight and sound must be different from that of humans, because animals merely react like robots to the stimuli they receive. Because he believed that humans, who possess souls, clearly have emotional responses to sights and sounds, Mersenne hoped to find a rational explanation for those moods and feelings. His explorations in optics included experiments on visual acuity (sharpness) and binocular vision. Concerning sound, Mersenne began by showing that the pitch of a note is proportional to the frequency of the sound wave that produces it. Thus, musical intervals, such as octaves, are always fixed ratios of the frequency of sound waves. He measured the frequency of sound waves by plucking very long strings on a musical instrument and timing their vibrations. He also developed calculations to determine the frequency of strings whose vibrations were too fast to count. Mersenne thus uncovered the mathematical laws for the production of sound waves that explained such phenomena as resonance* and dissonance*. He measured the speed of sound and realized that it was unrelated to pitch or loudness, and he determined that the intensity of a sound is inversely proportional to the distance from its source.

Mersenne's greatest contribution to the new science of the 1600s was his role as a clearinghouse for new ideas. He was in contact with many of the important scientists of his day and served as a conduit for the exchange of views between scientists who were often located at enormous distances from one another. Blaise PASCAL, Descartes, Galileo GALILEI, Pierre de FERMAT, and the philosopher Thomas Hobbes were part of Mersenne's influential circle of scientific correspondents.

* **resonance** intensification or prolongation of a sound produced by combining vibrations of a similar frequency

* **dissonance** harsh or inharmonious mixture of sounds

Mersenne had a vision of all sciences as an interlocking whole whose secrets are revealed when researchers from all fields share the knowledge they gain by closely studying the natural world. He said that it was almost impossible to separate the sciences, "for they would rather suffer than be torn apart; and if anyone persists in doing so, he gets for his trouble only imperfect and confused fragments." His most important contribution to science was this vision and his belief that knowledge could be realized only though a never-ending emphasis on precise experimentation and observation. He followed this philosophy in his own work, encouraged it in his colleagues, and inspired it in future generations of scientists.

Giovanni Battista
MORGAGNI
1682–1771
MEDICINE, ANATOMY

Giovanni Battista Morgagni was one of the leading anatomists of his day, whose close observations with the microscope led to a new interpretation of the workings of living organisms. In 1706 he published a work in which he noted many new discoveries about very small structures, such as the glands of the trachea (windpipe) and the human reproductive organs. However, his most important work was a book he published much later in life. In it he declared that every living organism is comprised of several mechanical systems, all of which must operate in harmony for the smooth functioning of the organism. Morgagni also stated that organisms, like machines, will deteriorate and break down. Physical symptoms are the evidence of such breakdowns, which often occur at such a minute level that they can be investigated only with a microscope.

In discussing the origin and course of diseases, Morgagni also considered environmental and psychological factors as well as physical ones. For his work in this field, Morgagni is sometimes called the founder of pathological anatomy.

Isaac
NEWTON
1642–1727
MATHEMATICS, PHYSICS, ASTRONOMY

* **optics** scientific study of the properties of light

* **calculus** advanced form of mathematics that involves computing quantities that change as functions of different variables

The English physicist and mathematician Isaac Newton is widely regarded as the most important figure in the scientific revolution. As a physicist he formulated the three fundamental laws of motion that form the basis of modern physics. These laws also led him to develop a universal law of gravity. Newton was the first to determine that white light is composed of lights of various colors, and his investigations into light laid the foundations of the modern science of optics*. As a mathematician he invented calculus* (along with Wilhelm LEIBNIZ), permitting mathematicians to analyze physical phenomena. His ideas revolutionized notions about nature and have dominated scientific thought for hundreds of years.

Life and Career

Despite his scientific triumphs Newton displayed a lifelong insecurity and defensiveness in his dealings with other scholars. He engaged in bitter disputes with fellow scientists over credit for discoveries. He had a difficult time accepting criticism and often reacted to it with irrational rage. More than once he ended correspondence with colleagues because of comments that most would accept as valid and constructive. Newton's biographers have attributed much of this behavior to the circumstances of his childhood, whose influence he apparently never overcame.

Early Life and Career. Newton began life in a single-parent household in Woolsthorpe, England, his father having died just three months before his birth. In addition, Newton was a premature baby who was given little chance of survival. He later remarked that he could have fit into a quart-sized mug at birth. When Newton was two years old, his mother remarried, and shortly thereafter left the young Isaac in the care of his aged maternal grandmother and moved to another village with her new husband. Newton was thus abandoned by both his parents early in life, and few doubt that this had a permanent impact on his relations with others in later life.

As a boy Newton attended local schools, where he showed an early interest in mechanical devices. He constructed model clocks and lanterns and even built a replica of a mill, powered by a mouse. After her husband died, Newton's mother returned to Woolsthorpe and decided that her son should take care of the family farm. He proved to have no aptitude for or interest in such work, and at the urging of his uncle and his schoolmaster, he was permitted to prepare for a university education.

At age 19 Newton entered Trinity College at Cambridge University, during the height of the scientific revolution. However, instruction at Trinity was firmly entrenched in the outdated theories of the Greek philosopher Aristotle, including his belief that the earth was at the center of the universe. Trinity also neglected the mathematical approach to studying nature embraced by the new generation of European scientists. During this time Newton began to read the works of prominent scholars, such as the German astronomer Johannes KEPLER and the French mathematician and philosopher René DESCARTES. He compiled a set of notes, titled *Questiones quaedam philosophicae* (Certain Philosophical Questions), in which he recorded his thoughts and observations about the different ideas he encountered. These notes reveal that Newton was beginning to question and challenge the Aristotelian theories promoted in his university courses. Around this time he also began the close study of mathematics that eventually resulted in his discovery of calculus.

Newton received his bachelor's degree in 1665. Later that year, because of an outbreak of the plague that lasted nearly two years, the university was closed. Although Newton was forced to return home and continue his studies on an informal basis, it was an important time for the development of his ideas. During these years he did the work that led directly to the invention of calculus. He also performed the experiments that resulted in his theories of color and light. It was also at this time that perhaps the most celebrated story in the history of science took place. Newton claimed that the idea for the theory of gravity came to him when he saw an apple fall from a tree near his home. Almost all of his greatest ideas trace their roots to this period of Newton's life, but it was years before any of them became known to the public.

Productive Years. Newton returned to Trinity after the plague had subsided, and in 1668 he received his master's degree. The following year he was appointed Lucasian professor at the college. He was required to give at least one lecture a week in every term and to deposit his lectures (in written form) in the university library. Newton lectured in mathematics, optics, arithmetic, and algebra. However, he was not a successful lecturer, and as one colleague recalled, "so few went to hear him and fewer that understood him, that ofttimes he did in a manner, for want of hearers, read to the walls." His brief lectures (he often spent less than five minutes in an often empty lecture hall) gave him more time to pursue his other areas of inquiry. It was during these years that he worked on the books that would establish his reputation—*Opticks* and *Philisophiae Naturalis Principia Mathematica* (Mathematical Principles of Natural Philosophy). He also invented a telescope based on the reflection of light by mirrors rather than its refraction* through lenses. Although he was unknown in the scientific community at the time, his demonstration of the telescope to London's Royal Academy of Sciences resulted in his election to that organization in 1671.

During the next 15 years, Newton devoted his energies to studies in mathematics, optics, and mechanics*. He published notes in all of these fields that often led to disputes with fellow scientists. For instance, he engaged in a nasty, long-running argument with Robert HOOKE after Hooke dismissed Newton's original theory of color. Hooke later accused Newton of stealing ideas that appeared in his paper about the properties of light. The two men settled this particular dispute, but they again came into conflict when Newton submitted the manuscript of the first book of the *Principia* to the Royal Society. Hooke claimed, without merit, that Newton had plagiarized* an essential element of his theory of gravity. Newton responded by taking out of the manuscript every mention of Hooke and Hooke's contributions to the *Principia*.

Later Life and Career. Publication of the *Principia* established Newton's reputation internationally. Although defenders of the mechanistic philosophy of René Descartes resisted Newton's ideas, they admired his scientific abilities. In England, Newtonian ideas completely captured the learned community, and Newton's followers were installed in the scientific professorships at all the universities. It was around this time that the seeds of Newton's second great academic dispute were sown.

During the 1670s Newton had worked on calculus, leaving notes of his results with the Royal Society. However, he did not publish the methods that he used to obtain those results. Meanwhile, the German scientist Wilhelm Leibniz had also been working independently to develop calculus. Newton sent Leibniz a letter outlining some of his results, but again he mentioned nothing of his methods. Leibniz, realizing how similar Newton's ideas were to his own, rushed to publish his methods to secure credit for being the first to come up with the idea. When Leibniz published his methods in 1684, Newton cried foul, claiming that Leibniz had taken his ideas from Newton's previous work.

Newton began a campaign to smear Leibniz's reputation, writing articles attacking Leibniz and publishing them under the names of his colleagues

* **refraction** deflection of a light ray or energy wave as it passes at different speeds through media of different densities

* **mechanics** science that studies how energy and force affect objects

* **plagiarize** to steal and use the writings or ideas of another as if they were your own

in England. Newton, who by this time was president of the Royal Society, handpicked a committee to determine who deserved credit for the discovery. He also determined what evidence the committee should see and even wrote the final report himself; it was published anonymously. Not surprisingly, the report found in favor of Newton. Even this, however, did not reduce Newton's ill feelings toward Leibniz. He held a grudge about the matter for nearly 25 years, and only his death brought it to an end.

Newton's scientific creativity waned considerably after the release of the *Principia*. With the exception of two important revisions of the *Principia,* which appeared in 1713 and 1726, he published no more important papers for the remainder of his life. He became increasingly involved in politics, serving as a member of Parliament. He successfully opposed the attempt of the Catholic king James II to force the admission of a Benedictine monk to the university. In 1696 he was appointed warden of the royal mint to oversee coinage and prosecute counterfeiters. Seven years later he became president of the Royal Academy, a position in which he continued to make enemies. Late in his career he had a running argument with the astronomer John FLAMSTEED, and at one point he tried to force the publication of Flamsteed's star catalog. Newton even stole his work and gave it to Flamsteed's enemy, Edmond HALLEY, for publication. Flamsteed sued and won the return of his materials and the right to burn the copies that had already been printed. Newton, in a typical response, rewrote later editions of the *Principia* to remove any references to the help that Flamsteed had given to its preparation.

Toward the end of his life, Newton devoted much energy to studies of alchemy*, theology*, and religious prophecy. Some have suggested that Newton's earlier scientific works were influenced by such mystical and religious beliefs. Although there have been some promising starts, scholars have yet to work out any deep connections among Newton's alchemical, religious, and scientific works. Others have said that his late interest in these areas was a product of his increasingly agitated state of mind and suggested that he may have suffered from severe psychological problems. It is true that he suffered at least one nervous breakdown, and possibly two, during his life. However, it is difficult to know to what extent, if any, his later activities were driven by mental problems. He continued to serve as president of the Royal Society and warden of the mint until his final days. He died in 1727 after a brief illness.

Scientific Accomplishments

Newton's greatest contribution to science lies in his discovery of the laws of motion as outlined in his masterpiece, the *Principia*. The discoveries that he sets forth in the *Principia* were possible largely because of his use of calculus, which he also invented.

Development of the Principia. Newton's undergraduate notebooks reveal that he had begun to think about the problems of dynamics* and planetary motion from an early age. They show that he was familiar with the work of early astronomers, such as Kepler and Galileo GALILEI, as well

* **alchemy** medieval form of chemical science, especially one that sought to turn base metals into gold or silver or transform something common into something special

* **theology** study of religion

* **dynamics** study of the relationship between motion and the forces affecting motion

Newton the Mystic

Newton displayed a long-standing interest in mystical studies, such as alchemy and prophecy, much of which is in stark contrast to his scientific writing. Some of the projects he pursued included an attempt to decipher what he considered the "figurative language" used by the biblical prophets. He also explored the question of whether Jesus sent his apostles out to teach metaphysics to his followers. In all, his writings contain some 650,000 words on alchemy and 1,300,000 on theology and prophecy.

as the laws of motion set forth by Descartes. They also show that he had begun to question the accuracy of some of these theories. He was particularly critical of Descartes's principles of motion, which assumed that motion was caused by an external force, because Newton was convinced that all bodies possess an inherent tendency toward motion. He also objected to Descartes's laws of impact because they assumed that colliding bodies were perfectly hard, meaning that when they collided, they made contact at only a single point. Descartes also maintained that at the time of impact, a moving body transfers its entire motion to the object with which it collides. Newton, however, recognized that "bodyes here amongst us" have "a relenting softnesse and springynesse," so that when they collide, they are touching at more than one point for a short time. He also realized that the body being struck not only receives a force at impact but also imparts an equal force to the body striking it. This gave rise to one of the laws of motion stated later in the *Principia,* that every action is countered by an equal and opposite reaction.

Another event, mentioned earlier, led Newton to the idea of gravitation, an integral part of the *Principia.* Newton was aware of the phenomenon of centrifugal force, in which a body moving in a circular path has a tendency to move away from the point around which it rotates. The body tends to move along a tangent to its circular path—that is, along a straight line that touches the outside of the circle but does not intersect it. For example, the moon exhibits the effects of centrifugal force in its orbit around the earth. However, some other force opposes centrifugal force, clearly pulling the moon toward the earth, keeping it in orbit, and preventing it from flying off into space. One day, when Newton saw an apple fall from a tree, he realized that the same force that pulls the moon toward the earth attracted the apple as well. This gave him an insight into one of the basic laws of planetary motion, called the inverse square law. That law states that the acceleration of a falling body is inversely proportional to the square of the distance from the center of the body toward which it is falling. Consequently, as an orbiting body moves farther from the body it is orbiting, the force attracting it to that body becomes weaker. As it approaches the center, the force becomes stronger.

Newton made this discovery by combining the law of centrifugal force with Kepler's third law of motion. Using Kepler's law, he calculated the distance from a planet to the sun, based on the duration that it takes the planet to revolve once around the sun. Using a formula he derived by combining these two laws, Newton set out to determine the acceleration of the moon toward the earth and measure the force of gravity. Knowing the radius of the earth and the distance from the earth to the moon, Newton calculated that the apple was 60 times closer to the center of the earth than the moon was. Thus, the acceleration of the moon toward the earth was $1/(60 \times 60)$ or 1/3,600 the acceleration of the apple. He then measured his result against the time it takes the moon to make one full revolution around the earth and found that the two figures were in general agreement. The numbers did not match exactly because Newton's measure of the radius of the earth was inaccurate.

It was not until nearly 20 years later that Newton came to fully understand dynamics, which then enabled him to discover the basic laws of motion and gravity. The stimulus for this event was a correspondence with Hooke in which Newton claimed that a body falling freely toward the earth would move in a spiral motion. Hooke countered with his argument that such a body would follow an elliptical (oval) path, not a spiral one. Newton refused to accept this argument, but at Hooke's insistence he decided to seek out the answer. To this end Newton first imagined a body moving from one point to another along an elliptical orbit. He then determined the position of the body after a short time if it continued to move on a path that was tangential to the ellipse rather than remaining on the elliptical path. He knew that the attractive force of the object around which the body was rotating would deflect the orbiting body from the tangent; that is, it would force the body to keep moving along the ellipse. Newton assumed that the distance of the deflection of the body would be proportional to the inverse square of its distance from the object it was orbiting. He then measured the distance between the object the body was orbiting and the point on the tangent where the body would be if it were not deflected by the attraction. Calculations based on these assumptions yielded results that matched Newton's predictions and showed that the orbit was indeed an ellipse. This provided mathematical confirmation of the inverse square law.

Newton's announcement of his discovery of the inverse square law set off a furious controversy between himself and Hooke. In earlier correspondence Hooke had proposed something similar but had assumed that it was necessary to measure the distance from the position the body occupied while in its orbit around the object. Newton proved that the measurement required was not from the orbit itself but from the tangent—the position the body would have occupied if the attractive force did not deflect it toward the object it was orbiting. Hooke's lack of mathematical skill prevented him from arriving at the correct solution. Nevertheless, he remained convinced that Newton had stolen his idea.

Laws of Motion. Newton was now ready to compile his ideas into a full treatise of motion—*Principia*. The book begins with a series of definitions, including the first proper definitions of mass, a quantity of matter in proportion to its bulk and density; momentum, the combined velocity and mass of an object; and inertia, a force that causes a body to resist a change in state. Newton also provided a definition of centripetal force along with several measures of the force. Building on his definitions, Newton outlined three basic laws of motion. The first is the law of inertia, which states that an object will resist any change in state unless acted on by an outside force. Thus, objects at rest tend to remain at rest, while objects moving in a particular direction tend to continue moving in that direction. The second is the law of conservation of momentum, which states that the change in a body's motion is proportional to the force applied to that body. If one object strikes another object, the combined motion of both objects after the collision will be equal to the total force at impact. The third law states that for every action there is an equal and opposite reaction.

What truly distinguished the *Principia* from previous treatises on planetary motion was that earlier works considered only the attraction of bodies toward a fixed center. However, Newton recognized that all bodies exert such an attractive force on each other. Consequently, when one body orbits another, they attract each other mutually because the bodies orbit around a common center of gravity located somewhere between them. Earlier laws of planetary motion failed to consider this fact. Newton also noted that this mutual attraction causes the earth to wobble on its axis and is responsible for observed irregularities in the orbit of the moon. Both of these phenomena had been noted long before Newton's time, but he was the first to offer a mathematical model whose predictions matched actual observations.

Book II of the *Principia* deals with the motion of bodies in resisting media. In this book Newton examines such topics as the elasticity and compressibility of gases and fluids. He also describes fluids as being composed of "particles fleeing from one another," although he ultimately admitted that he could not prove it was so, even by using the mathematical approach he adopted throughout the *Principia*. Other topics examined in Book II include the motion of fluids and the propagation of waves in a fluid medium, such as air or water. In this section Newton shows that vibrations in the air cause sound. In the next section of the book, he examines the motion of waves and concludes that although a wave moves forward, the particles of the medium in which it moves do not move with the wave front; instead, they vibrate around a fixed position. The last section of Book II deals with vortices and addresses the question of whether planets travel in their orbits because of the action of vortices, as Descartes had argued. Newton showed that "the hypothesis of vortices is utterly irreconcilable with astronomical phenomena."

Isaac Newton's three laws of motion form the basis of modern physics. He also discovered the universal law of gravity, invented calculus, and created theories about the properties of light and color. This illustration shows Newton presiding at a meeting of England's Royal Society.

The System of the World. In the final book of the *Principia,* Newton brings together the observations of the first two books to propose a "system of the world" that attempts to explain the motions of the planets, comets, and the tides. He stated that a single force, called gravity, causes all these types of motion. Newton proposed a universal law of gravitation, according to which there is a power of gravity that causes planets to be pulled (gravitate) toward their satellites. This force also causes all planets to gravitate toward one another and causes falling objects to accelerate toward the earth. He then showed that tides occur as a result of the gravitational pull that the sun and the moon exert on the oceans on the earth's surface. The gravitational pull of the moon has two additional effects on the earth—it causes the earth to bulge slightly at the equator and to wobble on its axis.

Toward the end of Book III, Newton showed that the movement of comets through the solar system indicates that "the celestial spaces are void of resistance" and that comets move in an elliptical orbit around the sun. Book III represents the first attempt to construct a unified system to explain all of the phenomena of celestial motion as the result of a single force—gravity. This monumental achievement formed the basis of modern physics, and Newton's laws and systems remained largely unchanged until the discoveries made by Albert Einstein some 200 years later.

Scientific Accomplishments: Mathematics and Optics

The laws and propositions in the *Principia* relied on accurate mathematical calculations that were made possible by the second of Newton's great achievements, the discovery of calculus. His other great contribution to science was *Opticks,* a book in which he sets forth the basic principles of light.

The Calculus. Accurately determining the basic laws of motion, particularly planetary motion, was complicated by the limits of the available mathematical procedures. Measuring any type of curved or circular motion requires the accurate determination of the slopes of curves as well as the areas enclosed by circles and various types of curves. The classic approach to solving such problems employed a method known as the use of infinitesimals. This involved inscribing a large square in a circle and then inscribing other squares in the area of the circle not covered by the first square. Eventually, so little of the space in the circle was not filled by squares that any additional squares one attempted to inscribed would be infinitely small, and thus insignificant. By summing the area of all the inscribed squares, one could approximate the area of the circle. To calculate the area of a circle, the area under a curve, or the volume of a curved solid, it was necessary to go through this painstaking, and usually approximate, process.

Newton's discovery of the calculus began with his reading of Descartes's classic work *La Géométrie,* which contains the techniques of analysis used in algebra to solve problems in geometry. He then moved beyond Descartes to develop his own method of analysis that used the method of infinitesimals to find the slopes of curves and the area under curves. Newton applied this new calculus to his study of the problems of planetary motion. Although the mathematics of the *Principia* is presented in the familiar geometrical style of the day, the book's triumph would have been impossible if not for the use of calculus.

Optics. Newton's work in optics first gained notice when he invented and demonstrated the first reflecting telescope for London's Royal Society. The invention came about because of an experiment in which he shone light through a prism and noticed that it broke up into different colors. This result was expected, but Newton noticed that the image was oblong, not circular as he had expected. He then passed a beam of light of a single color through a second prism. To his surprise, it did not break down the beam into any additional colors. This led him to propose a theory of colors that stated that white light is comprised of a combination of all the colors of the rainbow. Until then it was assumed that sunlight was pure white and that colors, such as in a rainbow, were caused by reflection or refraction of white light from the objects it struck. Newton also concluded that refracting telescopes would always suffer from difficulties related to the tendency of their lenses to distort light like a prism. This led him to invent a telescope that enlarged images by reflecting them through curved mirrors rather than passing light through a lens.

Newton compiled his observations and theories about light into a book titled *Opticks,* in which he showed that the lights of different colors have different degrees of refraction. He demonstrated this by passing a beam of light through two prisms placed back-to-back and directing the refracted light of each color through a third prism. By turning the third prism in different directions, he was able to eliminate various colors, starting with blue and violet and continuing with green, yellow, orange, and red. The experiment led to the formation of the theory that the colors of the rainbow are produced when sunlight is refracted through raindrops at different angles. Newton also worked out the index of refraction for each type of colored light.

Through the description of another experiment in *Opticks,* Newton helped revive the wave theory of light. He observed that light passing through a pair of glass plates created a pattern in which concentric rings of color alternated with rings of darkness. The colors of the rings, known today as Newton rings, corresponded to the thickness of the layer of air between the plates. In addition, some colors, such as red, caused circles of light to extend to the edge of the lens, while others, such as blue and violet, did not. He concluded that the alternating light and dark rings indicated regions where the light was either reflected or transmitted. Thomas Young would later propose that the rings were produced by waves of light—the dark areas were places where light waves interfered with each other, canceling each other out. From this theory Young calculated the wavelengths of the main colors of the spectrum. His results were close to the values accepted today by modern physicists.

In addition to studying refraction of light, *Opticks* also examines questions on the relationship between light and heat as well as the nature of vision. Newton proposed that heat was caused by vibration and studied

The Eccentric Genius

Even when Newton was not warring with a rival, he displayed behavior that was considered quite strange during his day. One colleague recalled some of his odd habits. He ate little and often forgot to eat at all. He rarely dined with his colleagues at Cambridge, but when he did appear in the dining hall, he did so with "shoes down at heels, stockings untied, surplice [gown] on, and his head scarcely combed." He went to chapel quite seldom but often went to the local church. In a country known for its suspicion of foreigners, Newton received overseas guests "with a great deal of freedom, candor, and respect."

the question of why black bodies generate more heat that light-colored ones. He also discussed the causes of heat and speculated about heat and vapors in the sun and stars. Newton claimed that sight was the result of vibrations of the optic nerve, caused when the nerve is struck by light. The *Opticks* covers binocular vision and other aspects of sight. It also presents Newton's theory that light is emitted as particles or corpuscles. However, his experiment with concentric rings of light led him to suggest that waves were somehow involved in the propagation of light. His contradictory stance on this issue anticipated, albeit unintentionally, the modern notion that light exhibits properties of both particles and waves.

Opticks, the *Principia,* and the invention of calculus stand as monuments to Newton's scientific genius. No other scientist of his era, and few of any age, made so many important discoveries in as many fields as Newton. Modern science owes Newton a debt that has been repaid in the only way possible, by embracing and building on his theories and observations for the continuing advancement of scientific knowledge.

PARACELSUS

ca. 1494–1541

MEDICINE, CHEMISTRY,
NATURAL PHILOSOPHY

Paracelsus was one of the strangest and most controversial figures of Renaissance science. He barged loudly into the medical profession, outraging doctors and delighting students with his bold—sometimes obscene—rants against the reigning practices of the day. Finally forced out of several respectable academies, Paracelsus took to wandering through Europe, spreading his knowledge, ideas, and treatments where he could. His thought and practice were a remarkable mix of the rational and the mystical. He was a keen observer and experimenter who made important progress toward modern medicine, yet at the same time he developed complex theories about spiritual essences linking human health to the cosmos.

Family Background. "Paracelsus" is a nickname given in later life to the man born Theophrastus Philippus Aureolus Bombastus von Hohenheim. Scholars are uncertain about the origin and meaning of the nickname, but it may have meant "surpassing Celsus," a reference to the ancient Roman scholar Aulus Cornelius Celsus, whose works on illness, surgery, nutrition, and drugs made him a famous authority on classical medicine.

Paracelsus's father was William of Hohenheim, of the Bombast family of Swabia, a region in present-day Germany. William had an affair in Switzerland—with a slave who worked as a servant at an abbey there—resulting in the birth of a son. William was a practicing physician, and he took charge of Paracelsus's early education in mining, mineralogy, botany, and natural philosophy*. Paracelsus also studied with an abbot who introduced him to mystical theological* ideas. He found time as well to practice basic medicine in the mines of central Europe.

A Turbulent Career. Paracelsus probably studied medicine at various Italian universities, but it is uncertain whether he actually received a degree. He traveled often and found jobs as a military surgeon in Venice,

* **natural philosophy** development of theories to explain the natural world

* **theological** referring to theology, the study of religion

Scandinavia, the Middle East, and Rhodes. In his early 30s he drifted through the Germanic states of central Europe. During this time he practiced medicine and narrowly escaped trouble for sympathizing with the Peasants' War, in which rural laborers took up arms to demand the abolition of serfdom* and their right to hold common land.

His break came in Strasbourg (in present-day France), where he set up a practice. In 1527, called into Basel for a consultation, Paracelsus cured an important citizen's infected leg, for which local physicians had recommended amputation. He won the post of physician to the city of Basel and professor of medicine at the university, despite the disapproval of the university officials. They refused to accept him as a colleague because they believed that he showed disrespect by not swearing a required oath or submitting documents to prove his qualifications. Moreover, he lectured in German instead of Latin and allowed unlicensed doctors, known as barber-surgeons, into his classes. Paracelsus also spoke and wrote mightily to attack the traditional medicine taught by the other physicians. Rejecting the official doctrines and textbooks, he promised a new set of lessons based on his own firsthand experience as a researcher and physician.

A loud, rude, and imposing man, Paracelsus offended and alienated many people. He was angry, resentful, and uncompromising. He was often seen in lower-class taverns, drinking heavily and gathering knowledge

* **serfdom** form of slavery in which medieval European peasants were bound to work on the lands owned by aristocrats

Paracelsus was the first physician to reject the authority of ancient medical texts. Rather than search for a cause of an illness within the body, he looked for external causes that had entered the body.

about folk medicine. He would treat the poor for free but charged high rates for the rich. He criticized organized religion, attacked academic medicine as wasteful, and called on the world to follow his new ways of thinking. In 1528 he denounced a church official who refused to pay one of his enormous bills for treatment, and the authorities of Basel decided that they had had enough. Paracelsus was forced to leave town, and he never again received a professorship or even a steady job.

He moved on to other cities, finding work and patrons and writing the *Opus paramirum* (A Work Beyond Wonder). His stays were always tumultuous and brief. When he was able to set up a laboratory or lodge with prominent aristocrats who requested his help, Paracelsus continued his research and wrote papers about his findings. His own health failed him in 1541, and he died in Salzburg, Austria.

A Medical Revolution. In Paracelsus's time the medical profession was based on the work of the ancient Greek physician Galen, who held that the body had four natural humors, or fluids, that had to be in balance for an even temperament and good health. Treatments were usually attempts to restore this balance—for example, by draining blood.

Paracelsus was the first physician to reject the authority of ancient medical texts. Rather than search for a cause of an illness within the body's supposed natural state, he looked for external causes that had entered the body. Centuries later, modern medicine would equate this idea with viruses and bacteria. Paracelsus also looked outside the body for treatments, administering prepared doses of medicine. He took a careful, conservative approach to treatment, emphasizing the body's natural ability to heal with little intervention. A dedicated chemist, he often prescribed chemically prepared drugs in preference to the herbal medicines of ancient times. He invented laboratory techniques and chemical substances and was the first to attempt to organize chemicals according to their properties.

Paracelsus's influence on the development of science in the 1600s was his chemical philosophy, which was based on three fundamental elements—salt, sulfur, and mercury. This *tria prima* represented the principles of solidity, combustibility, and liquidity, which are inherent in all substances. However, Paracelsus was not really a scientist in the modern sense of objective inquiry and logical reasoning; he was a visionary, a spiritual mystic who developed a complex philosophy of the universe. He believed that all matter and living things had a vital spirit, a force of existence that was related to the light of stars. He found links of essence between each star and specific herbs, minerals, body organs, diseases, and remedies. Many of Paracelsus's ideas were influenced by folk rituals, certain early Christian philosophies, and other ways of thinking that were shunned by the religious and medical establishment.

Although Paracelsus was a fine doctor and an able chemist, resistance from authorities and his own uncompromising attitude prevented him from accomplishing much in his lifetime. However, he helped revive and reinterpret parts of scientific tradition that the authorities had previously suppressed. In doing so he made important progress in medicine and chemistry, and his influence on future scientists was profound. His ideas attracted naturalists and physicians including Johannes Baptista van HELMONT, Robert BOYLE, and Georg Ernst STAHL.

Ambroise PARÉ

ca. 1510–1590

SURGERY

* **cauterize** to seal and numb a wound by burning with high heat

Ambroise Paré, the son of an artisan, rose to become chief surgeon to the kings of France. In his youth he served as an apprentice to a barber-surgeon, a physician who lacked a university degree in medicine. Paré continued his studies in Paris and, when still in his 20s, became a master barber-surgeon and entered the French army, serving in Italy for two years.

During this tour of duty, Paré revolutionized the treatment of gunshot wounds. Until then doctors believed that bullet wounds were poisonous and had to be cauterized* with hot oil. But during one battle Paré ran out of oil, so he used a dressing made of egg yolk, oil of roses, and turpentine. The next day he realized that the soldiers who had received the dressing were healing better than those who had been cauterized. His paper on the subject, published in 1545, made him instantly famous.

Paré's other pioneering work included a new device for closing off blood vessels during amputations, as well as techniques for surgical births. His understanding of contagious infections and public health measures was crude by modern standards but advanced for his time. However, he labored under the ancient theories of human health, which were still held as true.

During his career Paré encountered great resistance from the French academic medical profession, which tried to exclude and humiliate barber-surgeons. However, Paré's skills were so great that he won the support of his aristocratic clients, and he was appointed chief surgeon to the kings Charles IX and Henry III. During the great religious and civil struggles that wracked France in his lifetime, Paré remained a Roman Catholic and a member of the royal court, but his concern for those who suffered always rose above politics.

Ambroise Paré revolutionized the treatment of gunshot wounds and developed a device for closing off blood vessels during amputations. This illustration shows Paré helping a wounded soldier.

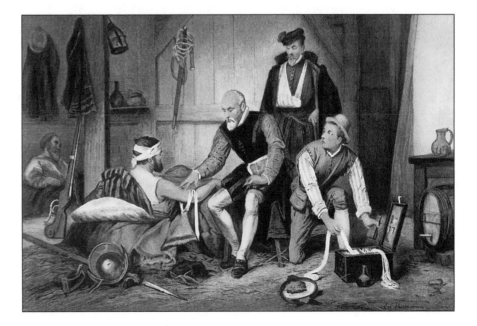

Blaise PASCAL

1623–1662

MATHEMATICS, PHYSICS, PHILOSOPHY

* **conic sections** geometric curves and shapes created by the intersection of a cone and a plane

* **projective geometry** field of mathematics that studies the properties of shapes viewed from different perspectives

* **analytic geometry** field of mathematics that uses algebra to study the properties and relations of points, lines, and shapes on a coordinate grid

Blaise Pascal was a brilliant, complex, and troubled man who began his astonishing career while still in his teens. He solved difficult problems in mathematics and physics and was the first to invent and sell a mechanical calculator. Meanwhile, he also struggled with illness, depression, and profound religious experiences. He participated in aggressive debates about religious controversies while privately writing a series of deeply personal reflections. Pascal accomplished all of this work by the age of 39, when a painful cancer ended his life and career.

A Child Joins the Scientific World. Pascal was born in the French village of Clermont-Ferrand. His mother, Antoinette Begon, died when Blaise was only three years old, and his father, Étienne, raised him and his two sisters. In 1631 the family moved to Paris. Pascal's father took charge of his education, and at 12 Pascal was mastering *Elements,* the classic work by the ancient Greek mathematician Euclid. By the age of 15, Pascal was participating in an academy founded by the prominent mathematician and philosopher Marin MERSENNE.

First Achievements in Geometry. Like others in the scientific circles of Paris, the young Pascal read the work of Girard Desargues on the study of conics, or conic sections*. Desargues's text was baffling to most—the ideas were highly original, and the writing style was uniquely personal. Yet Pascal appreciated its richness and potential and was inspired to work at exploring the field of projective geometry*.

In 1640 Pascal published a pamphlet called *Essay pour les coniques* (Essay on Conics), presenting his initial discoveries and outlining a grand plan for a major text on the subject. Pascal worked on this project in fits and starts over the next few years, developing a powerful vision of the capabilities of projective geometry. His work made a strong argument that, at least in the area of conics, projective geometry was as effective as analytic geometry*, which was favored by the influential French mathematician René DESCARTES. However, Pascal's pamphlet was not easy to obtain, and the larger work was never published, hindering the progress of projective geometry while analytic geometry became ever more dominant.

New Circumstances. In 1640 the family moved to the city of Rouen, where Pascal's father worked for the king. Pascal made a few brief visits to Paris over the next several years but continued his work in geometry and maintained his contacts with other mathematicians. In 1641 he began to suffer serious health problems that would return often for the rest of his life. During one period of ill health, he agreed to a suggestion that he spend some carefree time in Paris. At this time he doubtless tried his hand at the pastime of gambling, and some biographers suggest that these games inspired his later interest in the mathematics of chance.

While juggling these troubles and activities, Pascal turned much of his attention in Rouen to helping his father. Étienne's job required a great deal of arithmetic and accounting, and Pascal set out to invent a machine that could perform simple addition and subtraction. He pursued this goal with originality, practical sense, and stubbornness, despite frustrations and delays over the course of more than 50 rejected models. He finally chose a successful one in 1645. For the next few years, he supervised the manufacture, marketing, and sale of these complex and expensive machines, but historians are unsure how popular they were.

Pascal's restless mind also latched onto the current controversies in Christian religious philosophy. He had been a practicing Roman Catholic all his life, but in 1646 he became attracted to the doctrines of Jansenism, a controversial sect whose followers insisted that they were Catholics but whose beliefs closely resembled Protestantism. In its French form Jansenism called for a strict and pure life of the mind and body. This religious conversion had a great impact on Pascal's later life.

Experiments on Pressure and Vacuums. Just a few months after his religious upheaval, Pascal took up another scientific question—the study of pressure and vacuums recently pursued by the Italians Galileo GALILEI and Evangelista TORRICELLI and Pascal's old colleague, Mersenne. These scientists had conducted experiments in which they used a suction pump to create a vacuum that pulled columns of water or mercury up a glass tube. They found that the column would not exceed a certain height, yet this height changed depending on the altitude and weather at the trial site.

These experiments led to the invention of the hydraulic press and the syringe. They sparked debate among scientists across Europe. The main questions were whether vacuums really existed and whether air had weight. In 1647 Pascal conducted his own trials, but his work was interrupted by sickness. He left Rouen for Paris, where he wrote a report on his experiments and announced his affirmative answer to both questions. He argued that the weight of the surrounding air determined how high the mercury rose in the tube, even if a vacuum still existed at the top of the tube. He would prove to be on the right side of the controversy.

With the help of his brother-in-law, Pascal pursued experiments that led to the invention of the barometer. Pascal began to write a major text about vacuums, but this was never finished, and only a few fragments survive. He did complete a shorter work in early 1654. Although it was not highly innovative, it summed up the evidence with clear language and tight logic and remains a classic of scientific literature from the 1600s.

Late Concerns in Mathematics and Religion. In 1654 Pascal began to carry on a correspondence about games of chance with the French mathematician Pierre de FERMAT. Imagining a gambler throwing a die several times, they discussed how to calculate the probabilities of possible results. They also took up the more complex question of how to divide the stakes among several players if the game were interrupted at any point. Fermat solved the problems by analyzing all the possible combinations, while Pascal explored more theoretical solutions that drew on how the scenario developed with each repetition of the die throw. Pascal also took a philosophical approach—he pondered the link between decisions and chance, and the moral consequences of both.

Pascal again became troubled and dissatisfied with his worldly life and scientific pursuits. He was shaken by another powerful religious experience

Pascal's Contest

Late in his career, a prideful and mischievous Pascal started a contest for his fellow mathematicians. Anonymously, he challenged them to solve a difficult problem that he believed he had already mastered. The leading minds of the day took interest, including John Wallis, Christiaan Huygens, and Christopher Wren. With some bias, Pascal eliminated some responses from the contest, drawing heated protests. But the responses also fed his own ideas and helped him to develop solutions that were even more advanced.

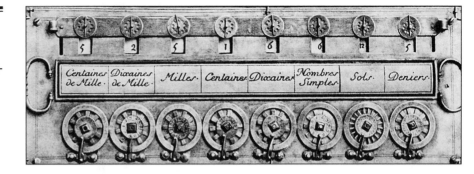

Blaise Pascal solved difficult problems in mathematics and physics. He also invented the barometer and the calculator. This illustration shows a design for a calculation machine, which Pascal produced and sold during the 1600s.

that he called a "night of fire," and he retreated to the Jansenist monastery to focus on religion and meditation. He never again published under his own name, always using a pseudonym. In 1657 he published a series of 18 letters attacking the religious order of the Jesuits. Although he left the monastery the following year, he continued to publish other religious writings. In private he worked on a defense of Christianity intended for nonbelievers and on a collection of literary and philosophical fragments. The latter was published after his death under the title *Thoughts* and became his most famous book.

As Pascal's friends in Paris encouraged him to return to scientific work, he turned to a last series of brilliant studies. He devoted more than a year to an idea called the theory of indivisibles, which enabled him to study problems involving infinitesimals, or very small values. He applied the theory to calculating the lengths of curves, the areas and volumes of shapes and forms, and their centers of gravity. As he prodded his colleagues to work on these problems and learned of their results, he added to his own work and developed the complexity of his ideas.

Pascal's work was a crucial influence on the discovery of integral calculus* by the German mathematician Wilhelm LEIBNIZ. But Pascal never made that leap himself, partially because he refused to use the algebraic methods of Descartes, and also because he abandoned his work just as it was flowering. He fell ill again in 1659 and threw himself back into prayer and charitable service. Two years later Pascal had a falling out with his Jansenist friends. He seemed to yearn for solitude, but oddly, he also involved himself in a business plan to provide public transportation on the streets of Paris. A final illness struck when a cancerous growth in his stomach spread to his brain; Pascal died in terrible pain.

* **integral calculus** advanced method of mathematics that finds the expression of a function from the description of how the function changes

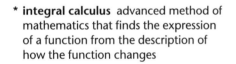

Joseph
PRIESTLEY

1733–1804

CHEMISTRY, ELECTRICITY

During his lifetime the English minister Joseph Priestley acquired a reputation for his unorthodox theological* and political views, but as a scientist he is best remembered for his discovery of oxygen. In addition to his work with gases, Priestley also published comprehensive accounts of recent investigations into electricity and optics* and several important books on English grammar and the art of public speaking. Priestley's scientific explorations also laid the foundations for many important discoveries in the field of chemistry.

* **theological** referring to theology, the study of religion

* **optics** scientific study of the properties of light

* **natural philosophy** development of theories to explain the natural world

Life and Career. Priestley spent his early childhood in the house of his maternal grandparents. When he was six, he was sent to live with his aunt after his mother's death. A very bright child, he was encouraged to study for a career in the ministry. In addition to his courses at school, Priestley taught himself ancient languages, mathematics, and natural philosophy*. At age 19 he entered the academy at Daventry, where he was introduced to methods of investigation based on the comparison of texts with conflicting information. At Daventry he developed a philosophy that emphasized reducing phenomena to their most basic elements. As a utilitarian one of his main goals was to determine the practical benefits of scholarly research. This philosophy guided his work.

After completing his education, Priestley took up preaching, but he encountered difficulties because of a speech impediment and his independent views about theology. He later established a successful school in the town of Nantwich, which landed him an invitation to teach at a newly founded academy in Warrington. He was 28 at the time. At Warrington he published several books on grammar and language that greatly influenced the great English poets Samuel Coleridge and William Wordsworth. He also published treatises on education, history, and law that inspired the work of the philosopher Jeremy Bentham. It was at Warrington that he began his scientific career by writing *The History of Electricity*, with the assistance and encouragement of Benjamin FRANKLIN.

In 1767 Priestley moved to Leeds, where he lived near a brewery and began a series of experiments on the fixed air (carbon dioxide) that was produced in the brewery. He invented soda water with the supply of carbon dioxide from the brewery. Around the same time Priestley was elected a fellow of London's Royal Society, and he became minister of a Presbyterian congregation in Leeds. In 1772 he published his second major work, *The History of Optics*. The following year he entered into private service as a librarian and resident intellectual to the earl of Shelburne.

Priestley stayed with Shelburne for seven years, after which he moved to Birmingham. During his time at Shelburne, he performed most of the experiments with gases that earned him his scientific reputation. In Birmingham, Priestley joined the famous Lunar Society, whose members included the physician and naturalist Erasmus Darwin and James WATT, inventor of the modern steam engine. The society and its members were interested in the application of scientific advances to practical uses, an orientation that fit in well with Priestley's utilitarian philosophy. However, Priestley focused most of his energies at this time on questions of theology and politics. He acquired a reputation for views considered antagonistic toward the monarchy and the church. In 1791 a mob destroyed his house, laboratory, and all his books and papers. He then moved to London, but continued political persecution forced him to emigrate to the United States, where he joined his sons, who had moved there three years earlier. He settled in Pennsylvania, where he spent the rest of his life.

Scientific Writings. Priestley first came to the attention of the scientific community with the publication of *The History and Present State of Electricity, With Original Experiments*. To prepare this work he consulted the

Distorting the Record

There has grown up around Priestley a legend about his methods that makes it appear as if his investigations were haphazard. The accounts of others, as well as quotes from his own writings, suggest that he was ignorant of the work of other chemists, that he used crude apparatus, and that his discoveries came about largely by accident. Although these claims are exaggerated, it appears that Priestley himself actually encouraged them in order to emphasize the difference between his career and that of his rival, Antoine Lavoisier.

* **conductivity** ability of a substance to transmit electricity

original works of contemporary scientists who had conducted research into electricity. Priestley often repeated the experiments described in these sources, and he soon began performing his own original experiments. His main accomplishment was discovering the conductivities* of many substances. He also studied the motion of the electrical fluid as well as other electrical phenomena. Interpreting an experiment performed by Franklin, Priestley deduced the inverse square law of force between electrical charges. This work likely inspired the experiments by Henry CAVENDISH that formally established the law.

The *History of Electricity* was so popular that Priestley decided to compile a multivolume history of all the experimental sciences. The second book in this planned series was *The History of Optics*. This was the only work on the subject for 50 years and the only one in English for 150 years, but it was not a financial success. Probably the most important contribution of the book is the account of an experiment by a fellow scientist that provided evidence that light takes the form of a particle. However, optics at this time was a science based on principles of mathematics, a subject in which Priestley had very little training. The revenue from sales of the book failed to pay for the cost of its preparation, and Priestley abandoned plans for the grand scientific history he had hoped to write.

Research into Gases. Priestley did not begin his most important work, the investigation of gases, until he was 37. He read works on chemistry as a student and continued to read accounts of the work of other chemists while writing his scientific histories. But the work that influenced him the most was Stephen Hales's *Vegetable Staticks,* in which Hales showed that air was fixed or trapped in certain substances. After reading Hales's book, Priestley confined his experimentation almost exclusively to the study of different kinds of air. By heating and mixing various substances and by working with the residue from such experiments, he produced several types of airs, or gases. These he subjected to a number of tests, asking such question as: Would they burn or support combustion? How did they look and taste? How long would a mouse live in a container filled with each gas? The outstanding result of these experiments was the "accidental" discovery of oxygen in 1774–1775. Priestley heated mercuric oxide in an apparatus and expected to produce carbon dioxide. However, unlike carbon dioxide, the gas he produced supported life and caused a candle to burn even more brightly than it did in regular air. Priestly believed that combustion was caused by a substance called phlogiston and that gases containing less phlogiston burned better than did gases that were saturated with the substance. Since the new gas, oxygen, supported combustion so well, he believed that it must be low in phlogiston. He called it dephlogisticated air. The French chemist Antoine LAVOISIER would later coin the term *oxygen* for the gas.

Other fruits of Priestley's research were the isolation of ammonia, sulfur dioxide, and other compounds containing oxygen; gaining early knowledge of photosynthesis; and discovering the role of the blood in respiration. Because of his contributions to science, Priestley was elected a member of nearly 20 scientific societies and was known as the foremost chemist of his day. However, Lavoisier and his French colleagues soon ushered in a new age of chemistry that changed the face of the field.

Priestley believed that the types of air he produced were all the same substance and differed only in the amounts and types of impurities they contained. To him the properties of air were physical and mechanical, not chemical, and he believed that the nature of substances could be altered or understood through purely physical processes, such as heating or compression. Later, French scientists realized that air and many other materials were chemical compounds composed of other substances. What Priestley failed to appreciate was that only by identifying the chemical nature of a substance and classifying it according to its chemical properties could one fully understand it. Although his brand of chemistry was replaced by the work of Lavoisier and others, Priestley's contributions to science and his influence on future scientists remain undiminished.

John RAY

1627–1705

NATURAL HISTORY

* **naturalist** student of natural history, the systematic study of natural objects, especially in their natural settings

* **taxonomy** classification of organisms that reflects their natural relationships; science or technique of classification

* **herbalist** person who collects or deals in herbs, especially medicinal herbs

One of the leading naturalists* of the 1600s, John Ray spent a lifetime studying and writing about nature. Ray made important contributions to the study of biology and botany, particularly in the area of taxonomy*. The first to fix the species as the fundamental unit in the taxonomic hierarchy, he established systematic methods for classifying plants and animals that helped make possible the work of the Swedish naturalist Carl LINNAEUS in the 1700s.

Early Life and Career. Born in Black Notley in Essex, England, Ray was the son of the village blacksmith. His mother was well known in the local area as a skilled herbalist* and medical practitioner. Ray attended grammar school in nearby Braintree. In his later writings he recalled that he had become very much interested in botany from an early age.

In 1644 Ray entered Trinity College at Cambridge University on a scholarship. Four years later he graduated with a bachelor's degree and accepted a fellowship at the college. During the next decade Ray lived quietly in Cambridge, teaching Greek, mathematics, and humanities. However, his life was interrupted suddenly in 1662 by the Act of Uniformity, a law that required people to take an oath that they would conform to the beliefs and practices of the Church of England. Ray's refusal to take the oath lost him his fellowship, and he was forced to leave Cambridge.

Ray found a wealthy patron named Francis Willughby, who became his student and colleague. For more than a decade, Willughby's various estates served as Ray's bases for scientific expeditions throughout England and parts of Europe to study plants and animals. Their most ambitious expedition, which lasted from 1663 to 1666, took them through Germany, Italy, France, Switzerland, and the Low Countries.

Willughby died suddenly in 1672, but he left money in his will so that Ray could complete the work they had started together. Ray married the next year and eventually returned to Black Notley. He remained there for the rest of his life, engaged in his writing, studies, and correspondence. In addition to his own work, which focused on plants, Ray undertook to

The English naturalist John Ray made important contributions to the study of biology and botany. He established systematic methods for classifying plants and animals.

---

* **physiology** science that deals with the functions of living organisms and their parts
* **morphology** branch of biology that deals with the form and structure of plants and animals

complete Willughby's work on animals. Together their goal had been to produce a systematic study of nature based on firsthand observations and critical evaluation of the works of other scientists and scholars.

Studies and Research. Ray's primary interests were botany and plant anatomy. While at Cambridge he took frequent walks in the countryside to study plants. His studies led to the publication of two catalogs of English plants. The catalogs, which contained descriptions of hundreds of different plants, set new standards for the composition and classification of British plants. They marked the first phase of Ray's botanical work. Thereafter, he turned his attention to plant physiology*, morphology*, and taxonomy.

In 1668 Ray composed tables of plants for a book by another scholar, John Wilkins. In completing this task he began searching for consistent principles for the classification of plants. His work on classification continued, and in 1682 Ray published a work that summarized his ideas on taxonomy. In this work, *Methodus plantarum* (Systematics of Plants), Ray became the first botanist to make a distinction between monocotyledons (plants with one seed leaf) and dicotyledons (plants with two seed leaves).

Ray's masterwork was *Historia plantarum* (History of Plants), a three-volume work published between 1686 and 1704. This work was Ray's contribution to his and Willughby's goal of producing a systematic study of nature. The aim of *Historia plantarum* was to classify, list, and describe all known plants in Europe. In addition to information gained from his own observations, Ray compiled material from a wide range of sources. He derived his discussion on plant anatomy and morphology from the writings of scholars such as Marcello MALPIGHI and the English botanist Nehemiah Grew.

For each plant species in *Historia plantarum,* Ray not only provided names, classifications, and descriptions; he also gave details of the habitat, distribution, and medicinal uses of each plant. However, unlike some earlier books on plants, *Historia plantarum* contained no illustrations. This was probably due largely to the financial and technical difficulties of adequately illustrating such a comprehensive work.

Attempting to complete Willughby's survey of the animal kingdom, Ray published *Ornithologioe* in 1676. An important feature of this work was Ray's pioneering attempt to classify birds according to habitat and anatomy. Divided ecologically into land and water birds, the book contains descriptions concentrated on plumage and behavior patterns. Ray also completed books on fish, reptiles and quadrupeds (four-footed animals), and insects. The book on insects was the first such work published on this subject in nearly 100 years.

In addition to his work in science, Ray published several books on religion. The most popular of these, *The Wisdom of God,* discussed science from a religious perspective. Beginning with the solar system, it included discussions of the theory of matter, geology, the plant and animal kingdoms, and human anatomy. Ray argued that the fundamental relationship that is found between form and function throughout nature is proof that God created everything in the universe.

René-Antoine Ferchault de
RÉAUMUR

1683–1757

MATHEMATICS, TECHNOLOGY,
NATURAL HISTORY

* **naturalist** student of natural history, the systematic study of natural objects, especially in their natural settings

* **entomology** science that deals with insects

* **mollusk** marine animal with a shell of one or more pieces enclosing a soft body

Bee Man of France

Réaumur was especially interested in bees. He spent an enormous amount of time observing these creatures, and he conducted many ingenious experiments. Réaumur discovered that he could anesthetize the insects by immersing their hive in cold water. He could then handle the bees, count them, and separate them into different classes. In his many studies Réaumur measured the amount of pollen the bees gathered each day, estimated the number of eggs laid by a single queen, kept track of the bees' activities, and observed the function of the queen in bee society. He also tracked individual bees by tinting them with unique dyes.

One of the greatest naturalists* of his time, René-Antoine Réaumur conducted research in natural history, biology, physics, and entomology*. He also made significant and original contributions to industrial technology through his investigation of various industries in France.

Early Life and Career. Born in La Rochelle, France, Réaumur was a member of an old and illustrious family that prospered in trade and entered the ranks of the lesser nobility. His father, a judge in a provincial court, died when Réaumur was less than two years old. The young boy was raised by his mother with the aid of several aunts and uncles. Nothing is known with certainty about Réaumur's early education. He probably studied at a school run by the religious order of Jesuits, most likely in the city of Poitiers. In 1699 one of his uncles summoned Réaumur to Bourges to study law. He remained there for three years, after which he went to live in Paris.

Soon after arriving in Paris, Réaumur met a cousin who was studying mathematics with a young instructor from the Académie des Sciences. Réaumur decided to take classes too, and after only three lessons he knew more than his cousin and as much as his instructor. Through his teacher Réaumur became acquainted with the great mathematician Pierre Varignon, who became his friend, teacher, and guide. In 1708 Varignon nominated his young friend to be his assistant at the Académie des Sciences.

Réaumur made three presentations dealing with geometry to the academy. His presentations revealed a remarkable degree of mathematical knowledge and sophistication. Had Réaumur continued to pursue mathematics, he might have become one of the greatest mathematicians of his day. The following year he suddenly changed the course of his scientific career after reading a paper on the growth of animal shells, which stimulated his interest in natural history. Réaumur never again devoted himself to pure mathematical research. Thereafter, his interests diversified.

Natural History. Réaumur was among the greatest naturalists of his age because of the breadth and range of his research, his detailed observations, and the ingenuity of his experiments. His reasons for pursuing natural history were a strange mixture of practicality and delight in the many curiosities of nature.

After reading the paper on the growth of animal shells, Réaumur began investigating the shell growth of mollusks*. He showed that the shells of these creatures grow because of the addition of successive layers rather than by the incorporation of new material into an already existing structure. An investigation into the formation of pearls led him to study the substance that makes the scales of fish appear shiny. During his investigations Réaumur also rediscovered the secret of making a famous purple dye that was highly prized by the ancient Romans.

Réaumur's greatest work in natural history was *Mémoires pour servir à l'histoire des insectes* (Memoirs Serving as a Natural History of Insects), published in six volumes between 1734 and 1742. A milestone in the history of entomology, the work describes and classifies many types of insects. Réaumur's approach was to classify them based on animal behavior

* **crustacean** class of animals that typically have a body covered with a hard shell or crust, such as lobsters, shrimp, and crabs

* **physiology** science that deals with the functions of living organisms and their parts

The Fiercest Insects

In the early 1700s the term *insect* was used for almost any small invertebrate, or animal without a backbone. The word referred primarily to creatures that had segmented bodies, including not only spiders, ants, and bees but also worms. Réaumur extended the concept of insects even further. Among the animals he considered insects were clams and other mollusks, lobsters and other crustaceans, and even reptiles and amphibians. "The crocodile is certainly a fierce insect," Réaumur once proclaimed, "but I am not in the least disturbed about calling it one."

rather than on their form and structure. Réaumur also focused on the usefulness of insects and discussed the economic value of insect research—for example, in the production of silk, honey, and other products.

Biology and Genetics. Réaumur's ideas in biology and animal generation were dominated by the ideas of the preformationists—scientists who believed that the form of each living thing was preformed in the eggs of preceding generations. Some of Réaumur's observations supported these ideas. His studies of butterflies, for example, suggested that preformed biological structures remained in a state of suspended animation until conditions became suitable for development.

Réaumur never accepted all the theories of the preformationists, however, and as early as 1712 he began to reject some of their ideas. In a paper published the same year, he showed that certain crustaceans* had the power to regenerate, or regrow, missing legs or parts of legs. This suggested that specialized tissues did not develop from preformed matter, a finding that contradicted preformationist ideas. Later discoveries about regeneration, announced by Réaumur in 1741, caused a sensation among European naturalists and challenged commonly accepted biological ideas.

Another area of biology in which Réaumur made significant contributions was physiology*. In a brilliantly conceived experimental investigation of the process of digestion in birds, he demonstrated the digestive power of the gizzard—a muscular portion of a bird's stomach. Réaumur later investigated the role of gastric juices in digestion.

Technology. Early in his career Réaumur was placed in charge of writing an industrial encyclopedia for the Académie des Sciences that would cover all the arts, industries, and professions of France. He began this enormous task in 1713 and continued working on it for a number of years.

Réaumur investigated the arts of dealing with gold and precious stones, the tinplate industry, and various industrial processes. His most significant contribution to industrial technology was his investigation of the iron and steel industry. In researching the production and composition of iron and steel, Réaumur learned a great deal about the properties of these metals, and he devised improved techniques for manufacturing them to increase their strength and resilience—the ability to be shaped, bent, and stretched and still return to their original form.

Réaumur also undertook an extensive investigation of the porcelain industry. Chinese porcelain was in great demand in Europe in the early 1700s, and European workmen had been unable to create porcelain of the same quality. Réaumur researched processes for making porcelain and experimented with various substances for use in its composition. Although he did not learn the secrets of Chinese porcelain making, his discoveries helped later chemists develop techniques that made French porcelain among the finest in the world. During the course of his experiments, Réaumur also invented a new type of ceramic that proved useful in the late 1900s for protecting the nose cones of rockets from overheating.

Réaumur was perhaps best known for a thermometer scale that he invented and that bears his name. Thermometers had been in use for about

100 years, but there was no standard scale to enable scientists to compare their thermometer readings. Réaumur devised an alcohol thermometer with a standard measurement for the freezing and boiling points of water. This scale enabled scientists to compare the temperatures referred to by others.

Francesco REDI

1626–ca. 1697

ENTOMOLOGY, PARASITOLOGY, TOXICOLOGY

* **tourniquet** tight bandage that restricts the flow of blood

Francesco Redi was a pioneer of experimental toxicology (the study of poisons) who also made significant contributions in entomology (the study of insects) and parasitology (the study of parasites). The son of a famous Italian physician, Gregorio Redi, Francesco served as the head physician and counselor to the powerful Medici family of Florence. Working with poisonous snakes, Redi identified the source of the snakes' venom and discovered that the venom is harmful only when it enters the bloodstream. Because of this knowledge, he recommended applying a tourniquet* above a snakebite wound to prevent the venom from circulating and infecting the blood. He also recognized that it is safe to suck the venom from a wound because swallowing the venom is not harmful. These were the first investigations into experimental toxicology and were published in his 1664 letter titled *Osservazioni intorno alle vipere* (Observations on Vipers).

Redi is best known for designing a series of tests for William HARVEY's theory that flies are not generated spontaneously but develop from eggs too small to be seen. Using a microscope, Redi identified the egg-producing organs in insects, proving that they reproduced like many other animals. He then argued that decaying matter was an ideal source of food for insect larvae and that maggots only appear there because insects, knowing that such material is a source of nourishment, lay their eggs in it. He then proved his theory by placing decaying organic matter in containers that could not be penetrated by insects. When no maggots appeared on the organic matter, Redi's theory was proved correct, and he published his findings in *Esperienze intorno alla generazione degli insetti* (Experience in the Generation of Insects). Redi nevertheless supported the idea of spontaneous generation in the case of intestinal worms and gallflies. The doctrine of spontaneous generation was not conclusively discredited until the work of Louis Pasteur.

George Joachim RHETICUS

1514–1574

MATHEMATICS, ASTRONOMY

George Joachim Rheticus was the son of the town physician of Feldkirch, Austria, who was also his first teacher. When Rheticus was 14, his father was beheaded for practicing witchcraft, and George later moved to Zurich to complete his studies. At the age of 22 he was named professor of arithmetic and geometry at the University of Wittenburg, and two years later he took a leave of absence to meet with Europe's leading astronomers.

A year into his travels, he met Nicholas COPERNICUS, who had proposed a heliocentric model of the solar system, which placed the sun, not the earth, at its center. Because his theory disagreed with the teachings of the Catholic Church, Copernicus had resisted the efforts of his colleagues to persuade him to publish it. However, after meeting Rheticus, Copernicus agreed to allow the youth to publish a preliminary report of his findings under Rheticus's name. When the paper did not generate the hostility that Copernicus feared, he released his groundbreaking work, *De revolutionibus orbium coelestium* (On the Revolutions of the Heavenly Spheres).

In 1542 Rheticus accepted a professorship of mathematics at the University of Leipzig in Austria. There he published an important new table of trigonometric functions. Based on material that appeared in *De revolutionibus,* it was the first table to give the cosine* directly, although Rheticus did not use that term. After three years in Leipzig, Rheticus traveled to his hometown and then on to Milan and Zurich. He returned to Leipzig in 1548 but was forced to leave the university three years later because of a drunken encounter with a student. In 1551 Rheticus published the *Canon of the Doctrine of Triangles,* in which he produced the first extensive table of tangents, the first printed table of secants (straight line that intersects a curve at two or more points), and the first table to give values for all six trigonometric functions.

Three years later he received an invitation to teach at the University of Vienna, but he declined the offer. Instead, he moved to Poland and later to Hungary, where he lived and worked until his death in 1574. In a sort of replay of his dealings with Copernicus, all his work in trigonometry was finally compiled and published by one of his students more than 20 years after Rheticus's death.

* cosine in trigonometry, the ratio of the adjacent side to the hypotenuse

Santorio
SANTORIO

1561–1636

MEDICINE, PHYSIOLOGY,
SCIENTIFIC INSTRUMENTATION

S antorio Santorio, also known as Sanctorius, was noted for his experimental approach at a time when most physicians relied unquestioningly on the medical doctrines of the ancient Greek philosophers Hippocrates and Aristotle and the ancient anatomist Galen. Although Santorio supported many of the accepted ideas on anatomy and medicine, he stressed the importance of reaching conclusions based on observation and reasoning. He said, "One must believe first in one's own senses and in experience, then in reasoning, and only in the third place in the authority of Hippocrates, of Galen, of Aristole, and of other excellent philosophers."

The son of a Venetian nobleman, Santorio received a classical education in languages and literature before studying medicine at the University of Padua in 1575. He graduated in 1582, set up a private medical practice, and almost immediately began to study the change in weight that occurred in his own body as a result of eating and eliminating waste. This work resulted in the publication of his most famous work, *De statica medicina* (On Medical Measurement). He argued that health was dependent on a balance of substances ingested by an organism and those expelled by it. His measurements indicated that a large part of excretion takes place invisibly, through the skin and lungs. He studied the size of this excretion, its relationship to visible excretions, and its dependence on diet, sleep, and exercise. He concluded that invisible excretion varies according to several internal and external factors. His ideas about the relationship of health to the balance of material taken in and expelled were later disproved, but his emphasis on quantitative experimentation was a great leap forward in medicine.

Santorio invented several measuring instruments and medical devices, including a thermometer, a device for measuring atmospheric humidity, a pendulum for timing the pulse rate, a trocar (an instrument for making precise incisions), a special syringe for extracting bladder stones, and a bathing bed. He spoke of these inventions in his lectures and demonstrated their uses. For example, he publicly used the trocar while performing surgery on the abdomen and trachea. Although Santorio promised to reveal the methods of construction of his apparatus in a book titled *De instrumentis medicis* (On Medical Instruments), the work never appeared.

Santorio modified traditional medical ideas according to his findings. For example, the accepted authorities did not differentiate between different ailments produced by the same causes, but Santorio defined a continuum of illness from mild to severe. He also attempted to deduce the total number of possible diseases, which according to his calculations was about 80,000. Santorio published his arguments in 1602, in a book titled *Methodi vitandorum errorum omnium qui in arte medica contingunt*. The book examines the methods a doctor should follow to avoid making mistakes in medical practice and contains descriptions of many diseases as well as examples of diagnoses for different illnesses.

Santorio later took up a professorship at the University of Padua, where he remained until 1624. Thereafter, he retired from this post and moved to Venice, where he lived until his death from a disease of the urinary tract. While in Venice, he published a work in which he revealed the principles of construction of various instruments. In 1630 he was given the task of organizing measures against an epidemic of the plague. The same year he was elected president of the Venetian College of Physicians. His emphasis on experimentation and research was one of the foundations on which modern medicine was built.

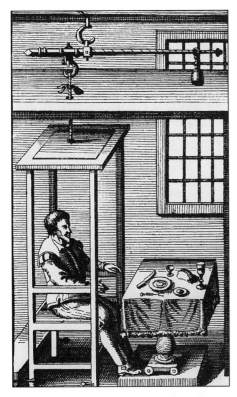

Santorio Santorio spent much time in his weighing chair to study the change that occurred in his body weight from eating food and eliminating waste. He also invented instruments for measuring temperature, humidity, and pulse rate.

Carl Wilhelm SCHEELE

1742–1786

CHEMISTRY, PHARMACY

The Swedish pharmacist Carl Wilhelm Scheele was unequaled in the history of chemistry. In spite of inadequate laboratory facilities, he successfully isolated a number of organic and inorganic compounds, including the toxic gases hydrogen sulfide, hydrogen fluoride, and hydrogen cyanide. Scheele's greatest achievements, however, were his discoveries of various chemical elements, including manganese, nitrogen, tungsten, barium, molybdenum, and chlorine. Scheele also discovered oxygen. However, credit for that discovery is given to English chemist Joseph PRIESTLEY, although Scheele preceded him by two years.

Life and Career. Scheele was born in Stralsund, Pomerania, a region once controlled by Sweden that later became a part of Germany. He became interested in pharmacy at an early age and decided to pursue it as his career. According to some sources, two friends of his family—a physician and a pharmacist—taught Scheele how to read prescriptions and write chemical symbols while he was still just a young boy.

After finishing grammar school in Stralsund, Scheele went to Göteborg, Sweden, where he began an apprenticeship at the pharmacy of Martin Bauch. Bauch, who enjoyed a reputation for competence and knowledge, had a significant influence on Scheele, encouraging the young apprentice to do experiments and pursue developments in chemistry. Scheele remained with Bauch until 1765, when he left Göteborg and began to travel. He first found work in a pharmacy in the city of Mälmo, where he was allowed to work in the pharmacy laboratory because of his preference for experimental work. His stay in Mälmo was especially important because Mälmo was close to the university city of Lund. This gave Scheele his first contact with the academic world, which he gained through a friendship with Anders Retzius, a lecturer in chemistry at the University of Lund. Mälmo was also close to Copenhagen, Denmark, a center of culture and trade where Scheele had access to recently published literature.

After three years in Mälmo, Scheele went to Stockholm and took up a position in a pharmacy. Allowed only to prepare prescriptions and not to perform chemical experiments, Scheele was unhappy in that position. In 1770 he moved to a new pharmacy in Uppsala, the site of the best-known university in Sweden. There Scheele gained a reputation as an able chemist, made several important discoveries, and was elected a member of the Swedish Academy of Sciences.

Despite his achievements in Uppsala, Scheele had to content himself with subordinate positions that allowed him limited opportunities for experimental research. Eager for more independence, Scheele moved to the small town of Köping in 1775 because of an opportunity to manage a pharmacy on his own. He remained in Köping for the rest of his life, becoming one of the town's most popular and respected citizens. Scheele left Köping only once, in 1777, to travel to Stockholm to take his pharmacist's oath and take his seat as a member of the Royal Swedish Academy of Science.

Work and Discoveries. Scheele performed thousands of experiments during his career. He questioned the dominant theories of the day, leading him to pursue new directions in research. His experiments resulted in the discovery of various acids, gases, and chemical compounds. One of his more important discoveries was chlorine, but because Scheele failed to recognize it as an element, credit for that discovery went to English chemist Sir Humphry Davy in 1810. Scheele's discovery of oxygen resulted from experiments with air and fire and the phenomenon of combustion (burning). In the only book he published, *Chemische Abhandlung von der Luft und dem Feuer* (Chemical Observations and Experiments on Air and Fire), released in 1777, Scheele concluded that the atmosphere is composed of two gases: vitiated air (nitrogen), which prevented combustion, and fire-air (oxygen), which supported combustion. Scheele's book included detailed descriptions of oxygen, including its properties and different methods of producing it. Unfortunately, its publication was delayed, enabling Priestley to announce his own findings first.

Among Scheele's other discoveries were glycerin (a colorless, sweet liquid derived from oils and used to make medicines and explosives), a green pigment sometimes known as Scheele's green, the presence of calcium phosphate in bone, and the art of preserving vinegar by heating a vessel containing it in a kettle of boiling water. This last discovery was made nearly a century before French chemist Louis Pasteur performed similar experiments and developed the process of preservation known today as pasteurization.

Michael SERVETUS
ca. 1511–1553
BIOLOGY, PHILOSOPHY

* **pharmacology** science that deals with the preparation, uses, and effects of drugs

* **theological** referring to theology, the study of religion

Michael Servetus lectured on various subjects, practiced as a doctor, and is remembered in the history of science for his insight into the roles of the lungs and heart in the circulation of the blood. Religion, however, was Servetus's first subject of study and a lifelong concern. At a time when heresy was punishable severely, Servetus paid the ultimate price for disagreeing with the religious authorities of his day.

Servetus's date and place of birth are not known, but he was probably born in 1511 in Villanueva de Sixena in Spain's Huesca province. His parents were nobles, and one of his brothers was a priest. The young Servetus learned Latin, possibly at the University of Zaragoza, which was not far from his home. At age 15, Servetus entered the service of Juan de Quintana, a friar of the Franciscan religious brotherhood who was also a learned and influential man. Quintana became confessor to Emperor Charles V of the Holy Roman Empire, whose coronation Servetus witnessed. In 1530, however, Servetus left Quintana's service because his studies of the Bible had raised doubts in his mind about the rightness of Roman Catholic religious doctrine, especially the idea that God is a Trinity, or threefold deity. Servetus moved to Switzerland, where he published works that denied the Trinity, outraging both Catholics and Protestants.

Assuming the name Michel de Villeneuve, Servetus moved on to France. As an employee of a publishing house in Lyons, he prepared several new and successful editions of the *Geography* of Ptolemy, a Greek scientist of the ancient world. He also read many medical books and developed an interest in the subject. In the late 1530s, he published two books on the topics of healing herbs, medicinal syrups, and diet, both considered noteworthy contributions to modern pharmacology*. Servetus also spent several years studying medicine in Paris, where he lectured on geography, astronomy, and the use of astrology in medicine and in forecasting the future. However, he was charged before the Faculty for Medicine for teaching astrology.

Although he lived outwardly as a Catholic, Servetus had not abandoned his beliefs or his theological* studies. In 1553 he published his major work on theology, *Christianismi restitutio* (Christianity Restored), which contains Servetus's lasting claim to scientific fame. To explain how the divine spirit enters the blood and is spread through the body, Servetus described circulation as blood traveling from the right to the left side of the heart via the lungs—not through minute holes in the dividing wall of the heart (the septum) as Galen had argued. Servetus's religious ideas, however, caused such protest that the authorities seized and burned nearly all copies of his book. Not until 1694 was Servetus's scientific discovery recognized and accepted. Long before that time, however, the Italian anatomist Realdo COLOMBO had made the same discovery and published his findings. In fact, an Arab scientist named Ibn al-Nafis had discovered circulation through the lungs in the 1200s, but neither Servetus nor Colombo knew of his work.

The publication of *Christianismi restitutio* was the undoing of Servetus, who had been living under an assumed name since the publication of his works denying the Trinity. He was arrested and imprisoned for heresy, but he escaped. As he fled through Switzerland toward Italy, he was recognized and turned over to the authorities, who burned him at the stake.

Lazzaro SPALLANZANI

1729–1799

NATURAL HISTORY, BIOLOGY, PHYSIOLOGY

The Italian scientist Lazzaro Spallanzani is considered one of the founders of experimental biology. Famous throughout Europe for his experiments in animal reproduction, Spallanzani also made important contributions to the study of bodily functions, such as blood circulation, digestion, and respiration. His work helped disprove the theory of spontaneous generation—the idea that living organisms could be produced from inanimate, or lifeless, matter. Spallanzani also was a pioneer in the science of vulcanology, the study of volcanoes and volcanic phenomena.

Early Life and Work. Born in Scandiano, Italy, Spallanzani was the son of a distinguished and successful lawyer. He attended local schools until age 15, at which time he went to a Jesuit college in the nearby town of Reggio Emilia, where he studied philosophy, languages, and the classics. Invited to join the Jesuit religious order, Spallanzani chose instead to study law at the University of Bologna. There he became interested in science and mathematics through the influence of his cousin Laura Bassi, a professor. Spallanzani broadened his education and began studying physics, chemistry, natural history*, and other subjects. With Bassi's support he also gained permission from his father to abandon law and pursue his other interests.

* **natural history** systematic study of natural objects, especially in their natural settings

Around 1753 Spallanzani became a doctor of philosophy. Soon afterward he also was ordained a priest and became attached to churches in the city of Modena. Although he performed his priestly duties irregularly, he remained attached to the church throughout much of his life. At various times financial assistance from the church enabled him to pursue his scientific investigations. Early in 1755 Spallanzani began teaching at the College of Reggio Emilia, and two years later he was appointed lecturer of mathematics at the recently founded University of Reggio Emilia. In 1761 he set out on the first of many scientific excursions to various parts of Italy. Such trips became a regular part of his scientific research because they enabled him to investigate unexplained natural occurrences and collect numerous specimens of plants and animals, which he later gave to museums.

Early Discoveries and New Directions. While teaching at Reggio Emilia, Spallanzani was introduced to the work of the French naturalist* Georges-Louis BUFFON and the English biologist John Turberville Needham. Buffon and Needham believed that all living things contained inanimate

* **naturalist** student of natural history, the systematic study of natural objects, especially in their natural settings

matter as well as special particles called animalcules that serve as the elementary building blocks of life. They argued that when an organism dies, the animalcules play a role in the spontaneous generation of new life from nonliving matter.

Equipped with a microscope, Spallanzani began to conduct experiments to investigate spontaneous generation. Scientists had long held that simple living things, such as the microorganisms* revealed by Antoni van LEEUWENHOEK's research with a microscope, could be generated spontaneously through the reorganization of inorganic material. Spallanzani showed that the solutions in which microorganisms ordinarily reproduce are not conducive to breeding when the solution is boiled for 30 or more minutes and then placed in a sealed flask. Proponents of spontaneous generation dismissed Spallanzani's work, arguing that prolonged boiling merely destroyed a vital principle in the air. In 1765 Spallanzani reported his findings to the Bologna Academy of Sciences.

Spallanzani's work on spontaneous generation led to new avenues of research. In 1765 he began to study the ability of some lower, less complex animals to regenerate, or regrow, lost parts of their bodies, such as tails or legs. By studying earthworms, salamanders, toads, and frogs, he discovered that lower animals have a much greater capacity to regenerate than higher, more complex animals, that the ability to regenerate decreases with the age of the organism, and that internal organs cannot regenerate.

Further Studies. Spallanzani's scientific accomplishments and discoveries brought him fame throughout Europe. In 1768 he was elected a fellow of the prestigious Royal Society of London, and the following year he accepted a position as professor of natural history at the University of Pavia in Italy. He remained there for the rest of his career.

A popular teacher and lecturer, Spallanzani spent much of his time conducting scientific research. He continued to study regeneration and found further evidence to disprove more of the theories of Buffon and Needham. In experimenting with the idea of transplantation, he eventually succeeded in transplanting the head of one snail onto the body of another.

Spallanzani broadened his studies to investigate the blood circulation and digestion of animals. Through his work with circulation, he established the existence of connections between the arteries and veins of warm-blooded animals. He also studied the effect of growth on circulation as well as the influence of gravity and the effect of wounds on different parts of the circulatory system. Finally, Spallanzani showed that the pulse of warm-blooded animals is caused by the pressure that the blood exerts on the walls of the arteries as it is pumped through the body by the heart.

In studying digestion, Spallanzani concluded that the basic factor in the digestive process is the action of *gastric juice*—a term he introduced. He discovered that gastric juice helps dissolve food in the digestive system and that the speed at which it dissolves any given food is related to the quantity of the juice. Spallanzani also found evidence that gastric juice contains chemicals that are suited to particular types of foods. Despite some errors and gaps in his work, Spallanzani successfully explained many phenomena of gastric digestion.

---

* **microorganism** tiny living thing that generally can be seen clearly only through a microscope

---

Dressed for Results

Spallanzani and other scientists knew that semen stimulated, in some way, the expansion of an organism within a female egg. However, they did not fully understand the function of semen and sperm or know if actual contact between egg and semen was necessary.

In one of his experiments, Spallanzani fitted tight pants on male frogs and brought them into contact with frog eggs. When no tadpoles developed, he concluded that contact between egg and semen was essential for the formation of a new organism.

Lazzaro Spallanzani made important contributions to biology in the areas of reproduction, circulation, digestion, and respiration. Later in his life, he conducted research in the field of vulcanology.

Spallanzani also studied fertilization in both plants and animals. In his work with animals, he showed that contact between a female ovum (egg) and a male sperm is necessary for fertilization. Spallanzani also performed the first successful experiments in artificial insemination, in which he used artificial means to cause a dog to become pregnant.

Other Accomplishments. Early in his career at the University of Pavia, Spallanzani was placed in charge of the Museum of Natural History there. Charged with acquiring new exhibits for the museum, he undertook many expeditions to various parts of Europe to gather new specimens of plants, animals, minerals, and other objects. Through his labors the collections of the museum became among the finest in Italy.

Spallanzani's specimen-gathering expeditions gave him an opportunity to investigate new and different life forms and study natural phenomena. During one such trip he founded Europe's first marine zoological laboratory and conducted studies on deep-sea phosphorescence*. He also demonstrated the animal nature of corals and other tiny marine organisms.

* **phosphorescence** property of some organisms to give off a natural glow or light

Among Spallanzani's better-known studies of natural phenomena are those dealing with volcanoes. He visited active volcanoes in Italy, including Etna in Sicily as well as Stromboli and Volcano on islands off the Italian coast. Making perilous climbs to the craters of these volcanoes, he observed and measured lava flows and noted the gas explosions that forced up red-hot lava and ejected huge rocks. His observations of volcanic activities proved fundamental to the emerging science of vulcanology.

During the last years of his life, Spallanzani conducted further research on microscopic plants and animals. He also engaged in research that contributed greatly to the understanding of plant and animal respiration. Through his experiments he determined that the blood carried carbon dioxide through the body and that oxygen was converted to carbon dioxide in the tissues rather than in the lungs. This work laid the foundation for modern ideas about respiration and established the basic uniformity of the respiratory process throughout the animal kingdom.

Christian Konrad
SPRENGEL

1750–1816

BOTANY

Christian Konrad Sprengel was a pioneer in the study of the relationship between plant structure, insect activity, and the mechanisms that control pollination in plants. In his late 30s, he made important discoveries while studying geraniums. Sprengel said that the structure of a flower can only be interpreted according to the role it plays in relation to its insect visitors. He noted that flowers use color and scent to attract insects and that the markings on each flower provide a guide to the location of its nectar. He also recognized that a plant develops male and female organs at different times, which means that it cannot pollinate itself. This was one of his most important discoveries. By combining this observation with his study of insect activity, Sprengel came to realize that the structures of flowers are designed to encourage and assist insect visitors, which are responsible for carrying pollen from male plants to female ones. His discovery of the insects' role in pollination later had a major impact on Charles Darwin's theory of evolution by natural selection.

Georg Ernst
STAHL

1660–1734

MEDICINE, CHEMISTRY

The German physician and chemist Georg Ernst Stahl is a controversial figure in the history of science. Stahl devoted much effort to developing distinctive theories about the nature of matter and of biological processes. He is remembered today for his theories about phlogiston, a principle or element of fire that he believed formed part of every substance that could be burned. Stahl also had a successful medical practice and was regarded in his day as an important scientific figure. However, he was out of step with the intellectual trends of his time, and by the end of the 1800s, new research and experiments had disproved or overturned many of his theories as well as his system of medicine. Nevertheless, modern historians of science are becoming increasingly aware of the influence that his decades of teaching and writing had on the course of medical thought in the 1800s.

Education and Career. Stahl was born in Ansbach, Germany. Beyond the fact that his upbringing was shaped by Pietism, a movement within the Lutheran Church that called for moral reform, little is known about his background or early life. As a young man Stahl was interested in chemistry. He attended the university at Jena, a city in eastern Germany, where he studied medicine. A friendship that Stahl formed with a fellow student, Friedrich Hoffmann, later became a major element in his career. After his graduation in 1684, Stahl spent the next several years on research. He also lectured on chemistry at the university and became a reputed scientist and teacher. He then spent seven years in Weimar as the court physician to the duke.

Stahl, Georg Ernst

The German physician and chemist Georg Stahl developed theories about phlogiston, a principle or element of fire, which he believed to be part of every combustible substance.

* **mechanics** science that studies how energy and force affect objects

* **physiology** science that deals with the functions of living organisms and their parts

* **pathology** study of diseases and their effects on organisms

In 1694 Stahl's friend Hoffmann was appointed professor of medicine at a new university in the city of Halle, and he arranged for Stahl to receive the second professorship of medicine. Although Stahl lectured on a variety of scientific topics at Halle, his favorite subjects were chemistry and the theory of medicine. Hoffmann and Stahl formed a strong teaching staff, and the university at Halle became a leading medical school. It was also a center of Pietism.

Stahl's friendship and professional relationship with Hoffmann weakened over time. The two men held very different ideas about the nature of living things, and their disagreement over scientific issues became profound. In addition, personality conflicts may have come between them—Stahl was proud, reserved, and stern, Hoffmann more easygoing. The two men became rivals, even enemies. Stahl suffered other misfortunes as well. His first and second wives died, as did his daughter. In 1715 Stahl left Halle for Berlin, where he became the court physician to Frederick William I of Prussia. He spent the rest of his life in Berlin.

Major Scientific Theories. Stahl produced a great quantity of writings on many subjects. Although he never prepared a straightforward overview of his theories, his work contains recurring themes and formed the foundation of his thinking.

One of these themes is the belief that living and nonliving things are fundamentally different. This belief was the basis of Stahl's difference of opinion with Hoffmann. Hoffmann adopted a view called iatromechanics, which said that the simple laws of mechanics*, which explain the properties and movements of machines, were sufficient to explain how living organisms function. Stahl, on the other hand, based all his work on the belief that life is a nonmaterial quality or principle that cannot be explained in purely chemical or mechanical terms.

According to Stahl, both living and nonliving things are made of matter, but living things also possess something more, a vital principle or life force that separates them from the world of nonliving things. Stahl called that life force "anima." In fact, the term *animism* refers to this concept of a life force that cannot be studied or observed directly. Although Stahl was not the only scientist to hold such views, he was the only one who took the effort to explain the anima's relationship with the body. He argued that life depends on motion, such as the motion of the heart and the blood, and he concluded that motion comes from the anima, not from matter. However, he never clearly explained how motion could link the nonmaterial anima and the material body.

In his writings on medical subjects and in his treatment of patients, Stahl was hardheaded and practical. He taught that the proper study of medicine involves the thorough examination of the body's functions, and he wrote about the specifics of physiology*, pathology*, and the treatment of illnesses. Stahl placed all these subjects within the framework of his theory that the body, whether in health or in disease, is controlled by the directing force of the anima. Although he was one of the leading chemists of his time, Stahl believed that chemistry and detailed anatomical study drew attention away from medicine's proper concern—the body as a whole, presided over by the anima.

In chemistry as in medicine, Stahl strongly disagreed with the purely mechanical interpretation of nature. Following a traditional idea that matter consists of basic elements that are distinct from its atoms, Stahl agreed with a scientist named Johann Joachim Becher, who claimed that substances were made of combinations of elements, or earths. One earth made objects solid; another gave them weight; and a third gave them color, odor, and combustibility, or the property of being able to burn.

Stahl used the term *phlogiston* to refer to the combustible earth. He believed that through processes such as rusting and burning, phlogiston separated from the materials—such as plants and minerals—in which it existed. Stahl also explored the relationship between phlogiston and air, seeking to determine what happened to the phlogiston liberated by combustion. He developed a theory of recycling in which phlogiston in the air entered into plants and then, through plants was consumed as food, into animal bodies. Phlogiston provided chemists with the first reasonable explanation of combustion. Stahl's theory enjoyed enormous support until the late 1800s, when French chemist Antoine-Laurent LAVOISIER demonstrated that it was in fact the element oxygen that was involved in combustion.

Niels STENSEN

1638–1686

ANATOMY, GEOLOGY, MINERALOGY

* **physiology** science that deals with the functions of living organisms and their parts

Niels Stensen, one of the most important early investigators of human anatomy, made key discoveries about glands, the role of the heart in human physiology*, the study of muscles, and the workings of the reproductive system. He also contributed to the field of geology, especially the study of fossils and the history of the earth.

Born in Copenhagen, Denmark, Stensen was the son of a goldsmith, and some have suggested that his father's work spurred his early interest in technical, mechanical, and scientific matters. Stensen studied medicine at the University of Copenhagen but traveled widely during his time as a student and attended several institutions. His journeys took him to France, Holland, Germany, and Italy, where he converted to Catholicism. He served as royal anatomist in the Danish court and as tutor to the crown prince of Florence. Stensen was eventually ordained a priest and later served as a bishop in Northern Europe. During this time he also pursued his scientific investigations into anatomy and geology.

Stensen's first anatomical investigations concerned the glands and the lymphatic system. While dissecting the head of a sheep, he found the duct of the parotid gland (Stensen's duct), which is a principal source of saliva for the oral cavity. After this discovery he began to work toward understanding the whole glandular lymphatic system. Stensen was the first to distinguish the lymph nodes from actual glands, such as the salivary glands, and to categorize them according to their function. His initial discovery led him to believe that every fluid in the body was a glandular secretion. His theory led him to discover glands in the cheeks, beneath the tongue, on the palate, and in the nose. He discovered the passage that runs from the eyelids to the nose and explained that the lachrymal fluid (tears) serves to cleanse and lubricate the eyeball. He also located concentrations of lymph nodes in the small intestines.

Stensen determined that certain glands carry fluids from the veins to the other parts of the body, and that other glands bring fluids back to the veins where they mix with blood and are carried back to the heart. He also studied the structure of muscles, showing that they contained arteries, veins, fibers, nerves, and membranes. He argued that all muscles possess the ability to contract. He then demonstrated that the heart possesses all the characteristics of a muscle and argued that it was not, as most others believed, the seat of the soul or the source of the body's life and heat. Stensen tirelessly questioned the views of those who tried to explain nature using philosophical speculation or analogy* rather than thorough experimentation and observation. For example, he demonstrated that the pineal gland, which the philosopher René DESCARTES had declared to be the seat of the human soul because of its uniqueness to humans, was found in animals other than humans.

Stensen's own anatomical investigations at this time led to important discoveries about the female reproductive system. He discovered the oviduct and realized that it was a tube designed to carry eggs. He also realized that the "female testes" were really ovaries whose purpose was the production of eggs. Before that time, most physicians believed that their purpose was to produce semen. Stensen also studied the anatomy of rays and sharks and discovered that they do not lay eggs, but that their embryos remain connected to the uterus by a placenta*.

The last period of Stensen's scientific activity began when he studied the head of a large shark he had received while in Florence. He paid particular attention to its teeth, which led him to wonder if they were related to similar-looking rocks called tongue stones that were found on the island of Malta. Stensen concluded that the stones were actually fossilized shark teeth, which led him to study geology in more detail. He hoped to find information that would indicate how fossils were formed and would help to determine the origin of individual fossils. Stensen studied the relationship between fossilized bodies and the materials in which they are enclosed. He also examined the role of fluids in geological processes.

Stensen presented a theory of sedimentation*, examined when and of what materials different layers of sediment were formed, and collected data on the areas where stratification* occurs. He even introduced the idea of a natural chronology and history of the earth suggested by his research, although he had no sense of the immense duration of geological time. His work in geology, like his work in anatomy, was based on rigorous observation rather than the speculation that characterized natural philosophy*. For example, his study of quartz crystals revealed that they all have the same angles between corresponding faces—a result known as Steno's law.

* **analogy** form of reasoning based on the assumption that if two things are alike in some respects, then they are alike in all other respects as well

* **placenta** flattened organ in pregnant mammals that connects the fetus to the maternal uterus and facilitates the exchange of nutrients

* **sedimentation** process in which water or wind moves suspended particles of soil, sand, or other matter and deposits them in a new location

* **stratification** separation of rock or other material into layers

* **natural philosophy** development of theories to explain the natural world

Simon
STEVIN

1548–1620

MATHEMATICS, ENGINEERING

Simon Stevin spent most of his professional life serving as an engineer and military quartermaster (in charge of supplies) for the Netherlands. During the course of his duties, he published in a variety of subjects including mathematics, astronomy, mechanics*, navigation, engineering, military science, music theory, and geography. The illegitimate son of a wealthy Dutch citizen, he attended the University of Leiden, matriculating

* **mechanics** science that studies how energy and force affect objects

in 1583. Thereafter, he held a series of financial posts in the city governments of Bruges and Antwerp. During this time he did most of his work in mathematics and mechanics. After becoming quartermaster-general, he began to focus on astronomy, engineering, and navigation.

Stevin's work on mathematics focused primarily on its application to practical problems. One of his most influential works was a 29-page booklet titled *De Thiende* (The Tenth), which was published in 1585. In this work he showed that decimal fractions could replace fractions with integers for most purposes. Until this time, decimals had only been used occasionally in trigonometric tables. Stevin eliminated all difficulties in handling decimal fractions and he promoted the use of decimal notation for weights, measures, coinage, and geometric measurements. Later, he applied mathematical principles to solve problems in perspective, a subject much studied by artists and architects, as well as mathematicians.

* **Renaissance** period that marked the beginnings of modern science and the rebirth of interest in classical art and literature that occurred in Europe from the late 1300s through the 1500s

In mechanics, Stevin was the first Renaissance* scientist to continue the work of the ancient Greek scientist Archimedes. His main work on mechanics, published in 1586, discusses the theory of the lever and presents the law of the inclined plane. In perhaps his most famous discovery, he demonstrated that as the length of an inclined plane increases, the pull of gravity on a body on that plane decreases. Stevin also produced the first systematic work on hydrostatics* since Archimedes. In other works, he applied the principles of mechanics to machines, balances, the hauling of ships, and other problems. Related to his work on mechanics were his writings on engineering, in which he designed and described new types of canal locks and sluices*. He also proposed the construction of a new type of windmill and devised calculations that enabled him to determine the minimum wind pressure on a windmill sail needed to lift water to a particular height. In addition, Stevin developed a formula to determine how much water is raised by each revolution of the sails of a windmill.

* **hydrostatics** field of physics that deals with the properties and behavior of fluids at rest

* **sluice** human-made channel for conducting water and regulating its flow by the use of a valve or gate

Stevin was an early supporter of the sun-centered theory of the solar system devised by Nicholas COPERNICUS. He also proposed a theory of tides that anticipated the work of Isaac NEWTON by some 50 years. Stevin also proposed a method of determining longitude based on measurements of the earth's magnetic field taken from many places around the globe. Although the method was sound, it suffered because he, like earlier scientists, assumed that the earth's magnetism was uniform throughout. The range of Stevin's interests and publications, and his ability to combine theory and applications, make him one of the most versatile scientists of the early modern age.

Jan
SWAMMERDAM
1637–1680
BIOLOGY

* **entomology** science that deals with insects

Jan Swammerdam was a Dutch physician and researcher who was extremely skilled at observing natural objects through microscopes, or magnifying lenses. He also invented clever experiments and laboratory techniques that let him observe subtle biological processes and fragile organisms. Swammerdam focused his energies on two areas of biology—anatomy and entomology*—and made significant discoveries in each.

Life and Career. Swammerdam was born in Amsterdam, in the Netherlands. His family was associated with medicine—both his father and his brother were apothecaries, practical chemists who prepared and sold medicines. As a child, Swammerdam helped tend his father's collection of objects from around the world, including such natural history specimens as minerals and animals. At this time he began his own collection of insects.

In 1661 Swammerdam entered the University of Leiden, also in the Netherlands. His fellow students included Niels STENSEN (Steno), Frederik Ruysch, and others who became well-known scientists. Swammerdam completed his formal studies in 1663, and after several years of additional study in France, Amsterdam, and Leiden, he was qualified to practice medicine. Although there is no evidence that he had a regular medical practice, in his writings Swammerdam mentions being kept from his research by the demands of seriously ill people.

Swammerdam wanted to devote his life to scientific research, but illness and periods of severe depression and anxiety interrupted his work. He also suffered from poverty after his father, insisting that Jan earn his own living, cut off financial support. In the mid-1670s Swammerdam became attracted to the teachings of a religious mystic. He wrote to the mystic for spiritual comfort and to ask permission to publish his research, and he later visited her in Germany. Around the same time Steno, fearing that Swammerdam had rejected the sciences, wrote to another friend and colleague, Marcello MALPIGHI, that Swammerdam was searching for God and had destroyed some of his scientific manuscripts. Consequently, Steno sent some of Swammerdam's work to Malpighi. However, Swammerdam had valued his research enough to leave instructions in his will that his work be published posthumously*. His research was published in the 1730s under the title *Biblia naturae* (Book of Nature).

*** posthumous** occurring after the death of an individual

Anatomical Researches.

Anatomical Researches. Swammerdam's studies of human and animal anatomy were well known to medical researchers of the time. Because Swammerdam conducted some of these studies in the company of his colleagues, the letters and papers written by some of the leading medical scientists of the day contain accounts of his work.

Swammerdam earned his medical doctorate for his research on respiration, or breathing. To observe respiration he submerged a dog in water, making it breathe through a tube. He then recorded the mechanical process of breathing by measuring the rise and fall of the water as air entered and left the dog's lungs.

He also created an ingenious experiment to disprove the widely held notion that muscles increased in volume when they contracted. First, he demonstrated that a frog's leg muscle could contract even when separated from the frog's body, brain, and blood. He then placed the muscle in a glass tube filled with water and sealed the top with a drop of colored water. When the muscle contracted, the colored water did not spill over the tube, proving that muscle volume does not increase during contractions.

Among Swammerdam's other achievements in technique were the use of wax injections to make blood vessels distinct, his method of dissecting delicate material underwater so that it did not collapse or disintegrate, and his outstanding skill in observing things through the microscope. Swammerdam was the first to notice oval particles, later known to be red blood cells, in blood. He made this important discovery in 1658, before he went to university. Another of his significant finds was the discovery that the soft material inside the spine consists of fibers that end in the brain. Another concerned the very nature of human reproduction. Swammerdam was one of several researchers of the 1600s, Steno being another, who put forward evidence that female mammals, including people, have ovaries and eggs.

Studies of Insects. Unlike Swammerdam's medical or anatomical work, his lifelong study of insects was carried out privately. Much of it remained unpublished during his lifetime, although *Historia insectorum generalis* (General History of Insects), published in 1669, was recognized as a work of major importance. It offered a profoundly new and important view of insect life. Before Swammerdam, scientists believed that insects lacked internal organs, arose spontaneously out of organic matter rather than being born, and changed from one form to another through a process of metamorphosis rather than by any observable series of stages. Swammerdam, who had been interested in entomology since his days as a young collector, undermined those notions with his observations and experiments.

To prove that insects evolve from one form to another, such as from a caterpillar to a chrysalis to a butterfly, Swammerdam performed delicate dissections that showed that caterpillars contain structures that develop into the butterfly's wings and legs. Believing that the laws of nature are regular and simple, he disproved the idea that insects change through abrupt and incomprehensible metamorphoses. He also opposed the idea of spontaneous regeneration because he believed that it led to atheism* and allowed chance and accident to rule instead of law and regularity. Instead, he argued that they grow gradually through processes much like those that are observable in other organisms, although those processes may be much harder to see in insects than in chickens, frogs, or carnations.

Concerned principally with development and not origin, Swammerdam maintained that the most important phase of insect life was the pupa. It is the stage in which an insect prepares to change its size or form by growing a new inner skin that will appear when it sheds the outer skin. He divided insects into four groups. Insects in one category are born in their adult forms and simply grow larger. Those in the other three categories undergo various kinds of changes in form, always passing through the pupa stage.

According to Swammerdam, all living things come from parents of the same kind by means of eggs. In this manner he contributed to the development of the ideas of preexistence and interconnectedness.

* **atheism** belief that no god or supernatural force exists

---

Niccolò
TARTAGLIA

ca. 1499–1557

MATHEMATICS, MECHANICS,
MILITARY SCIENCE

Niccolò Tartaglia is best known for his work in mathematics and geometry and for his translation of famous ancient scientific works. He was also accomplished in military sciences and made several advances in the science of ballistics*. But events early in his life almost prevented him from making any contributions at all. Born into a poor working-class family in Brescia, Italy, Tartaglia suffered a mouth wound that left him with a speech impediment as well as a nickname that he later adopted as a

* **ballistics** study of the dynamics of projectiles

surname (*tartagliare* means "to stammer" in Italian; his actual surname was probably Fontana). He later received several serious head wounds that almost claimed his life.

Tartaglia began formal schooling at 14 but ran out of money to pay his teacher and, therefore, was largely self-taught. Nevertheless, he made a name for himself as a mathematician by rediscovering and popularizing a method for solving the general cubic equation (a third-degree equation with one unknown). His other contributions to mathematics included calculating the volume of a tetrahedron (a solid geometrical figure with four triangular faces) from the lengths of its sides, and contributing to the theory of division of areas. He also produced some of the first modern translations of the works of the ancient Greek mathematicians Euclid and Archimedes.

* **projectile** body projected by an external force and continuing in motion by its own inactivity

Tartaglia applied his mathematical skills to the art of warfare, producing pioneering works on the motions of projectiles. He determined that the trajectory of a projectile* is always a curved line. He also calculated that the maximum firing range of a projectile could be obtained by elevating any gun to a 45° angle. Based on his study of gunnery, Tartaglia devised instruments for determining heights and distances that were impossible to reach physically. These instruments are considered the beginnings of modern tachymetry, the science of making quick and accurate measurements. The historian Pietro Riccardi credited Tartaglia with producing "the major advances in practical geometry of the first half of the sixteenth century." He died in Venice, Italy, in 1557.

Evangelista TORRICELLI

1608–1647

MATHEMATICS, PHYSICS

* **calculus** advanced form of mathematics that involves computing quantities that change as functions of different variables

During his brief career the Italian mathematician and physicist Evangelista Torricelli produced only one published manuscript that included important contributions to mathematics, including geometry and calculus*. However, Torricelli's fame rests not on his published works but on the results of an experiment in which he demonstrated that air has weight. The experiments led to the invention of the barometer and acceptance of the theory that air exerts pressure on the objects it surrounds. His discovery also provided stimulus to experimentation and theoretical activity that fundamentally changed the world of physics.

Life and Career. When Torricelli was a young boy, his father, a textile artisan, sent him to study with an uncle who was a member of an order of monks. In his late teens Torricelli attended courses in mathematics and philosophy offered by the Jesuit school in his hometown of Faenza. His performance was so impressive that his uncle sent him to study under Benedetto Castelli, a fellow monk in Rome. Castelli, a mathematician and hydraulic engineer, quickly realized Torricelli's potential. Castelli was a former pupil of the great scientist Galileo GALILEI, with whom he kept up a correspondence. When Torricelli was 24, he wrote to Galileo, acknowledging Castelli's receipt of an earlier letter from Galileo. In his note to Galileo, Torricelli took the opportunity to introduce himself and point out that he was familiar with the geometry of the ancient Greeks. He also said that he had studied the astronomical ideas of the ancient and modern scientists and declared himself a follower of the ideas of Galileo and Nicholas COPERNICUS. Several years later Castelli showed Galileo a commentary that Torricelli had written on one of Galileo's essays on motion. Galileo was considering adding new sections to the essay, and Castelli recommended that he take on Torricelli as an assistant. Galileo agreed, and in late 1641 Torricelli joined him at his home in Arcetri. Torricelli stayed and worked there until Galileo's death the following year.

Torricelli then moved to Florence at the invitation of Galileo's patron, the Grand Duke Fernandino II of Tuscany. He remained there for the rest of his life, conducting research and corresponding with other scholars. His only published work, the *Opera geometrica* (Geometrical Work), appeared in 1644. Two years later, while preparing a draft of his correspondence for publication, he contracted a serious illness and died within a few days.

Scientific Accomplishments. In the first part of the *Opera geometrica,* Torricelli discusses his knowledge of the new geometry of indivisibles developed by the Italian mathematician Bonaventura Cavalieri. He applies Cavalieri's principles and develops a universal theorem that is still in use. Using this theorem, Torricelli could determine the center of gravity of any object. The *Opera* also made important contributions to the new calculus developed by the German mathematician Wilhelm LEIBNIZ and the Englishman Isaac NEWTON. In the second part of the book, Torricelli examines Galileo's studies of the motion of projectiles*. He demonstrates that if a projectile is relaunched in the opposite direction and at the same speed at which it was originally launched, it will follow the same trajectory in the opposite direction. In other words, he proves that any dynamic phenomenon is reversible. Torricelli also produced tables to calculate the trajectory of a projectile using only the original speed and angle of firing. Another table determines the angle at which the gun should be elevated, given the distance to the target and the range of the weapon. These firing tables were of great practical use in making weapons to discharge missiles.

In another section of the work, Torricelli calculates the velocity at which a jet of liquid would flow out of a small opening at the bottom of a container. This and other observations about the flow of water led the scientist Ernst Mach to proclaim Torricelli the founder of hydrodynamics*. Torricelli was also active in other areas, including the grinding of telescope lenses. He determined that the key to making a fine lens was to make its surface as spherical as possible. He produced some of the finest lenses in the world at the time and earned a comfortable living by selling them. Torricelli also presented lectures at the Accademia della Crusca, the most important of which concerned impact and wind. He argued that bodies themselves contain energy (which he called "force and impetus") that they transmit during collisions. He also stated that energy is not a separate force supplied from outside the bodies themselves.

In his lecture on wind, he proposed a new theory, later proved correct, that wind is produced by the difference in the temperatures (and density) of air between two regions of the earth. His most famous scientific contribution

* **projectile** body projected by an external force and continuing in motion by its own inactivity

* **hydrodynamics** scientific study of the motion of liquids

stems from a dispute related to this idea. The dispute took place between Galileo and Giovanni Batista Baliani and centered on the question of whether air has weight. Baliani believed that it did, while Galileo said that it did not. To determine who was correct, Torricelli designed an experiment that was executed by his colleague, Viviani. In the experiment Viviani partially filled a glass tube with mercury and covered the open end with a finger. He then set the tube, open end down, in a bowl that was also filled with mercury. Instead of draining into the bowl, the mercury in the tube fell slightly but stopped at a certain point. Torricelli argued that the pressure of the air weighing on the mercury in the bowl was transmitted to the mercury in the tube and prevented it from falling farther. He also said that if the tube was filled with a liquid lighter than mercury (such as water), then the liquid in the bowl would have been forced farther up the tube by the weight of the air.

The French scientist Blaise PASCAL confirmed this hypothesis many years later. This experiment led to the invention of the barometer, a device for measuring changes in air pressure. One scholar later wrote that the invention of the barometer had changed physics just as the telescope had changed astronomy. Although he lived only a short time, Torricelli played a major role in the birth of the modern science of physics.

Andreas
VESALIUS
1514–1564
MEDICINE, ANATOMY

The physician Andreas Vesalius is often considered the founder of the modern practice of anatomy. His revolutionary ideas about the structure of the human body completely overturned principles of anatomy that had been accepted for over 1000 years. Perhaps more significantly, his insistence on the importance of dissection in the study of human anatomy changed the conduct of anatomical research and even today remains fundamental to that field.

Life and Career

Vesalius was born in Brussels, Belgium, to a family that had been prominent in the medical profession for several generations. His father was apothecary* to the Holy Roman Emperor Charles V. Andreas was destined not only to follow in his family's footsteps but also to blaze new trails for others to follow.

Education and Early Work. Vesalius studied at the University of Louvain, Belgium, and later chose to pursue medicine at the prestigious University of Paris in France. At age 19 he began his medical education in the tradition developed by the ancient Greek physician Galen, whose ideas he later challenged. In 1536 war between France and the Holy Roman Empire forced Vesalius to return to Louvain. There he successfully convinced the university administration to reintroduce anatomical dissection into the medical curriculum after it had not been taught there for many years. The following year he received his bachelor's degree, and a year later he enrolled at the University of Padua in Italy, Europe's most famous medical

* **apothecary** individual trained to fill prescriptions; pharmacist or druggist

school. He received his doctorate after two days of examinations, and the next day he was appointed lecturer in surgery and anatomy. It was at that time that Vesalius's different approach to anatomy became apparent.

Instead of reading from ancient texts while a barber-surgeon performed the dissection, Vesalius performed the dissections himself. He produced large, detailed anatomical charts for his students to use when no cadavers (dead bodies intended for dissection) were available for study. He also prepared a dissection manual in which he first publicly expressed ideas that disagreed with those of Galen. As he performed more dissections, Vesalius became convinced that Galen had based his ideas about human anatomy on nonhumans (animals) and that these ideas were often incorrect. In a series of anatomical demonstrations in Bologna, Vesalius declared that human anatomy could be learned only by dissecting the human body. He also demonstrated that Galen's description of bones fit the bones of apes but not of humans.

Later Work. Prompted by the success of his investigations, Vesalius began work on a book titled *Fabrica,* in which he presented his ideas about anatomy. The book was published in 1543, the same year as the publication of Nicholas COPERNICUS's great work on the revolutions of heavenly bodies. Vesalius's book immediately sealed his reputation as the greatest of Renaissance anatomists. Soon after its publication Vesalius suddenly abandoned his anatomical studies to take a position as physician to Emperor Charles V. Part of his duties included serving as a surgeon on the battlefield, where he increased his knowledge of anatomy and developed several successful surgical techniques. His fame as a surgeon spread, and he was in great demand throughout Europe. After Charles gave up his throne, Vesalius took a post as physician at the court of Charles's son, Philip II of Spain. He served in this capacity for the rest of his life. In 1564 Vesalius left Spain for a trip to the Holy Land. Sometime during the return voyage, storms forced his ship to land at the island of Zákinthos, off the western coast of Greece. Vesalius died there and was buried in an unidentified site.

Scientific Achievements

Vesalius's sole work of note was the *Fabrica,* but its importance to the development of anatomy cannot be overestimated. Before Vesalius, all anatomy was based on the teachings of Galen. With the *Fabrica,* Vesalius revolutionized not only basic knowledge of human anatomy but also the philosophy underlying teaching in that field.

Purpose. Vesalius argued that to practice medicine properly, a physician had to acquire hands-on knowledge of the human body. Until that time physicians had engaged only in research and theorizing; actual surgery and dissection were performed by surgeons, who had less training and education. Vesalius hoped that the *Fabrica* might convince physicians to appreciate the fundamental importance of anatomy to all aspects of their profession. He also wanted to demonstrate the errors of Galen's approach to anatomy. These included Galen's reliance on animal specimens, which

The Best Physician in the World

Best known for his revolutionary work in anatomy, Vesalius was also an accomplished physician who learned much of his art on the battlefield. While serving as an army surgeon, he developed a technique to drain pus surgically from wounds to prevent infection. He later correctly diagnosed an internal aneurysm (abnormal blood-filled dilatation of a blood vessel) and accurately predicted the course of the ailment, a remarkable feat at the time. His reputation was so great that a contemporary called him "the best physician in the world."

Vesalius considered worthless for explaining human anatomy. Vesalius stressed that animal dissection was valuable only as a way to compare animal and human anatomy. However, he thought it desirable that human dissection be accompanied by a parallel dissection of animals, mainly to show the source of Galen's errors.

He also said that a physician should perform the same dissection several times on different bodies to make sure that his observations were not based on cases that represented anatomical abnormalities. Finally, Vesalius argued that it was important for a physician to become skilled at dissection to reach his own conclusions, rather than accepting the conclusions of others. To this end he included detailed descriptions of techniques for dissecting various parts of the body.

Contents. The *Fabrica*'s greatest contribution to anatomy is its detailed illustrations, particularly those that depict the skeletal and muscular systems. The illustrations, which were likely completed at the Titian school in Venice, were astonishingly detailed, complete, and accurate and included captions as well as numerical and alphabetic notations that referred to and clarified some of the accompanying text. This work marked the first time that a scholarly work integrated with illustrations was used as an effective teaching tool. Vesalius's muscle men illustrations, beginning with the outer skin and revealing the underlying layers of muscles, were particularly novel.

Of course, the *Fabrica* does not just offer new illustrations of the human body but also incorporates the new ideas that Vesalius had formulated based on his studies. The section on bones emphasizes the importance of the skeleton as the foundation of the body's structure and demonstrates Galen's errors on this subject. In the section on the nervous system, Vesalius shows that the nerves are not hollow, as Galen had claimed. The *Fabrica*'s coverage of the abdominal organs disputes Galen's claim that the liver had several different lobes. Contrary to Galen, Vesalius argued that the cavities in the brain called ventricles had nothing to do with intellectual activities and that their function was merely the collection of fluid. He also disproved the notion that sensation and motion were controlled by a series of arteries near the base of the brain. The *Fabrica* contains descriptions of many previously unknown structures, and many of the terms that Vesalius coined for various structures are still in use.

The *Fabrica* is not without blemish. It follows Galen's physiological system and repeats some long-standing errors. For example, Vesalius describes the supposed pores in the septum (dividing wall) of the heart, despite his admission that he could not detect them. His treatment of the female reproductive organs is inadequate largely because of the scarcity of female cadavers. Still, his true accomplishment with the *Fabrica* was to change accepted attitudes about his field. Medicine and anatomy had long depended on the uncritical acceptance of Galen's theories. Although individuals had occasionally cited Galen's errors, none had offered a way to check systematically the accuracy of his ideas. By arguing for the importance of dissection and demonstrating how it could be used to correct errors and discover new truths, Vesalius charted a new course for later

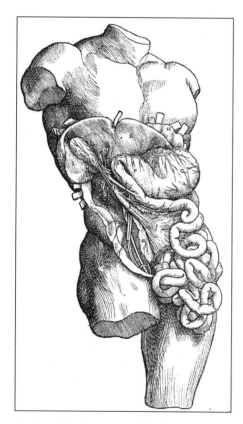

Andreas Vesalius stressed the importance of dissection in studying human anatomy. His book *Fabrica*, published in 1543, contains many medical illustrations of internal organs and the muscular and skeletal systems. This illustration from *Fabrica* shows the anatomy of the abdomen.

anatomical investigators. His work inspired the discoveries of Realdo COLOMBO, Gabriele FALLOPPIO, William HARVEY, and other great physicians of the next generations.

François VIÈTE

1540–1603
MATHEMATICS

The French mathematician François Viète introduced the use of letters for known and unknown quantities in mathematics. This innovation, considered one of the most significant advances in the history of mathematics, paved the way for the development of modern algebra. Viète devoted his career to recovering the basic analytic methods by which ancient Greek mathematicians, such as Euclid and Archimedes, had solved equations and developed mathematical theorems.

Life and Career. Born in Fontenay-le-Comte, France, Viète was the son of an attorney. After receiving his basic education in Fontenay, Viète entered the University of Poitiers to study law. He received a bachelor's degree in law in 1560. However, four years later he abandoned the legal profession to supervise the education of Catherine of Parthenay, the daughter of Antoinette d'Aubeterre, and to serve as an adviser to the family. When d'Aubeterre was widowed in 1566, Viète accompanied her to the city of La Rochelle. From there, four years later, he went to Paris. In 1573 King Charles IX appointed Viète counselor to the *parlement,* or assembly, of the region of Brittany, which met at the city of Rennes. Viète remained in Rennes for six years, after which he returned to Paris and took a position as a counselor in the royal administration.

Between 1584 and 1589, Viète was banished from the royal court by political enemies, and he spent some time at Beauvoir-sur-Mer. Thereafter, he was recalled to the royal court by King Henry III. When Henry was forced to leave Paris and move the government to Tours because of growing religious conflicts between Catholics and Protestants, Viète accompanied him and served as counselor of the national *parlement.*

During the religious wars between France and Spain, Viète performed a crucial service to King Henry IV of France. In 1589 the French intercepted a coded letter intended for their Catholic enemy, King Philip II of Spain. It took him several months, but Viète successfully deciphered the difficult code used in the letter. His accomplishment helped reinforce his growing reputation as a mathematician.

By 1593 Viète had gained repute as a mathematician. Shortly thereafter, when the ambassador from the Netherlands remarked to King Henry that France did not have any mathematicians capable of solving a problem posed by Adrian Romanus, the king summoned Viète and told him of the challenge. Within minutes, Viète solved the problem and presented his answer to the king. By the following day, he had found 22 additional solutions.

After an absence of several years, Viète returned to Paris in 1594. The following year he published his answers to the problem posed by Romanus. Romanus was so impressed by Viète's solutions that he traveled to France to meet the mathematician, and the two soon became close friends.

In 1597 Viète went to live in his hometown. In 1602 he was dismissed from the service of Henry IV and he died the following year in Paris.

Accomplishments. Viète's first scientific works were the lectures he gave to his student Catherine of Parthenay. Only one of these works has survived—*Principes de cosmographie* (Principles of Cosmography)—which contains essays on the sphere, elements of geography, and some elements of astronomy. One of Viète's major works was *Canon mathematicus, seu ad triangula cum appendicibus* (Mathematical Laws Applied to Triangles). Begun in 1571 and published partially in 1579, this work was probably the first in Western Europe to systematically develop methods for computing different types of triangles using the basic elements of trigonometry.

Canon mathematicus contains a table of trigonometric lines with some additional tables, the computational methods Viète used in constructing his theorems, and explanations of the calculation of triangles using basic trigonometry. To construct his table of trigonometric lines, Viète applied a method used by the ancient Greek astronomer Ptolemy, which was improved by the Arabs and later introduced to Western Europe through translated works.

The most important of Viète's many works on algebra was *In Artem analyticem isagoge* (Introduction to the Analytical Arts). The work introduced the use of letters for known quantities—denoted by consonants—and for unknown quantities—denoted by vowels. Viète drew from several Greek sources, including *Arithmetica* by the Greek mathematician Diophantus, and *Elements* by Euclid. This innovative work paved the way for the development of algebra.

In 1593 Viète published *Zeteticorum libri quinque,* which continued his investigations in algebra. Of the five books of the *Zeteticorum,* the first contains ten problems that seek to determine quantities for which the sum, difference, or ratio is already known. The problems contained in the second book give the sum or difference of the squares or cubes of unknown quantities, their product, and the ratio of this product to the sum or the difference of their squares. In the third book, the unknown quantities are proportional, and the reader is required to find these quantities if the sum or the difference of the extremes or averages is given. The remaining books give solutions to other algebraic problems.

Although completed in 1593, *De aequationum recognitione* (Concerning the Recognition of Equations) was not published until more than a decade after Viète's death. This work contains 25 propositions, or theorems, that present methods for solving second-, third-, and fourth-degree equations. In *De numerosa potestatum* (Concerning Numerous Powers), published in 1600, Viète presents a method of approximating the roots of numerical equations.

Viète also had a role in the improvements of the Julian calendar, the calendar adopted by the ancient Romans and named after Julius Caesar. For centuries, the annual determination of dates for religious festivals had caused problems and confusion. The rapid progress of astronomy in the 1500s and 1600s led many to reconsider these problems, and many new calendars were proposed. The adoption of a new Gregorian calendar, named after Pope Gregory XIII, met with opposition from many scientists, including Viète. Viète valued the studies involved in reforming the calendar, and toward the end of his life he became involved in formal arguments over these reforms.

John WALLIS

1616–1703

MATHEMATICS

* **calculus** advanced form of mathematics that involves computing quantities that change as functions of different variables

* **theology** study of religion

* **archivist** person responsible for preserving and caring for manuscripts and other documents

The most influential mathematician before Isaac NEWTON, John Wallis made significant contributions to the origins of calculus* and the development of modern algebra. He was the first to show the usefulness of the exponent (power of a number), and his application of negative and fractional exponents was an important advancement in mathematics. Wallis invented and introduced the ∞ symbol for infinity, and systematized the use of formulas as a form of mathematical notation.

Life and Career. Born in Ashford in Kent, England, Wallis was the son of a respected minister. His father died when Wallis was just six years old and he was raised by his mother. In 1625 Wallis was sent to a grammar school in the nearby town of Tenterden, where he received training in Latin. He later attended school in Felsted, Essex, where he continued his studies in Latin and studied Greek and Hebrew as well. Wallis also was introduced to the elements of logic at this time, but mathematics was not part of the regular grammar school education. In 1632 Wallis entered Emmanuel College at Cambridge University, where he took the traditional undergraduate courses as well as courses in theology*, physics, anatomy, astronomy, geography, and philosophy. He also studied mathematics, which at the time was not in fashion as a college subject.

Wallis received a master's degree in 1640 and was ordained a minister. For some years he earned his living as a private chaplain and as a minister in London. From 1644, two years after the outbreak of the English Civil War, Wallis also served as secretary to the Assembly of Divines at Westminster. The following year, Wallis moved to London, where he became seriously interested in mathematics after reading *Clavis mathematicae* (The Keys to Mathematics) by a well-known English mathematician named William Oughtred. Four years later Wallis was appointed professor of geometry at Oxford University. This appointment came as a surprise to many, since Wallis's accomplishments thus far had little to do with mathematics.

This appointment at Oxford determined the course of Wallis's career. He held this position until his death more than 50 years later. In 1657 he was elected the university archivist*, an office he also held for the rest of his life. When the English monarchy was restored three years later, Wallis received the title of royal chaplain to Charles II.

In 1692 Wallis was offered a position as dean of Hereford College in Oxford in recognition of his services to England, but he declined. In addition to his mathematical achievements, Wallis helped found the Royal Society, taught deaf people to speak, and assisted the university in its legal affairs. The first two decades of Wallis's career at Oxford were the most creative period in his life. During his later life, he turned increasingly to editing the works of other scientists.

A Quarrelsome Nature

Wallis had a quick temper and was not modest about his accomplishments. These traits brought him into conflict with many other scholars and led to bitter quarrels, some of which lasted for years. His longest and most bitter dispute, with the English philosopher Thomas Hobbes, dragged on for more than 25 years. Wallis feared that Hobbes's ideas would undermine respect for the Christian faith. However, the philosopher's greatest "sin" was that he dared to criticize Wallis's *Arithmetica infinitorum,* which Hobbes characterized as a "scab of symbols." Wallis never missed an opportunity to attack Hobbes's work, and the two men had a violent hostility toward each other that was often expressed in wild accusations and abusive language. This bitter quarrel ended only with Hobbes's death in 1679.

---

* **mechanics** science that studies how energy and force affect objects

Accomplishments in Mathematics. Wallis's earliest works in mathematics, presented in 1648, dealt with the solution of third- and fourth-degree equations. In 1655 Wallis introduced the sign for infinity in a work called *De sectionibus conicis* (On Conic Sections). Two years later, he published *Mathesis universalis* (Universal mathematics), a work on arithmetic, geometry, and algebra, in which he traced the development of mathematical notation and symbols and stressed their importance.

Wallis's most famous mathematical work is perhaps *Arithmetica infinitorum* (The Arithmetic of Infinitesimals), published in 1655. This book deals with the use of negative and fractional exponents. More important than the individual problems that Wallis presents in *Arithmetica,* however, is the novelty of his approach, which focuses on logical analysis rather than the traditional geometric approach to problems.

Arithmetica infinitorum had a great influence on Isaac Newton, who said that some of his own work was inspired by a careful study of Wallis's book. Publication of the work quickly brought fame to Wallis, who became recognized as one of England's leading mathematicians. However, the work also provoked a mathematical challenge from the French mathematician Pierre de FERMAT, who called on Wallis and other mathematicians to solve a number of questions using Wallis's methods and symbols. Their efforts proved to be only partially successful.

Between 1669 and 1671, Wallis published *Mechanica* (Mechanics), a three-part book in which he studied the behavior of elastic and inelastic bodies. Considered a very important and comprehensive work on those subjects, the book represented a major advance in the application of mathematics to the field of mechanics*.

Wallis's last great mathematical work was the *Treatise of Algebra, Both Historical and Practical,* published in 1685. The result of many years of work, it combined a full explanation of algebra with a complete history of the subject up to the time of the French mathematician François VIÈTE in the late 1500s. The book emphasizes the development of mathematical notation, and it relies heavily on the published works of many English mathematicians. Scholars elsewhere in Europe criticized the book as being too one-sided, and such criticisms continued long after Wallis's death. Wallis helped shape more than 50 years of mathematics in England. He also played a major role in raising the status of mathematics in England and other parts of Europe. Because of Wallis and his fellow citizen Isaac Newton, England was the center of mathematical research until the time of the Swiss mathematician Leonhard EULER in the mid-1700s.

Nonmathematical Works. Wallis had important accomplishments in other areas as well. He pioneered attempts to teach deaf people how to speak, and promoted other scientific research through his work with the Royal Society of London. As archivist at Oxford, Wallis organized the university's documents and prepared a catalog that remained in use until the 1900s. Although not a practicing musician, Wallis composed several papers on musical theory, and he edited works on music that had been translated from ancient sources. Wallis also was an accomplished theologian. His sermons and other theological works were praised by many for their simple and straightforward language.

James WATT

1736–1819

ENGINEERING, CHEMISTRY

James Watt's name is forever linked to his first and greatest invention, the first commercially viable steam engine. However, some of his other explorations led to commercial applications of chemical processes, including bleaching and dyeing. Born in Greenock, Scotland, Watt followed in the footsteps of his father and grandfather, both of whom pursued technical careers. He attended school occasionally while working in his father's shop, learning skills such as woodworking, metalworking, and instrument making. In the 1750s, he traveled to London to apprentice as an instrument maker but left the city the following year. He then went to Glasgow, where he obtained a post as the instrument maker for the local university. It was here, eight years later, that he perfected a separate condenser for the steam engine invented by Thomas Newcomen. In 1766 he closed his shop at the university to open a surveying and engineering practice, patenting his steam engine and developing it commercially. During the next 25 years, he devised many improvements to the engine that increased its performance and efficiency. This engine was used during the Industrial Revolution in flour, cotton, and paper mills.

Watt's chemical investigations were largely of a practical nature. He helped develop a process to bleach textiles with chlorine and also tried to commercialize a process to produce alkali from salt and lime. He was one of the first to propose that water was a compound of oxygen (what was then called "dephlogisticated air") and another, unspecified, gas. The French chemist Antoine LAVOISIER later identified the other gas as hydrogen. Watt's accomplishments resulted in his election to the scientific societies of London and Edinburgh. Watt profited greatly from the sale of his engines. He retired in 1800, and he spent his remaining years tinkering with minor inventions in his home workshop.

Christopher WREN

1632–1723

MATHEMATICS, ARCHITECTURE

In his role as an architect, Christopher Wren changed the face of London after the Great Fire of 1666. As a scientist he made important contributions to the fields of astronomy, mathematics, and anatomy. He was a founding member of the Royal Society, the most prestigious scientific organization in Europe during the 1600s.

Wren's upbringing gave him a strong religious background—his father and uncle were high-ranking church officials. Yet even as a boy Wren displayed a talent for science, math, and drawing that amazed the adults around him. He built several mechanical devices, including a gauge to measure rainfall, and later pursued higher education at Wadham College, part of Oxford University.

In 1657 Wren became a professor at Gresham College. It was an exciting and stimulating time for Wren, and his friends and colleagues from Oxford and Gresham shared in his enthusiasm. His circle included other talented scientists, such as Robert BOYLE, John WALLIS, and Robert HOOKE. This group decided to create a more formal organization, the Royal Society, approved by the Crown in 1662.

While at Gresham, Wren made an important advance in mathematics. He solved the problem of finding a straight line with the same length as a cycloid, a beautifully curved form that had long attracted mathematicians. After just four years at Gresham, Wren returned to Oxford as professor of astronomy. He studied anatomy and won praise for his fine drawings of body parts. In 1669 he published an important paper describing the physical laws of impact—the moment when one body strikes another.

Wren also turned his talents for mathematics and drawing to the field of architecture. His designs were accepted for a chapel at Cambridge and a theater at Oxford. After a devastating fire swept through London in 1666, Wren played a major role in reconstructing the city. With the official approval of King Charles I, Wren designed about 50 church buildings to replace those lost in the fire, including the new version of St. Paul's, one of London's grandest cathedrals.

Wren also pursued research in several other disciplines, including meteorology*, and was a pioneer in the study of insects with the use of a microscope. He even served as a representative in the English Parliament for several terms. Meanwhile, his professional honors continued to pile up, including a knighthood granted in 1673. He served as president of the Royal Society from 1680 to 1682. The influential scientist Isaac NEWTON also honored Wren as one of the greatest mathematicians of his time. Wren spent his last years in retirement in London.

* **meteorology** science that deals with the atmosphere, especially the weather and weather predictions; also known as atmospheric science

SUGGESTED READINGS

History of Science

Asimov, Isaac. *Asimov's Chronology of Science and Discovery*. New York: Harper Collins, 1994.

Boorstin, Daniel J. *The Discoverers: A History of Man's Search to Know His World and Himself*. New York: Random House, 1983.

Cohen, I. Bernard. *The Newtonian Revolution: With Illustrations of the Transformation of Scientific Ideas*. Cambridge, Mass.: Cambridge University Press, 1980.

Crombie, A.C. *The History of Science from Augustine to Galileo*. New York: Dover Publications, 1995.

Daston, Lorraine, and Katharine Park. *Wonders and the Order of Nature, 1150–1750*. New York: Zone Books, 1998.

Duhem, Pierre. *The Aim and Structure of Physical Theory*. Translated by P. Wiener. New York: Atheneum, 1962.

Hall, Maria Boas. *The Scientific Renaissance, 1450–1630*. New York: Dover Publications, 1994.

Hellemans, Alexander, and Bryan Bunch. *The Timetables of Science: A Chronology of the Most Important People and Events in the History of Science*. New York: Simon and Schuster, 1991.

Koyré, Alexandre. *From the Closed World to the Infinite Universe*. Baltimore, Md.: The Johns Hopkins Press, 1957.

Kuhn, Thomas S. *The Structure of Scientific Revolutions*. Chicago: University of Chicago Press, 1962.

Luck, Steve, ed. *The International Encyclopedia of Science and Technology*. New York: Oxford University Press, 1999.

Magner, Lois N. *A History of the Life Sciences*. New York: Marcell Dekker, 1994.

Mason, Stephen Finney. *A History of the Sciences*. New York: Collier Books, 1962.

Mount, Ellis, and Barbara A. List. *Milestones in Science and Technology: The Ready Reference Guide to Discoveries, Inventions, and Facts*. Phoenix, Ariz.: Oryx Press, 1987.

Rice, Tony. *Voyages of Discovery: Three Centuries of Natural History Exploration*. New York: C. Potter, 1999.

Schlager, Neil, ed. *Science and Its Times*. Detroit, Mich.: Gale Group, 2001.

Silver, Brian L. *The Ascent of Science*. New York: Oxford University Press, 1998

Spangenburg, Ray, and Diane K. Moser. *On the Shoulders of Giants: The History of Science From the Ancient Greeks to the Scientific Revolution*. New York: Facts on File, Inc., 1993.

Westfall, Richard Samuel. *The Construction of Modern Science: Mechanics and Mechanisms*. Cambridge, Mass.: Cambridge University Press, 1978.

Biographies

Alic, Margaret. *Hypatia's Heritage, A History of Women in Science from Antiquity Through the Nineteenth Century*. Boston: Beacon Press, 1986.

Christianson, J.R. *On Tycho's Island*. New York: Cambridge University Press, 2000.

Cook, Alan H. *Edmond Halley: Charting the Seas and the Heavens*. Oxford and New York: Clarendon, 1998.

Cooney, Miram P. *Celebrating Women in Mathematics and Science*. Reston, Va.: The National Council of Teachers of Mathematics, 1996.

Ehrman, Esther. *Mme. du Chatelet*. Leamington Spa, U.K.: Berg, 1986.

Gamow, George. *The Great Physicists From Galileo to Einstein*. New York: Dover Publications, 1988.

Gillispie, Charles C., ed. *The Dictionary of Scientific Biography*. 16 vols. New York: Charles Scribner's Sons, 1970–80.

Hollingdale, S.H. *Makers of Mathematics*. New York: Penguin Books, 1990.

Holmes, F.L. *Lavoisier and the Chemistry of Life*. Madison, Wisc.: University of Wisconsin Press, 1984.

Suggested Readings

Jardine, Lisa, and Alan Stewart. *Hostage to Fortune: The Troubled Life of Francis Bacon*. New York: Hill and Wang, 1999.

Kass-Simon. G., and Patricia Farnes. *Women of Science: Righting the Record*. Bloomington, Ind.: Indiana University Press, 1990.

Keele, Kenneth D. *William Harvey: The Man, the Physician and the Scientist*. London: Thomas Nelson and Sons, 1965.

Koerner, Lisbet. *Linnaeus: Nature and Nation*. Cambridge, Mass.: Harvard University Press, 1999.

MacLachlan, James. *Galileo Galilei: First Physicist*. New York: Oxford University Press, 1999.

Meadows, Jack. *The Great Scientist*. New York: Oxford University Press, 1987.

Muir, Nane. *Of Men and Numbers: The Story of the Great Mathematicians*. New York: Dover Publications, 1986.

O'Brian, Patrick. *Joseph Banks: A Life*. Chicago: University of Chicago Press, 1997.

Roger, Jacques. *Buffon: A Life in Natural History*. Translated by Sarah Lucille Bonnefoi. Ithaca, NY: Cornell University Press, 1996.

Shapin, S., and S. Schaffer. *Leviathan and the Air-Pump: Hobbes, Boyle, and the Experimental Life*. Princeton, N.J.: Princeton University Press, 1985.

Sobel, Dava. *Longitude: The True Story of a Genius Who Solved the Greatest Scientific Problem of His Time*. New York: Walker, 1995.

White, Michael. *Isaac Newton: The Last Sorcerer*. Reading, Mass.: Perseus Book Group, 1999.

Yount, Lisa. *A to Z of Women in Science and Math*. New York: Facts on File, 1999.

On-line Resources

The British Society for the History of Science. *Provides information about society and its members, professional and academic information, and links to journals and other history of science web sites.*

http://www.man.ac.uk/Science_engineering/CHSTM/bshs/

Catalog of the Scientific Community in the Sixteenth and Seventeenth Centuries, Rice University, Texas. *Contains a catalog of 631 biographies of scientists from the sixteenth and seventeenth centuries.*

http://es.rice.edu/ES/humsoc/Galileo/Catalog/catalog.html

French Academy of the Sciences. *Contains description of the organization and its members, recent press releases, lists of publications, upcoming events, and prizes. English language version is available.*

http://www.academie-sciences.fr/uk/index.html

History of Astronomy-Bonn University. *Contains a large number of links to other history of science web sites, including those for museums, publications, and societies.*

http://www.astro.uni-bonn.de/~pbrosche/hist_sci/

History of Science Society at Washington University. *Provides description of organization, links to publications, professional links, a database of subject matter, reading lists, and academic links.*

http://depts.washington.edu/hssexec

Indexes of Mathematician Biographies, School of Mathematics and Statistics, University of St. Andrews, Scotland. *Provides brief biographies of mathematicians from before 500 B.C. up until the late 1950s, and contains links to web sites related to history of mathematics.*

http://www-history.mcs.st-andrews.ac.uk/history/BiogIndex.html

Institute and Museum of History of Science in Florence, Italy. *Provides information about museum and its library, access to on-line exhibitions, description of research activities and publications, listing of events and news, and links to related web sites.*

http://galileo.imss.firenze.it/

Mathematicians of the Seventeenth and Eighteenth Centuries, Math Department, Trinity College, Dublin. *Contains biographies of mathematicians from the seventeenth and eighteenth centuries, as well as a few science biographies, all of which have been adapted from a book of mathematical history.*

http://www.maths.tcd.ie/pub/HistMath/People/RballHist.html

Max Planck Institute for the History of Science. *Contains description of the institute, notice of events, visitor information, description of research, publication and resource lists, and links to related web sites.*

http://www.mpiwg-berlin.mpg.de/ENGLHOME.HTM

Museum of the History of Science, Oxford. *Provides information about the museum, listing of events, access to on-line exhibits and collections database, archive of on-line newsletters, information about the museum library, and links to other history of science web sites.*

http://www.mhs.ox.ac.uk/

The National Museum of Science and Industry, England. *Provides information about museum, on-line features, descriptions of museum collections and research, information about exhibitions, resources for researchers, and links to related web sites.*

http://www.nmsi.ac.uk

The Royal Society. *Official site for this international academic organization; includes recent press releases, scientific commentary, lists of publications, and descriptions of resources.*

http://www.royalsoc.ac.uk/

Stephen Hawking's Universe: Cosmological Stars. *Provides brief biographies of important figures in the history of cosmology, as well as links to web sites providing related information.*

http://www.pbs.org/wnet/hawking/cosmostar/html/cos.html

Zoological Record, BIOSIS and the Zoological Society of London, Biographies of Biologists. *Provides links to numerous web sites with biographical information about important figures in the history of biology.*

http://www.york.biosis.org/zrdocs/zoolinfo/biograph.htm

PHOTO CREDITS

INDEX

Page numbers in **boldface** refer to the main entry on a subject.
Page numbers in *italics* refer to illustrations, figures, and tables.

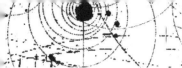

Index

Index

G

Index

Index

Index